PHILEMON

Readings: A New Biblical Commentary

General Editor
John Jarick

PHILEMON

Larry J. Kreitzer

SHEFFIELD PHOENIX PRESS

2008

Copyright © Sheffield Phoenix Press, 2008

Published by Sheffield Phoenix Press
Department of Biblical Studies, University of Sheffield
Sheffield S10 2TN

www.sheffieldphoenix.com

All rights reserved.
No part of this publication may be reproduced or transmitted
in any form or by any means, electronic or mechanical,
including photocopying, recording or any information storage
or retrieval system, without the publisher's permission in
writing.

A CIP catalogue record for this book
is available from the British Library

Typeset by Vikatan Publishing Solutions, Chennai, India

Printed by
Lightning Source

ISBN 978-1-906055-29-5 (hardback)
ISBN 978-1-906055-30-1 (paperback)

To the members of Mount Nebo Baptist Church,
in Louisville, Kentucky who tricked me into singing
'We're marching to Zion' solo one Sunday morning

Contents

List of Illustrations	viii
Preface	xi
Abbreviations	xiii
Introduction	1
1. Commentary	19
2. A Question of Characters	31
3. The Traditional Interpretation: The Case of the Runaway Slave	38
4. Traditions Re-thought: The Goodspeed and Knox Hypotheses	53
5. New Challenges to the 'Runaway Slave' Hypothesis	61
6. Philemon as a Morality Lesson: Christian Ethics and the Fight for Abolition	70
7. Pauline Biographies, Fictional Histories, and Contemporary Conversations	107
8. Philemon at the Movies	149
Postscript	169
Bibliography	174
Index of References	187
Index of Names	191

List of Illustrations

Opposite Preface: St Paul and Onesimus in prison

Figure 1: 13th-century drawing of Paul in prison addressing Philemon, Apphia and Archippus (New College MS 7, folio 278 verso)

Figure 2: Icon of Archippus, Apphia and Philemon from the Orthodox Church in America

Figure 3: Icon of Philemon, Apphia and Archippus from the Orthodox Church in America

Figure 4: Title page illustrations of *Onesimus; or, the Run-away Servant Converted* (1796, 1798)

Figure 5: Eleventh-Century Frescoe of Onesimus in Yilanli Church, Göreme in Cappadocia, Turkey

Figure 6: Jacques Callot's etching of the martyrdom of Onesimus (1636)

Figure 7: Icon of Onesimus from the Orthodox Church in America

Figure 8: Title page of *A Call to Archippus; or, An Humble and Earnest Motion to Some Ejected Ministers* (1664)

Figure 9: Title page of William Wilberforce's *A Letter on the Abolition of the Slave Trade* (1807)

Figure 10: A runaway slave is tripped up by the stumbling block of Scripture and caught by a Christian minister. An etching from John Greenleaf Whittier's *A Sabbath Scene* (1854 edition)

List of Illustrations   ix

Figure 11: *Life of St Paul* (1938)—A youthful Onesimus and his master Philemon

Figure 12: *Life of St Paul* (1938)—Paul signs the letter to Philemon promising to repay any debt owed by Onesimus

Figure 13: *Life of St Paul* (1938)—Tychicus teases Onesimus about his incessant reading

Figure 14: *Life of St Paul* (1938)—Philemon reads the letter from Paul as Tychicus and Apphia look on

Figure 15: *The Runaway* (2006)—DVD cover

Figure 16: *The Runaway* (2006)—Onesimus asks Philemon for forgiveness and declares his loyalty

Figure 17: *The Runaway* (2006)—Paul explains the nature of the Christian faith to Onesimus

Figure 18: *The Runaway* (2006)—With Paul's letter in hand, Philemon accepts Onesimus as his son and the two are reconciled

Figure 19: *Onesimus: A Quest for Freedom* (1992)—an arcade computer game released by Ark Multimedia Publishing

Figure 20: Slave Token from 1792 showing a chained slave with the inscription 'Am I Not a Man and a Brother?'

Figure 21: British £2 coin from 2007 issued to commemorate the 200th Anniversary of the Abolition of the Slave Trade

Preface

I first became interested in the Letter to Philemon while studying slavery and the Pauline epistles at seminary in Louisville, Kentucky. After finishing my degree there I was ordained at a small National Baptist church nearby which served a predominantly African-American community in the area. The church, rather small and poor, was situated, island-like, in the midst of a sea of surburban prosperity that was replete with large houses, manicured lawns, and tree-lined yards. That the socio-economic contrast was set out in such stark geographical terms always struck me as an unexpected legacy of the slave trade in Louisville during the mid-1800s. On the other hand, it is not surprising given that the city was a vital slade-trading centre that was strategically located on the Ohio River, and gave us the phrase 'being sold down the river' (a euphemism for slaves being transported downstream toward New Orleans and harsh conditions further south). Salutary reminders of life's injustices, and of the abiding relevance of the biblical text in addressing them, can come from the most unlikely places.

I am grateful to the Warden and Scholars of New College, Oxford for permission to reproduce the illustration from MS 7 (Figure 1); to the Orthodox Church of America for permission to reproduce the icons of Onesimus and Philemon, Apphia and Archippus (Figures 2, 3 and 7); and to Ark Multimedia Publishing for the illustration of the arcade game *Onesimus: A Quest for Freedom* (Figure 19).

Special thanks are due to Jos M. Strengholt and Arab Vision for permission to include stills from their film *The Runaway* (2006) (further details about this interesting project can be found on http://arabvision.gospelcom.net).

Finally, a word of gratitude to my Oxford colleague, John Jarick, is in order. He has supported and encouraged the project for a long time, and made various practical suggestions which enabled me, finally, to bring it to a conclusion and get it off my desk. The next visit to the pizzeria is on me, John!

LJK
Oxford
Trinity Term 2007

Abbreviations

ABD	*The Anchor Bible Dictionary* (6 vols.; ed. David Noel Freedman; New York: Doubleday, 1992)
ANRW	*Aufstieg und Niedergang der römischen Welt* (ed. H. Temporini and W. Haase; Berlin: W. de Gruyter, 1972–)
BZNW	Beihefte zur *Zeitschrift für die neutestamentliche Wissenschaft*
HTKNT	Herders theologischer Kommentar zum Neuen Testament
ICC	International Critical Commentary
JSNTSup	*Journal for the Study of the New Testament*, Supplement Series
JSOTSup	*Journal for the Study of the Old Testament*, Supplement Series
NICGT	New International Commentary on the Greek Testament
NRSV	New Revised Standard Version
REB	Revised English Bible
SBLDS	Society of Biblical Literature Dissertation Series
SNTSMS	Society for New Testament Studies Monograph Series
TNTC	Tyndale New Testament Commentary
WMANT	Wissenschaftliche Monographien zum Alten und Neuen Testament

Introduction

That the apostle Paul of Tarsus was the author of the Letter to Philemon has never been seriously questioned.[1] His authorship of Philemon was asserted by many of the earliest Christian writers. Not only is it mentioned within the Muratorian Canon (line 59), but also by Origen (*Homily in Jeremiah* 19), Marcion and Tertullian (*Against Marcion* 5.42), Jerome (*In Epistolam ad Philemonem*, Prologue), Eusebius (*Ecclesiastical History* 3.25), John Chrysostom (*Homiliae in Epistolam ad Philemonem*). and Theodore of Mopsuestia (*In Epistolam ad Philemonem*).[2]

However, does it really matter whether the epistle is genuinely from Paul or not? After all, someone reading the letter to Philemon for the first time might be tempted to think that it has little to offer in terms of theological discussion or critical debate. It does not appear to be concerned with, or even aware of, many of the key themes and ideas we have come to associate with Paul: there is no mention of the pivotal idea of justification by faith, nothing substantial is said about the Jewish Law or the struggle of Jew-Gentile relations within the church, and eschatological concerns are marginal at best. Philemon, in the words of one commentator, 'is the one of Paul's letters that does not deal with

---

1. F.C. Baur is a notable exception to the prevailing consensus of Philemon as a genuine Pauline letter. See Baur (1875: 80–84). Farrar (1913: 623) discusses Baur's rejection of the epistle, noting that he 'seems to blush for the necessity which made him declare this Epistle spurious.' Godet (1887: 153), says that Baur rejected Philemon simply because of its close association with the non-Pauline Colossians and in the process 'was compelled to sacrifice this innocent little Epistle, and to perpetrate a sort of critical murder.' For more on Baur's rejection of Philemon as a genuine Pauline letter, see Vincent (1897: 159–60); Bruce (1977: 394–96).

2. The comments on Philemon by these, and other early Christian writers, have been brought together in a convenient form in Gorday (2000: 309–18).

doctrinal or ecclesiastical issues.'[3] Other superficial features of Philemon also potentially give grounds for a challenge to it as a genuine letter of Paul. The epistle has ten words which do not appear elsewhere within the Pauline corpus, and two words (*apotiso* and *prospheilo*) in verse 19 are *hapax legomena* within the NT. Yet even when taken together these considerations are not enough to represent a serious challenge to its rightful place as a genuine letter of the apostle Paul.

In short, the case for Pauline authorship of Philemon seems assured, although other related considerations have a bearing on the overall intent and purpose of the letter and highlight the uncertainties about its interpretation. For instance, there are huge debates about the provenance of the letter. From where was Philemon written and under what circumstances? Most commentators agree that Philemon was written while Paul was in prison, and several places and times for that imprisonment suggest themselves. Three in particular have been suggested over the years: Ephesus (in 52–55 CE), Caesarea (in 58–60 CE), and Rome (in 60–62 CE). Since the time of Jerome and John Chrysostom, and perhaps even earlier (if the so-called anti-Marcionite prologue to Philemon[4] is deemed historically reliable), Rome has traditionally been the place most frequently suggested, although competent scholars have put forward good

---

3. Getty (1987: 503).
4. The Prologue reads: '*Philemoni familiares litteras facit pro Onesimo servo eius; scribit autem ei a Roma de carcere*'. It is found, for example, in *Codex Fuldensis* (written between 541 and 546) and based on the Latin Vulgate. Interestingly, the *Codex Fuldensis* also contains the apocryphal *Letter to the Laodiceans*.

arguments for the other two sites as well.[5] Much of the argument for Ephesus as the place of writing of the letter to Philemon rests on inferences about the relative geographical location of Colossae and the Lycus valley to Ephesus or Rome. The key point is that Ephesus is only 100 miles or so away from Colossae and thus seems to fit the reconstructed scenario involving a runaway slave much more readily than does Rome, which is nearly 1,000 miles away.

With a mere 25 verses, Philemon is the shortest of the letters within the Pauline corpus, and the form in which the Greek text of the letter has come down to us is fairly trouble-free, at least as far as variant readings or linguistic and grammatical difficulties are concerned. True, there is some debate about whether 'old

---

5. For Rome as the place of writing see Luther (1964: 108); Godet (1887: 142–43); Lightfoot (1885: 30–31); Vincent (1897: 58–62); Jones (1915: 315–16); Robertson (1920: 34); Scott (1930: 114); Knox (1932: 132); Cadoux (1933–34: 472); Dodd (1953: 94–95); Moule (1957: 21–25); Caird (1976: 214–15); Bruce (1977: 396–99); O'Brien (1982: 269); Patzia (1984: xx-xxi); Harris (1991: 241); Birdsall (1993: 630); Nordling (2004: 7–8). For Ephesus as the place of writing, see Winstanley (1915: 481–98); Deissmann (1922: 237–38); (1926: 20); Duncan (1929: 72–75; 1934–35: 293–298; 1956–57: 211–18; 1958–59: 43–45); Knox (1955: 555–56); (1960); Harrison (1950: 284); Leaney (1960: 136); Houlden (1970: 139–40); Lohse (1971: 188); Stuhlmacher (1975: 21–22); Gnilka (1982: 4–5); Koester (1982: 2.131–35); Wright (1986: 165); Lampe (1987: 21); Winter (1987: 2); Schenk (1987: 3841); Binder (1990: 28–29); Heil (2001: 189); Fitzmyer (2000: 11); Lüdemann (2002: 67); Wilson (2005: 326). For Caesarea, see Goguel (1926: 429–30); Dibelius (1953: 145–47); Johnson (1956–57: 24–26); Lohmeyer (1957: 172); Reicke (1970: 277–86); Robinson (1976: 61–85), and Ellis (2001: 266–75). Kümmel (1975: 347–48), wavers between Rome and Caesarea; Dunn (1996: 307–308), leaves the matter undecided between Ephesus and Rome; Barth and Blanke (2000: 126), favour Rome although they admit that the matter cannot be conclusively decided; Thompson (2005: 198) is similarly inclined. The Caesarean imprisonment has a sound textual basis in Acts 23:33–26:32; as does the Roman imprisonment in Acts 28:11–31. It is the Ephesian imprisonment that has to be inferred since there is no explicit mention of it in Acts, although Rom. 16:3, 7; 1 Cor. 15:30–32, 2 Cor. 11:23; and Clement's *Epistle to Rome* 5:6 are often invoked as an indication of such an incarceration. Occasionally, the imprisonment of Paul is denied altogether. For example, Goodenough (1929: 183), suggested that Paul was not literally in prison when Onesimus arrived, for his captivity was only figurative in nature.

4   Introduction

man' (*presbutes*) or 'ambassador' (*presbeutes*) is the proper reading in v. 9,[6] and those who delight in the unravelling the tangled nuances of Greek grammar can find at least one nice focal point for their interest. Here there is in v. 6 a sentence that has proved exceedingly difficult for translators to render into comprehensible English. Indeed, Moule describes it as 'notoriously the most obscure verse in this letter'.[7] But beyond these two minor considerations there is precious little else to capture the initial attention of a reader primarily concerned with textual-critical matters.

And yet it is amazing how many paths of contemporary New Testament scholarship do indeed converge on the short epistle of Paul to Philemon. If the old adage about all roads leading to Rome expresses an important socio-historical truth about the ancient Roman world, then it is equally fair to say that most scholarly explorations through the Pauline corpus make the letter we know as Philemon an important stopping point along their journey. Over the years students of the New Testament have continued to find Philemon to be a focus for their investigations. Scholarly studies of the letter over the last century or so can be grouped generally under five different, but interlocking, headings.

1. Form-Critical Analyses

Firstly, we note that many of the earliest scholarly investigations of Philemon in the twentieth century can be best described as pursuing an essentially form-critical approach to the epistle. They concentrated attention on the formal characteristics of the document as a genuine letter of the first-century world. What comes to the fore here is the recognition that Philemon is, above all else, a letter written by a particular man, to a particular person, at a particular time and place, and for a particular reason. It is the nature of Philemon as an occasioned letter that

---

6. See Hock (1995: 67–81) for a recent treatment of this. Petersen (1985: 101–102, 125–28) also discusses the point, arguing that 'ambassador' is the better option and gets closer to Paul's own understanding; Perkins (1998: 453) makes a similar point. Metzger (1971: 657) also discusses the two variants.

7. Moule (1957; 242). Reisenfeld (1982: 251–57) discusses the verse.

sets the agenda for, and helps determine the boundaries of, its interpretation.

At one level, it should come as no surprise that the contribution that Philemon makes to a discussion of the form of ancient letter writing has been very significant.[8] It is commonly agreed that the basic structure of the letter of Philemon conforms to a standard fourfold pattern common in antiquity: Introduction (vv. 1–3); Thanksgiving (vv. 4–7); Body (vv. 8–20); and Conclusion (vv. 21–25).[9] The letter has long been influential within discussions about the Christian adoption and adaptation of the standard patterns used in ancient letter writing, particularly as Philemon stands as the only clear and undisputed example of a personal letter written by one individual to another within the Pauline corpus.[10] Indeed, a number of scholars over the years have been keen to compare Philemon with similar personal letters penned by other ancient writers. Thus, papyrus letters which have survived from antiquity have been exhaustively analyzed and parallels to Philemon noted, both in terms of overall structure and form, as well as unusual ideas and phrases which occur within Philemon. In addition, some surprising, if not positively tantalyzing, parallels have been noted.

For example, one of the most intriguing parallels involves the unusual reference to Paul's promise to pay Philemon's debts in v. 19a ('I will repay [*ego apotiso*]'), which has been likened to an ancient version of an IOU. Scholars have frequently noted how Paul appears to take up the pen from his amanuensis at this

---

8. The work of White (1971: 1–47; 1972: 48–68), is foundational for such investigations. Kim (1972: 123–28), discusses the similarities that Philemon has to other examples of so-called 'letters of introduction' from the ancient world; Stowers (1986: 155) similarly describes Philemon as 'an intercessory letter', discussing it under the generalized heading of 'Letters of Mediation'. Also note Aune (1987: 211–12), on this point.

9. Porter (1999: 64) accepts this basic structure, but suggests that Paul expands the thanksgiving in such a way that distances Philemon from the conventions of Hellenistic letter-writing: 'In Philemon, Paul uses the thanksgiving to serve his linguistic discursive purposes, by separating his egalitarian words of greeting from the body of the letter, where he utilizes a set of variegated hierarchical words, beginning with bold words of authority and position'.

10. For a general introduction to this subject, see Doty (1973: 21–47).

point and, in accordance with the conventions of the day, finishes the letter by writing vv. 19a-25 himself.[11] Fascinating examples of other ancient letters using the verb *apotiso* (or its equivalents) have been identified, as have some cases where a validating signature has been affixed to a letter.[12]

Scholarly studies of ancient epistolary texts have also been usefully extended to include a consideration of how slaves were treated within them. For example, several letters from the ancient world shed light on how slaves who had run away were dealt with by their masters. A celebrated example is Pliny the Younger's letter to Sabinianus (*Epistula* 9.21), which at first glance appears to serve as a parallel to Paul's letter to Philemon, both in terms of its form and style, as well as its overall purpose.[13] The parallel with Philemon was noted as long ago as the 1640s and has remained a frequent point of discussion ever since.[14] But the points of comparison are not exact and the similarities can be overstated. For instance, it seems clear that within the letter to Sabinianus Pliny is addressing the situation of a freedman (*libertus*), and not a slave (*servus*), so the parallel may not be as relevant as is often argued.[15] Still, the parallel is sufficiently strong enough to persuade J.A. Fitzmyer to change his opinion as to the occasion which gave rise to Paul's writing to Philemon as he did. Fitzmyer originally held to the opinion that Paul wrote to Philemon because Onesimus was his slave who had run away—

---

11. Bahr (1968: 35–36) thinks Paul wrote vv. 17–18 as well.
12. Deissmann (1922: 331–34).
13. Knox (1960: 16–17), discusses the letter along these lines. Pliny's letter is frequently invoked as a parallel to Philemon by commentators. See Farrar (1913: 627–28, 734); Knox (1955: 556); Koch (1963: 184); Stuhlmacher (1975: 25); Harvey (1979: 684); Fitzmyer (2000: 20–23); Frilingos (2000: 91–92); Lüdemann (2002: 68–71); Thompson (2005: 196).
14. See Soards (1990: 210–11). Callahan (1997: 74), corrects himself via Soards article on this point having first identified Hugo Grotius as the initiator of this idea in 1646.
15. See Harrill (1993: 113); Pearson (1999: 276). Also see Koester (1982: 135), and Church (1978: 31–33), who argues that Pliny and Paul contrast sharply in their rhetorical approach. Vos (2001: 101) uses Pliny's letter to support his claim that manumission would not have achieved very much for Onesimus, just as a change of legal status made little difference for Sabinianus's freedman.

Onesimus was a *drepetes* or *fugitivus*.[16] The fact that the letter never *explicitly* describes Onesimus in such terms, together with the fact that Pliny the Younger wrote to Sabinianus in apparently similar circumstances, was sufficient to convince Fitzmyer that Paul was indeed writing to Philemon on behalf of Onesimus and interceeding for him. However, this intercession was *not* for Onesimus as a runaway slave as such, but as a concerned friend of Philemon, the owner-master.[17]

Another intriguing letter from antiquity that is sometimes invoked as a parallel to Philemon, is *PTurner* 41, a third-century papyrus from Oxyrhynchus in Egypt. It is from a woman named Aurelia Sarapias who wrote to a local official named Aurelius Protarchos about difficulties she had with one of her slaves. The details of the situation are not entirely clear, but it appears that the slave, whose name was Sarapion, made off with some of the possessions of the household and ran away. A number of inviting parallels with the situation involving Philemon and Onesimus are evident.[18]

2. Linguistic and Rhetorical Analyses

Secondly, in addition to such form-critical assessments, the letter to Philemon has been subjected to a variety of specialized linguistic and rhetorical analyses.[19] These have investigated everything from the chiastic structures which are thought to be contained within the letter, to its conformity to the styles of argumentation set forth in rhetorical handbooks of the first-century world, to the use made of exhortational strategies within the overall argument,[20] to the use of specialized vocabulary to

---

16. Fitzmyer (1968: 332–33; 1990: 869–70).
17. Fitzmyer (2000: 20–23).
18. Llewelyn (1992: 55–60) discusses the film.
19. See, for example, Church (1978: 17–33). Also worth noting are the discourse analyses of Snyman (1991: 83–99), who offers a study of the colons and concommitant paragraph divisions of the letter, and Allen (1992: 77–96), who argues that the culminating point of Paul's exhortation to Philemon comes in v. 17: 'Receive Onesimus as you would receive me.' Godet (1887: 148) made the same basic point over 100 years earlier, and Petersen (1985: 104–108), stressing the sociological implications of the verse, also sees it as a culminating point in the argument of the letter.
20. Russell (1998: 1–25).

sustain a particular rhetorical strategy.[21] Paul's letter to Philemon has also been the subject of sophisticated linguistic investigations,[22] and more recently by analytical techniques which make use of scientific and technological advances, notably corpus linguistics, that is, a computer-assisted discourse analysis of the Greek text of the epistle. These techniques offer the possibility, at least, of determining more precisely the original meaning and authorial intent of the letter, thereby resolving some matters of long-standing debate.[23] Specific features of Paul's epistolary style, such as his use of an introductory thanksgiving or intercessory prayer, have been thoroughly explored over the years.[24] In the main studies along these lines have tended to highlight how Paul subtly adapted his normal pattern of letter writing to fit the particular circumstances of his personal request to Philemon over the treatment of Onesimus. Recent publications demonstrate that Philemon still has the power to attract scholarly attention in each of these areas.

a. Chiastic Studies

One of the most elaborate examples of a chiastic reading of Philemon is that of the seventeenth-century divine Thomas Boys in his *Tactica sacra* (first published in 1824). Boys identified a nine-point chiasm arranged in what he described as 'an introverted parallelism of eighteen members' within the letter.[25] His arrangement was as follows:

---

21. Thus, Martin (1991: 332–37), suggests that the language about 'indebtedness' in v. 18 is an example of Paul's rhetorical skill, although it cannot necessarily be assumed to reveal anything about Onesimus actually owing money to Philemon.

22. Wilson (1992: 107–19) and Porter (1999: 47–70).

23. The epistle of Philemon is discussed as a test case for corpus linguistics in an engaging study by O'Donnell (2005: 444–85). He applies this discourse analysis technique to Philemon, and on the basis of it confidently asserts that the apostle did in fact intend that 'ownership' of Onesimus be handed over to him (2005: 480, 484).

24. Schubert (1939: 4–5, 12); Wiles (1974: 215–25, 281–84); O'Brien (1977: 47–61).

25. Boys (1824: 1.61–68; 2.vii-viii).

```
Aa - vv. 1–2
   Ab - v. 3
      B - vv. 4–7
         C - v. 8
            D - v. 9–10a
               E - v. 10b
                  F - vv. 11–12a
                     G - v. 12b
                        H - vv. 13–15
                           I - v. 15
                            *I* - v. 16a
                        *H* - v. 16b
                     *G* - v. 17
                  *F* - vv. 18–19a
               *E* - v. 19b
            *D* - v. 20
         *C* - v. 21
      *B* - v. 22
   *Ab* - vv. 23–24
*Aa* - v. 25
```

Moreover, Boys further identified a parallelism of six members within vv. 13–16 (letters H and I) which resembled each other in terms of construction and, perhaps more importantly, in their having a personal focus. Boys argued that each of these paired six members followed a pattern: the first related principally to Paul himself (v. 13), the second to Philemon (v. 14), and the third to Onesimus (v. 15). On the basis of these pairings Boys suggested that Paul's first thought was for himself, his next thought was for Philemon, and his third thought was for Onesimus. This three-step pattern is inverted in v. 16 (letters *I* and *H*). A system of correspondences, both verbal and conceptual, within the epistle was then developed by Boys for the rest of the letters of the chiasm (*H* to *Aa*).

In 1981 John Welch set out a reading of Philemon which similarly identified a ten-point inverted chiasm as the essential structure of the letter.[26] Verses 14 and 15 are presented by Welch as lying at the centre of this chiastic arrangement, and he suggested that it was here that the real reason for Paul's writing the letter was revealed. Welch suggested that Paul desired the return of Onesimus, but that he handled it in two ways. First,

26. Welch (1981: 225–26).

the apostle put the request into an ecclesiastical context and made Philemon bear the burden of willingly consenting to the return of Onesimus. Second, he suggested to Philemon that his difficulties with Onesimus were not all bad since they ultimately resulted in something positive and beneficial. These two points were identified as the heart of the chiasm insofar as they bind together the rest of the letter in a balancing pattern.

Nils W. Lund's influential study *Chiasmus in the New Testament* (1942) offered another suggestion about the chiastic structures thought to underlie Philemon.[27] Here Lund identified a 5-point inverted chiasm of the letter as a whole:

    A Salutation—vv. 1–3
        B Philemon's conduct towards all the saints
           He is the object of Paul's prayer—vv. 4–6
                C Paul had experienced much joy in the past, because his brother had refreshed the hearts of the saints—v. 7
                    D Paul refrains from pressing his claims on Philemon and prefers to ask a favor of him: The name Paul—vv. 8–11
                    E Paul and Onesimus: He is beloved by Paul—vv. 12–15
                    E' Paul and Onesimus: Philemon should love him also—vv. 16–17
                  D' Paul offers to reimburse Philemon, though he might have pressed his claim on him: The name Paul—vv. 18–19
                C' Paul expects much joy in the future in that his own heart will be refreshed through his brother—v. 20
        B' Philemon's conduct toward Paul, who is an object of the prayers of the saints—vv. 21–22
    A' Salutation—vv. 23–25

In addition, Lund went on to argue that the two central sections of this chiastic arrangement (that is, vv. 12–15 in E and vv. 16–17 in E') can themselves be arranged into a chiastic pattern of couplets. These couplets, he suggested, consist of a total of

---

27. Lund (1942: 219–20). Also see Jeremias (1958: 146).

twenty lines which contrast Paul and Philemon, at least as far as their dealing with Onesimus was concerned.

Another good example of a chiastic investigation is the recent study by John Paul Heil entitled 'The Chiastic Structure and Meaning in Paul's Letter to Philemon' (2001). He noted that Philemon has frequently been the subject of chiastic studies in the past, but that these have failed to convince because they have not been able to provide an explanation as to the reason why Paul was writing to Philemon in the first place. This fundamental weakness was tackled by Heil who proposed a new chiastic framework of nine units which is laid out as follows:

A Opening Address and Greeting (vv. 1–3)
  B Thanksgiving (vv. 4–7)
    C Appeal (vv. 8–10)
      D Onesimus (vv. 11–13)
        E Philemon's Consent (v. 14)
      D' Philemon's Beloved Brother (vv. 15–17)
    C' Philemon's Debt to Paul (vv. 18–19)
  B' What Philemon Will Do (vv. 20–22)
A' Closing Greetings (vv. 23–25)

As can be readily seen, Heil's analysis focused on v. 14, which he described as 'the central and pivotal point of the chiastic structure'.[28] According to Heil, Paul wanted to ensure that the whole matter with Onesimus was dealt with entirely with Philemon's consent. Paul desired Philemon's release of Onesimus, but he wanted that act to be a good deed performed out of love in response to the grace of God. His argument built up to him making this point in v. 14, and then proceeded from it until the concluding greetings.

b. Rhetorical Analyses

Paul's skill as a rhetorician, and his similarity to rhetorical styles and arguments which are well-known within Graeco-Roman writers, have frequently been noted in recent years. This is despite the fact that some earlier commentators, including J. B. Lightfoot, were rather negative about the contribution that rhetoric had to make to a study of the epistle.[29] In this regard, many recent commentators have highlighted the rhetorical skill and tact that Paul is able to bring to bear in writing to Philemon

---

28. Heil (2001: 188).
29. Lightfoot (1886: 317).

about such a delicate matter as his slave Onesimus. It is often noted that Paul did so in a way that genuinely took into account the social dynamics and proprieties in the world in which early Christians lived.[30]

In 1978 F. Forrester Church offered a study of Philemon which sought to explore the structure and design of Paul's letter to Philemon. Importantly, Church noted that Paul did *not* employ one of the standard conventions of rhetoricians within the letter, namely the use of diatribe. However, he suggested that this was not altogether a disadvantage. According to Church, the absence of a dialogical style does not prohibit us from seeing the importance of rhetoric for the structure of the letter, for its significance comes through regardless. Indeed, the epistle can be readily divided into standard rhetorical categories: vv. 4–7 are the *exordium*, vv. 8–16 are the *proof*, vv. 17–22 are the *peroration*.

Not surprisingly, opinions vary as to the motivations underlying Paul's request about Onesimus, as well as the degree in which he employed rhetorical strategies to get what he wanted. Some commentators stresses Paul's diplomacy and tactfulness in handling the delicate situation. Thus, Theo Preiss described Philemon as 'a case of tact and professional secrecy *par excellence*'.[31]

Not all have been so positive in their assessments of the Paul that is revealed through the letter to Philemon. Some view him as something of a manipulator, who threw his theological weight around and took advantage of his position as an apostle within the early church. Graham Shaw described Paul's letter to Philemon as a 'persuasive example of condescension' designed to get Philemon to come to share Paul's view of the runaway Onesimus. As Shaw sees it, 'Paul's primary concern in this letter is to establish his credibility in Philemon's eyes.'[32] Similarly, Gillian Feeley-Harnik argued that Paul's ultimate concern was to use the slave Onesimus as a means to force Philemon to obey him and thereby assist in the spreading of the Christian faith.[33]

30. Wilson (1992: 107–19) offers a study of the insights to be gained by examining Philemon against the conventions of how politeness functions within human relationships.
31. Preiss (1964: 32).
32. Shaw (1983: 137).
33. Feeley-Harnik (1982: 117–25).

She suggested that Paul was employing a strategy well-known among anthropologists, where the giving of a gift served as the means by which authority was achieved over the recipients of that gift. In this instance, Onesimus was the 'gift' that was given by Paul to Philemon, and the expectation that Philemon will 'do even more than I ask' (v. 21) was the expectation, not that Philemon will give Onesimus his freedom, but that Philemon will commit himself unreservedly to the fulfilment of the divine mission as revealed in Christ.[34]

3. Sociological Investigations into the World of Paul the Apostle

Thirdly, and closely connected to the scholarly investigations of the rhetorical techniques employed by Paul within the epistle, the letter to Philemon has had an important role to play within explorations into the social world of Paul the apostle.[35] The letter has proven itself to be particularly significant as a means for discerning the ways in which relationships involving power and authority functioned within the church concerned.[36] Philemon has also been the object of an innovative attempt to reconstruct Paul's narrative world, namely Norman Petersen's *Rediscovering Paul: Philemon and the Sociology of Paul's Narrative World* (1985). Understandably, the patriarchal nature of Philemon's role within the church at Colossae, and Paul's relationship to such a powerful figure, have been the subject of considerable scholarly interest in such explorations.[37] Thus, many interpreters have stressed the fact that the letter was not simply a private communication, and there is every reason to assume that it would have had a wider audience than just Philemon himself.[38] The reference to 'the church that meets in your house' in v. 2 makes this seem clear enough, as does the fact that (according to some

---

34. Feeley-Harnik (1982: 123) goes so far as to suggest that the real 'fugitive in the epistle is Philemon, not Onesimus, in that it is Philemon has run away from God's purposes, just as Jonah had done in the Old Testament.

35. See Horsley (1998: 155–60) for a methodological critique of such sociological approaches.

36. Thus, Polaski (1999: 59–72) applies Foucault's ideas about power relationships to a study of the letter.

37. Getty (1987: 503–508).

38. Wickert (1961: 235); Winter (1984: 206); Petersen (1985: 65–78).

14   *Introduction*

scholars) Paul, seems to stress his credentials as an elder statesman within the letter by describing himself as a *presbeutes* (or is it *presbutes*?) in v. 9, perhaps as a title replacing his customary use of *apostolos* at the beginning of his letters.[39] Other sociological focal points have been fastened upon by scholars in an attempt to understand the background and meaning of the letter to Philemon. Examples include the use of the family metaphor, such as the use of the idea of fatherhood expressed in the verb *egennesa* ('I fathered') in v. 10 where Paul described his role in bringing Onesimus to faith.[40] This idea of 'spiritual fatherhood' is found elsewhere in the uncontested Pauline letters (see 1 Cor. 4.15, 17; Gal. 4.19), but nowhere is it more powerfully presented than in the case of Onesimus.

4. Pauline Ethics: Slavery as a Test Case

Fourthly, and perhaps most importantly of all in terms of Philemon's abiding legacy to subsequent generations of readers, the letter has been viewed as providing something of a test case for examining Pauline ethics, particularly with regard to the question of Onesimus' emancipation from slavery.[41] In this sense Paul can be seen as performing a delicate balancing act between what is right (in principle) and what is achievable (in practice). Understandably, what Paul's letters have to contribute to our understanding of the place and practice of slavery within the early Christian church has been the subject of considerable scholarly interest. Several important studies in the past ten years of so have refocused attention on the subject.

---

39. So Moule (1957: 144); Wickert (1961: 235); Wright (1986: 180–81). The English classical philologist Richard Bentley (1662–1742) was the first to propose that *presbeutes* was the original reading in the verse (see Bentley (1862: 73), on this point). However, Birdsall (1993: 625–30) questions the need for an emendation of *presbutes* into *presbeutes*, and calls for its removal from the textual apparatus of critical editiions of the New Testament altogether. Barth and Blanke (2000: 107), state that 'Bentley's conjecture is ultimately superfluous', since *presbutes* can mean either 'old man' or 'ambassador'. Even so, most commentators accept *presbeutes* as the original reading, including Lohse (1971: 199); Hock (1995: 67–81). For more on *presbutes* and its significance for determining Paul's age, see below (page 46).
40. Frilingos (2000: 91–104).
41. Richardson (1968: 301–16).

A case in point is Dale Martin's *Slavery as Salvation* (1990) which sought to explore the ways in which the metaphor of slaves and slavery was used and developed within Pauline Christianity. Martin set this against the intriguing suggestion that slavery was sometimes seen in the ancient world as a means of social advancement.[42] Impressive though it is, Martin's work has not been without its critics, including those contributing to the *Semeia* 83/84 volume from 1998 entitled *Slavery in Text and Interpretation*. Here the tendency of New Testament scholarship in general to sanitize the horrendous, soul-destroying dimensions of the Roman slave system was castigated and the attempt to reduce it to a spiritual metaphor was called into question.[43] The question needs to be raised (so some of the contributors to the *Semeia* volume argue) about the legitimacy of dependence of New Testament interpreters upon studies of ancient slavery by classicists, studies which were overly optimistic and did not see the malevolent dimensions of the institution of slavery.[44]

5. Canonical Criticism: Philemon and the Formation of the Pauline Corpus

Fifthly, to step strictly speaking outside of the boundaries of the epistle itself for a moment, Philemon has also had an important role to play in discussions about the New Testament canon. More to the point, Philemon has figured significantly in scholarly debate about the formation and establishment of the Pauline corpus, particularly when it comes to establishing the order of

---

42. Also see Harrill (1998), Combes (1998: 79–82); Harris (1999: 128–31, 141).

43. The work of Patterson (1982) lies behind much of this renewed interest in slavery as a social institution. Interestingly, Patterson (1982: 72, identifies Paul as a key figure in 'the theological transmutation of the order of slavery' by Christianity. Thus, Christian theology interprets salvation not as emancipation in this life, but as spiritual re-enslavement to god. See Combes (1998: 22–24, 87–89); Harris (1999: 151–52), for a brief summary of Patterson's ideas.

44. See Horsley (1998: 19–66) for a survey of scholarship along these lines. Horsley (1998: 167–176) specifically addresses Martin's 1990 monograph, which concentrates on the Corinthian letters of Paul and only refers to the letter to Philemon in passing. Wire (1998: 288–89) and Stowers (1998: 295–311) offer a critique of some of Horsley's ideas, including the use made (or not) of Philemon. Also see Braxton (2000: 177–234).

the letters within the Pauline canon. The traditional close association between Philemon and Colossians is a key factor in these discussions. If, as many scholars suggest, the Pauline letters were arranged within the canon roughly in the order of their length, then the placement of Philemon at the end of the corpus following the relatively short letter to the Colossians makes sense.

Even more significantly, if, as John Knox suggested, Onesimus the bishop of Ephesus was responsible for the collation of the first Pauline corpus, and he was in fact the same Onesimus mentioned in the letter to Philemon, then the role of the letter in the formation of the canon is wholly disproportional to its size.[45] In other words, the brief letter of Philemon may offer a vital clue as to how and why the Pauline corpus first came to be compiled. Indeed, Philemon may be the key to solving one of the long-standing debates about the Pauline corpus, offering what is in effect a literary fingerprint of the person who put the collection together—Onesimus himself. As editor of the corpus, Onesimus appended the letter most intimately concerned with his own situation, Paul's personal letter to his fomer master Philemon, to the end of the collection.

One final methodological point about scholarly study of Philemon is worth noting. This concerns the relationship that the letter has traditionally been thought to have to Colossians, a matter which has tended to mean that the two letters have been treated together. This inevitably means that Philemon has been regarded as something of an afterthought, a mere appendage to Colossians, with the themes, preoccupations and concerns of Colossians setting the agenda.

On the other hand, the fact that Philemon has traditionally been associated so closely with Colossians has meant that the shorter letter has been seen as somewhat at odds with the teaching on slavery contained in Col. 3.22–4.1. The potentially liberating dimensions of Paul's teaching in Philemon simply lie unrecognized, or are at least subsumed, by the advice given to slaves and masters which appears to support the status quo. But what if our interpretation of Philemon is detached from the advice contained within Colossians, perhaps because we feel

---

45. For more on the formation of the Pauline corpus, see Mitton (1955); Finegan (1956: 85–103); Knox (1957: 311–14; 1960: 63–78); Schmithals (1972: 239–74); Gamble (1975: 403–18).

that Colossians does not represent the position of Paul on such matters but is the product of a later disciple? And what if we were to turn to a more authentically Pauline voice to help us determine what Paul's teaching to Philemon and Onesimus was? What if we were to use Galatians, for example, as our starting point, and accept the suggestion made by Neil Elliott in his *Liberating Paul: The Justice of God and the Politics of the Apostle* (1995) that Colossians and the so-called deutero-Pauline epistles represent a 'canonical betrayal' of Paul's teaching on the subject of slavery?[46] If we strike off the chain that has held the letter to Philemon shackled to the letter to the church at Colossae, are different ways of interpreting Philemon created? This is precisely what Lloyd A. Lewis attempts by reading Philemon against the backdrop of Galatians, for example.[47] Lloyd begins with the revolutionary re-definition of the nature of the Christian family that Paul offers to the churches in Galatia and applies that to a reading of Philemon. He suggests that the heavy stress on family relationships within Philemon makes much more sense and offers a clearer picture of what Paul's intentions were in addressing the relationship between Philemon and Onesimus.

This suggests that Philemon has potentially a valuable contribution to make as a letter in its own right. Little wonder then that in recent years several full scale English commentaries on Philemon, as a letter independent of Colossians, have been produced (German scholars have been producing independent commentaries on Philemon for some years).[48] This is an important methodological point, particularly if, as is frequently argued by modern scholars, Colossians is taken to be a *deutero-Pauline* document. However, the situation has changed somewhat with the turn of the new millennium. A number of recent commentaries, in German and English, illustrate this new-found status of Philemon as an independent document. Four of these are particularly worth highlighting briefly. The first is Joseph Fitzmyer's *The Letter to Philemon* (2000), his fourth contribution

---

46. Elliott (1995: 23–54). [Paul's letter to Philemon is specifically discussed by Elliott on pp. 40–48].

47. Lewis (1999: 232–46). Also see Jewett (1994: 64) for a remark along these lines.

48. Several German commentators have produce separate commentaries on Philemon, including Gnilka (1986); Stuhlmacher (2003).

to the prestigious *Anchor Bible* commentary series. Even more substantial is the 560-page volume by Markus Barth and Helmut Blanke entitled *The Letter to Philemon* (2000). A third example is John G. Nordling's *Philemon* (2004), published within the *Concordia Commentary* series and extending to 379 pages. These commentaries are a testimony to the value of Philemon as an independent letter with a distinctive contribution to make to Pauline studies. Also breaking new ground is Peter Arzt-Grabner's *Philemon* (2003), the first volume of the *Papyrologische Kommentar zum Neuen Testament*. This volume of 309 pages sets out to compare the Pauline letter with documentary evidence from the ancient world (notably papyri and ostraca). The aim was to arrive at a better understanding of the social and legal world in which Philemon and his slave Onesimus lived.

Of course the relationship with Colossians still has to be explored and explained within such commentaries, but not at the expense of the artistry of Philemon itself. Interestingly, the first two of these commentaries adopt different answers as to the question of the relationship with Colossians: Barth and Blanke argue for Pauline authorship of Colossians,[49] whereas Fitzymer holds that Colossians is a Deutero-Pauline document written perhaps fifteen years or so *after* Philemon was composed and sent by Paul.[50]

In 1887 Alexander Maclaren likened the connection between Colossians and Philemon as an expression of Paul's artistic abilities as a thinker and writer; he suggests the two letters can be compared to two pieces of art created by the sculptor Michelangelo (1475–1564):

> as if Michael Angelo had gone straight from smiting his magnificent Moses from the marble mass to incise some delicate and tiny figure of Love or Friendship on a gem.[51]

---

49. Barth and Blanke (2000: 130–31).
50. Fitzmyer (2000: 122).
51. Maclaren (1887: 271–72).

1. Commentary

Verses 1-2—Paul's opening description of himself as 'a prisoner' firmly places the letter among the so-called Prison Epistles (similar descriptions are found in Eph. 3.1; 4.1; 2 Tim. 1.8; also see Philemon 9). Where and when such imprisonment took place has been a matter of considerable scholarly debate. Cases have been made for an imprisonment in Ephesus in 52–55 CE, in Caesarea in 58–60, and in Rome in 60–62 (see pages 2–3 for a discussion of the various possibilities). The reference to 'brother Timothy' as a co-sender of the epistle recalls 1 Thess. 1.1; Phil. 1.1; Col. 1.1 and 2 Thess. 1.1, all of which describe him as such.

The named trio of addressees, 'Philemon, Apphia and Archippus', has prompted endless speculation about the precise relationship between them (see pages 32–34 for more on this). Commonly Apphia is taken to be the wife of Philemon, and Archippus their son, although this is not explicitly stated within the text of the letter. Apphia is sometimes taken to be the sister or daughter of Philemon. On the other hand, Archippus is often assumed to be one of the active agents in the establishment of Christianity in the region of the Lycus Valley in Phrygia; the term 'fellow-soldier' lends support to this interpretation (it is used only one other time in the NT, namely of Epaphroditus in Phil. 2.25). The exhortation to Archippus in Col. 4.17 ('See that you fulfill the ministry that you have received in the Lord') is generally regarded to indicate his place as an important leader in the area.

In short, a wide variety of suggestions have been put forward over the years as to what the precise family relationships between Philemon, Apphia and Archippus were, and what implications this has for our understanding of the life of the church in Colossae. Generally it is assumed that all three addressees are related and live under one roof. In this regard, it is perhaps most important to note that v. 2 speaks of the church 'in *your* house' in the singular, probably meaning Philemon's house as *pater familias*. The affectionate description of Philemon as 'beloved fellow-worker' appears to single him out within the apostolic greeting and it is hardly surprising that the church in Colossae is most commonly said to be the one meeting in his house. Interestingly, within this letter Paul similarly describes Mark, Aristarchus, Demas and Luke as 'fellow-workers' (see v. 24). Elsewhere he describes other named Christians as fellow-workers, including Priscilla and Aquila (Rom. 16.3); Urbanus (Rom. 16.9); Timothy (Rom. 16.21; 1 Thess. 3.2); Titus (2 Cor. 8:23); and Epaphroditus (Phil. 2.25).

Verse 3—The two-pronged greeting here offered ('grace and peace to you') is characteristally Pauline; the exact same words are found in Rom. 1.7; 1 Cor. 1.3; 2 Cor. 1.2; Gal. 1.3; Eph. 1.2; Phil. 1.2; Col. 1.2; 1 Thess. 1.2; and 2 Thess. 1.2. The 'you' is here in the plural (in contrast to the singular '*your* house' in v. 2), which probably means that the apostle's focus has shifted from Philemon, the leader, to the congregation at large.

Verses 4–7—Here Paul blends together a thanksgiving about and a prayer for Philemon, following an established pattern in ancient epistolary style. Paul assures Philemon that he is the subject of his prayers, boldly asserting that he makes remembrance of him (v. 4). The apostle also gives thanks to God for Philemon's faith and love, noting how this has been directed towards both the Lord Jesus Christ himself and his saints (v. 5).

The word 'always' appears strategically placed within the first part of the paragraph, although its meaning is not entirely clear. It could mean that Paul '*always* gives thanks to God', or it could mean that he '*always* remembers Philemon in his prayers'. Effectively the placement of the adverb means that it does double-duty within the thought.

Once again the 'your' in v. 5a ('hearing of your love and faith') is singular, focusing on Philemon's own individual faith and love. *How* Paul came to hear about Philemon's qualities in this regard is not made clear, although the phrase is generally taken to mean that Paul had some external source of information. It is possible that it was Onesimus himself who reported to Paul about Philemon's character as a Christian leader in the church at Colossae. A more likely possibility is that it was Epaphras who offered a report about Philemon. After all, Epaphras is mentioned in v. 25 as being present with Paul in his imprisonment, and Col. 1.7–8 and 4.12–13 intimate that Epaphras (not Paul!) had been instrumental in first bringing the gospel to the city of Colossae.

Verse 6 is notoriously difficult to interpret and represents the only serious challenge for textual critics within the letter (see page 4 on this point). The meaning of the Greek text itself is by no means clear, and the precise connection with what precedes in v. 5 is not easy to determine. Clearly the verse is meant to communicate the substance of Paul's petition, but what exactly was Paul wishing for within his prayer?

The opening phrases 'the sharing of your faith' and 'may promote' (as they are translated in the RSV) are very odd indeed. Some commentators interpret them to mean that Paul is voicing the hope that Philemon's faith might somehow prove to be an effective force within his own life. However, this seems to fly in the face of what Paul has been just declaring about Philemon's demonstrated character in vv. 4–5. Perhaps a better way of reading it is to take it as expressing Paul's hope for other Christian believers to find the kind of faith that characterized Philemon's life. This connects with the ending of v. 6, which appears to suggest that this will be 'acknowledged by everything that is good in you'. The concluding phrase of v. 6 is also awkward—it is strictly speaking 'into Christ', or 'with reference to Christ', and probably means 'for the sake of the Christian church'.

Verse 7 continues the positive description of Philemon's impact upon the believers with whom he has contact. Paul here again mentions in 7a Philemon's 'love' for the Christian faith (the same term was used earlier in v. 5). Interestingly, Philemon's love results in Paul's own 'joy' and 'comfort', two terms with rich association in Paul's letters. The phrase in 7a has been taken to hint at comfort which had been offered to Paul at some point during his imprisonment (the verb 'I have derived' is an epistolary aorist). This is a possible interpretation, but it is not certain that such practical support or consolation was necessarily what Paul had in mind.

In 7b Philemon is addressed as 'brother' a second time (see v. 1), and said to be the instrument of the 'refreshing of the hearts of the saints'. This is also the second time in the letter that the Christian believers are described as 'saints' (see v. 5). The term that is commonly rendered 'hearts' is somewhat unusual here; it is a physiological term meaning 'entrails' or 'inmost parts' (the AV renders it as 'bowels'). It is a term indicative of the intensity of emotion, and as such is an important means for Paul to communicate the depth of his feelings within the letter (he also uses the term in vv. 12 and 20). Paul elsewhere uses the term in 2 Cor. 6.12; Phil. 1.8; 2.1; and Col. 3.12. It is worth noting that the prayer and thanksgiving that Paul offers for Philemon in vv. 4–7 has as its final word in Greek the term translated as 'brother'. This fondly fraternal note paves the way for the body of the letter (vv. 8–20), wherein Paul's main reason for writing to Philemon about Onesimus is set forth. Understandably, the whole of this central section is addressed directly to Philemon himself and all the relevant pronouns ('you') are in the singular.

Verses 8–9—Paul here commences his appeal to Philemon for Onesimus, employing a range of complex rhetorical strategies in the process (see pages 7–8 for a discussion of the significance of rhetorical studies of Paul's letter). He does this first of all with a gentle assertion that he could *order* Philemon to do the proper thing, but that he has chosen instead to appeal to him to act out of love in the matter. At the same time, Paul also hints that his position in Christ gives him enough confidence ('boldness') to command Philemon to do what he wanted, should he have chosen to do so. Interestingly, Paul does not invoke his authority as an apostle in this regard, although that authority seems to be lurking just beneath the surface. It is probably significant that the term 'apostle' does not appear anywhere in the letter to Philemon. Perhaps Paul felt that in this instance the explicit invocation of such apostolic authority would have backfired and done more harm than good.

In 9b Paul injects two other ideas into his overall argument. First of all he intimates that his position as an 'old man' (the rendering of the NRSV) warrants some additional consideration by Philemon. In other words, the fact that Paul is in some respect Philemon's *senior* in the faith is brought to bear within the discussion. At first glance this seems straightforward enough, and makes good sense, particularly when it is noted that Paul strengthens the point by including his own name in the phrase ('Paul, an old man'). However, there is some basis for adopting an alternative reading in the verse (the RSV renders the crucial term as 'ambassador'). Within the Greek manuscripts of Philemon there is textual variation within the key term here; some manuscripts read *presbutes* ('old man') and others read *presbeutes* ('ambassador'). However, it is possible that a stronger distinction between the two alternatives can be made than is really justified. In practice, there was little difference between the two in Paul's day—ambassadors were invariably older, more mature men. There are some indications that ambassadorial language was used by Paul as a way of describing the Christian ministry (see 2 Cor. 5.20; also note Eph. 6.20). On the other hand, assuming for the moment that the term 'old man' was what Paul intended here, some commentators have attempted to determine Paul's age (and more precisely plot a chronology of the apostle's life) on the basis of the verse (see pages 46 for a discussion of this).

Secondly, Paul reasserts (see v. 1) the fact that he is 'a prisoner of Jesus Christ', stressing that he was currently ('now') in this state. This contrasts Paul's incarceration with Philemon's freedom, at the same time adding additional weight to Paul's rhetorical argument.

Verses 10-12—Paul here comes to the crux of the matter and states his reason for writing the letter to Philemon. In v. 10 he makes an appeal for Onesimus, whom he describes as 'my child, whose father I have become in my imprisonment'. The use of familial language is not unusual for Paul; he frequently used it to describe his relationship with his converts (see 1 Cor. 4.1, 4-15; 2 Cor. 6.13; Gal. 4.19; and Phil. 2.22). Several features of the verse have been hotly debated by commentators over the years, most notably the meaning of the prepositional phrase *'for my son'*. Generally this is take to mean that Paul is making an appeal *'on behalf of* my son', although some recent interpreters, notably John Knox and Sara B.C. Winter, have suggested that the true meaning is more literal than this. They take this phrase to infer that *Onesimus* is the object of the appeal and that Paul is asking for Onesimus himself, ie. that Philemon would in some sense give Onesimus to Paul (see pages 56-57 for a fuller discussion of this).

The circumstances of how and when Paul brought Onesimus to Christian faith are unclear. Much depends on the historical reconstruction that is accepted as to the time and place of Paul's imprisonment. A number of possible scenarios have been put forward, but a consensus has not been reached on the matter. Generally it is assumed that Onesimus visited Paul at some time during the apostle's imprisonment and that this was the catalyst for his conversion. It is possible that Onesimus himself was also in prison *with* Paul, although nothing within the letter confirms this, and it does make Paul's sending Onesimus (a fellow-prisoner!) to Colossae difficult to imagine.

Paul strategically withholds the name of his child in the faith, Onesimus, until the end of v. 10. This is the only time that he is named within the letter, although it is generally agreed that there is a word-play on his name in v. 20 (see below). The name 'Onesimus' ('Useful') was a common one in Paul's day, and there are numerous examples of it within surviving documents (examples of it being used for both slaves and freemen are extant).

Onesimus is mentioned only one other time in Paul's letters, in Col. 4.7–9 where the arrangements for the delivery of the apostle's letter to the church in Colossae through the agency of Tychicus are set forth. The parallel reference is significant, for in it Paul not only expounds upon his assessment of the character of Onesimus, describing him as 'a faithful and beloved brother', but notes that he is 'one of you' (ie. from Colossae). The identification of Onesimus as a Colossian is generally taken to carry with it the inference that Philemon was also a Colossian. It should be noted that such hypothetical reconstructions of the letter to Philemon assume a close historical relationship between Colossians and Philemon (a point challenged by those who take Colossians to be a Deutero-Pauline document).

In v. 11 Paul continues his assessment of Onesimus, injecting into a structured time-frame ('formerly' and 'now') a word-play on two Greek words that is difficult to convey into English. The two words *achreston* and *euchreston* have the same root (*chrestos*, meaning 'good'), but have different prefixes which set up the word-play. Commonly English translations attempt to convey the word-play by using the words 'useless' and 'useful' as equivalents to the two Greek terms. What is also interesting about this particular verse is the way that Paul again employs the rhetorical strategy of aligning himself with Philemon ('[Onesimus is now] useful *to you and to me*').

In v. 12 Paul states that he is sending Onesimus back to Philemon, emphasizing once again how close the tie is with Onesimus by describing him as part of his very 'heart' (see v. 7 above). It has been argued that the verb *anepempsa* means '*to send up* (to a higher authority)', as in Luke 23.7, where Pilate *sent* Jesus to Herod's jurisdiction. However, this is probably to read too much into the circumstances of the situation involving Onesimus and Philemon, and here it simply means *to send back*, as in Luke 23.11 where the same verb is used to describe Herod *sending Jesus back* to Pilate. There is some suggestion within the choice of the verb 'to send back' that Onesimus was originally sent to Paul, and that Paul is now returning him. *Who* might have sent Onesimus to Paul (was it Philemon? the church at Colossae?) is of course left open (see pages 63–65 for more on the scholarly suggestions about this).

Verses 13-14—Paul now moves to declare his own desires in the situation and offer a suggestion as to how the gift of Onesimus might become an extension of Philemon's support for the apostle's Christian mission. He admits that he wished 'to retain' Onesimus with him, although how advanced Paul's thinking was in working out the details of this arrangement is impossible to determine. However, Paul's stated desire seems to be at odds with the implied wishes of Onesimus; reading between the lines we detect that Onesimus wanted to return to Philemon in Colossae.

In v. 13b Paul's imprisonment in the service of Christ is again injected into the discussion ('in my bonds for the gospel'). This is the only time that the term *euangelion* appears in the letter, but it is not clear if Paul here means the gospel *message* he proclaims, or his *ministry* in preaching the gospel. Interestingly, Paul here seems to assume that Philemon wanted to serve him in this ministry, and identifies Onesimus as the means whereby this might happen. That Onesimus could substitute for Philemon in this regard is indicated by the phrase *huper sou*, which is translated 'on your behalf' (RSV) or 'in your place' (NRSV).

In v. 14 Paul brings the considerations of Philemon to the fore, declaring that he did not want to act without his (Philemon's) consent in the matter. Underlying this statement is the recognition that Philemon's rights over Onesimus have a higher legal priority than do Paul's. Yet, Paul hopes that Philemon's consent in the matter would not be forced, but be willing and voluntary. Occasionally, commentators have argued that the obtaining of such consent is the real reason for Paul writing the letter in the first place, and that a structural analysis of the letter highlights v. 14 as the central point in Paul's argument (see page 9–10 for an example of this).

Verses 15-16—These verses contain a veiled hint of the estrangement between Onesimus and Philemon, although it is delicately expressed by Paul. At the same time the apostle takes the argument in a surprising new direction by elaborating on the nature of the relationship between them as Christian believers, intimating that a profound change needs to be taken account of which is filled with new possibilities and challenges.

In v. 15a Paul suggests that Onesimus 'was separated for a time', the verb (*echorizesthe*) is cleverly put in the passive voice in order to leave open the question of who the instigator was in their separation. Many commentators see this as a divine passive, meaning that the hand of God was active in and through the process. Where and when the separation first occurred is not stated, but it does not need to be since the estrangement between Onesimus and Philemon is soon to be overcome. In v. 15b Paul contrasts the temporary separation with an eternal reconciliation between the two men, 'that you might have him back *forever*'. The use of *hina* ('in order that') suggests that Paul detected a theological dynamic of cause-and-effect at work here, which is perhaps reminiscent of Rom. 8:28 ('we know that God causes all things to work together for good') (NAS). It is worth noting that Paul avoids using the verb 'to flee' (*pheugein*—the root of our English word 'fugitive') when describing Onesimus's estrangement from Philemon. This has been seen by some commentators to undermine the traditional theory that Onesimus was a runaway slave (*fugitivus*) (see pages 62–63 below).

Verse 16 is in many respects the theological heart and soul of the letter, for here Paul lays out a challenge to Philemon to put the message of Christian reconciliation into practice. Philemon is to lay aside his previous way of regarding Onesimus, and adopt a new way of regarding him. Paul asserts that Onesimus is now no longer to be seen as a *slave*, but he is to be accepted as a *brother*. Much depends upon the meaning of the Greek term *doulos* in v. 16a, and nowhere is this more clearly seen than in the debates during the nineteenth century when advocates of slavery and abolitionists squared off against each other in acrimonious debate over this verse. Philemon became a popular proof-text for both sides of the argument, with abolitionists insisting that *doulos* did not mean 'slave' but 'servant', a point fiercely denied by supporters of the institution of slavery (see pages 101–103 for details). What is most striking about the passage is that it is ultimately only v. 16 that provides any textual basis for the traditional understanding of Onesimus as the slave of his master Philemon.

In recent years a similar similar interpretative debate has taken place about the meaning of the term *adelphos* ('brother') in v. 16a. Does Paul mean here, as is commonly assumed, that Onesimus is to be regarded as a *spiritual*, or *Christian* brother? Or is a more literal reading of the word to be adopted? Allen Dwight Callahan has done precisely this by suggesting that

Onesimus was the actual *physical* brother of Philemon (see pages 65–66 for more on this point).

In v. 16b Paul again brings his personal evaluation of Onesimus to bear in the matter, noting that he is a beloved brother 'especially to me'. He then goes on immediately to draw out the implications of this for Philemon, suggesting that if this was so for Paul himself, how much more it must be true for Philemon. The meaning of the concluding phrase of the verse, 'both in the flesh and in the Lord', is unclear. Generally it is taken to mean 'both as a human being and as a Christian'. The Greek phrase *en sarki* can carry such anthropological connotations (Paul uses it of his own life as a man in Gal. 4.4). Certainly the essential truth here about Onesimus's dual status as a human being and a brother within the Christian community was well captured by abolitionists in the debate over slavery. Beginning in 1792 the slogan 'Am I Not a Man and a Brother?' began to appear within literature and promotional materials associated with the abolitionist campaign (see page 171–173 for details).

Verses 17-18—Paul continues his advocacy on behalf of Onesimus by requesting that the treatment of Onesimus by Philemon be an extension of how Paul himself would be treated ('accept him as you would me'). Interestingly this appeal is based on an assumed relationship between Paul and Philemon, which he describes in 16a as a 'partnership'. The Greek term used here (*koinonon*) can mean a financial partnership, and it has been taken to infer that Paul had some sort of business relationship or commercial arrangement with Philemon.

Verse 17 hints at two possible grounds for the rift that has developed between Onesimus and Philemon, both of which Paul promises personally to address. Both moral offence ('if he wronged you') and financial indebtedness ('if he owes you anything') are specifically mentioned. Interestingly, the two ideas are commonly brought together in hypothetical reconstructions of Onesimus as a slave who stole from his master and ran away. *How* Onesimus offended Philemon, and *what* Onesimus owed him, are unfortunately not made clear. Perhaps Paul did not know, or simply wished to avoid mentioning painful details within this tactful letter. In any event, Paul asks Philemon to put these things on his (Paul's) tab. The verb used here ('charge') is a common term within the world of accountancy and sets up the declaration contained in v. 19.

28   Commentary

Verses 19-20—At this point Paul appears to take up the pen from his amanuensis Timothy and sign the letter, promising himself to repay whatever Onesimus owes (the 'I, Paul' is emphatic). This is not the only time that Paul signed one of his letters (see 1 Cor. 16.21; Gal. 6.11; and Col. 4.18), but it is the only time that he assumes financial responsibility for one of his converts. The Greek verb *apotiso* ('I will repay') is found only here in the NT, although there are rare instances of its use in other literature. For instance, there is an interesting instance of it being used by Josephus when he promises to repay twenty gold pieces taken from a royal palace in Galilee during the Jewish revolt (*Life of Josephus* 298).

In v. 19b Paul adds an aside which seems designed to quell any objections that Philemon might have had about the arrangements for repayment of Onesimus's debt. The apostle reminds Philemon that he owes his very self to Paul (the Greek verb *prospheileis* ('you owe') is a *hapax legomenon* within the NT). This is probably an allusion to Philemon's status as a Christian believer, although it could just as easily be a reference to some other agreement that Paul made with Philemon, perhaps in connection with a business arrangement (see v. 16 above). Perhaps the phrase is a gentle reminder to Philemon that Christianity had originally been brought to Colossae and the Lycus valley by Epaphras, who was acting as Paul's envoy at the time (see v. 5 above). The essential point is hinted at again in v. 23 where the figure of Epaphras is again mentioned.

In v. 20 Paul again underscores his close friendship with Philemon, addressing him as 'brother' for the third time within the letter (see vv. 1 and 7). Paul asks Philemon to 'refresh my heart', an appeal that recalls v. 7 where the ministry that Philemon had in refreshing 'the hearts of the saints' (presumably in Colossae) was noted. The most unusual feature of the verse is the request 'I want some benefit from you' (RSV). The word translated 'benefit' (the Greek term is *onaimen*) here is generally acknowledged to be related to the Greek name *Onesimus*, and may be a deliberate move on the part of Paul to recall the word-play contained in v. 11. If so, Onesimus himself is the 'Benefit' that Paul wishes Philemon to provide for him.

Verses 21-22—Paul now moves to enlarge the request he has made of Philemon, doing so on the basis of his confidence in the obedience of his friend. As Paul puts it, he is sure that Philemon 'will do even more than I say', although it is by no means clear precisely what this means as far as Onesimus himself is concerned. Frequently commentators suggest that Onesimus's manumission by Philemon is what Paul has in mind, although it needs to be stressed that the text (at best!) only hints at this as the action Paul expects. Some commentators are quick to invoke 1 Cor. 7:21b as shedding additional light on Paul's attitudes to slavery, but the verse is notoriously ambiguous. A comparison of how it is rendered in tne RSV ('But if you can gain your freedom, avail yourself of the opportunity') and the NRSV ('Even if you can gain your freedom, make use of your present condition now more than ever') illustrates the point.

In v. 22 more practical arrangements are addressed as Paul instructs Philemon to prepare a place for him to stay, presumably when he next visits Colossae. He further binds Philemon and the church of Colossae to himself by stating that he hopes to grace them with his presence, and that such a visitation might come about 'through your prayers' (the 'your' is plural).

Verses 23–25—In v. 23 Paul conveys the greetings of his colleague Epaphras, whom he describes as a 'fellow-soldier in Christ Jesus'. The Greek term translated 'fellow-soldier' (*sunaichmalotos*) is used only one other time in the NT (of Aristarchus in Col. 4.10). It is likely that Epaphras was with Paul in prison, although whether Epaphras was himself under house-arrest is not certain. The importance of Epaphras in bringing the Christian faith to the Lycus valley has already been noted (see vv. 5 and 19 above), and it is not without significance that Epaphras is the first person who is mentioned in the greetings.

In v. 24 the greetings of four others who are with Paul are conveyed: Mark, Aristarchus, Demas and Luke (they are collectively described as 'fellow-workers'). Each of the four appears elsewhere in the NT, notably in the greetings section of Col. 4.10–14. Mark is usually identified with the John Mark (the cousin of Barnabas) who is mentioned in Acts 12.12, 25 and 15.37–39. If this is correct, then the more positive references to Mark contained here and in Col. 4.10 (and 2 Tim. 4.11?) represent a reconciliation between him and Paul. Aristarchus, as just noted in the discussion of v. 23, is mentioned in Col. 4.10, although he also appears in Acts 20.4 where he is said to be from the port city of Thessalonica. Demas is mentioned in Col. 4.14 and 2 Tim. 4.10, although in the latter reference he is said to have deserted Paul and returned to Thessalonica (see page 60 below). Luke is mentioned in Col. 4.14, where he described as 'the beloved physician', and in 2 Tim. 4.11, where he is said to be the only remaining companion with Paul.

The concluding benediction in v. 25 ('The grace of the Lord Jesus Christ be with your spirit') is similar to those which close other letters of Paul. Indeed, all of the letters within the Pauline corpus conclude with a note of 'grace' (Rom. 16.20; 1 Cor. 16.23; 2 Cor. 13.13; Gal. 6.18; Eph. 6.24; Phil. 4.23; Col. 4.18; 1 Thess. 5.28; 2 Thess. 3.18; 1 Tim. 6.21; 2 Tim. 4.22; Tit. 3:15). The oldest surviving manuscript fragment of Philemon (P^{87}) has a shortened version of the benediction which is void of qualifying genitive phrases; it reads simply 'Grace be with you', exactly the same concluding benediction that is found in Col. 4:18. The papyrus dates from the mid-second century CE, and may be taken as evidence that there was a close association between Philemon and Colossians at a very early stage within the manuscript tradition of the two letters.

2. A Question of Characters

The letter to Philemon contains only 335 words in Greek, a brevity which has prompted one popular exposition of the letter to describe it as 'a postcard from Paul' (Cross 1999: 70). Yet, this briefest of the letters in the Pauline corpus has generated an enormous amount of scholarly speculation over the centuries. Debates rage over the letter's original historical setting and the connections between the various people named within it, notably Philemon and Onesimus. An astonishing range of reconstructions of the historical circumstances surrounding the relationship between Philemon and Onesimus have been put forward. Perhaps the most radical interpretation of all was that proposed by Carl von Weizsäcker, who in 1895 denied that there was any real personal relationships to be deduced from the letter at all. Instead, he suggested that Onesimus need not even have been a real person, but merely a figurative one. On the basis of the pun in v. 10 on the name of Onesimus as 'Useful', Weizsäcker (1895: 245) argued that the letter of Philemon was simply an allegory aimed at presenting new teaching for the Christian life. Generally, less reductionistic opinions have prevailed, and attention has focused on the human figures whose enigmatic existence is conveyed to us through the words of the epistle.

So who are the people mentioned in the letter? Who is contained in the cast of characters of this one-act drama from the pen of Paul? The statistical evidence contined in the 25 verses of the letter is quite surprising. In addition to threefold mention of Paul himself (vv. 1, 9, 19), and the eight references to the Lord Jesus Christ (vv. 1, 3, 5, 8, 9, 20, 23, 25), there are ten, and possibly eleven, other personal names recorded within the letter. These are: Timothy (v. 1), Philemon (v. 1), Apphia (v. 2), Archippus (v. 2), Onesimus (v. 10), Epaphras (v. 23), Mark (v. 24), Aristarchus (v. 24), Demas (v. 24), Luke (v. 24), and perhaps Jesus Justus (v. 24). The last of these names (Jesus Justus) raises some unusual questions, notably the possibility of its absence being due to a simple mistake by an early copyist. This is the argument of Ernst Amling

(1909: 261–62), who suggested that the omission of the name of Jesus Justus in v. 24 was a result of scribal error (the parallel in Col. 4.11, where Jesus Justus *is* named, is crucial for his argument). On the other hand, E.F. Scott (1930: 115) and G.B. Caird (1976: 223), suggested that Jesus Justus was not mentioned in Philemon simply because he was not known to Philemon personally. In any event, compared to Paul's other letters these eleven names represent a disproportionately high number of named individuals for a letter of this size. Not surprisingly, an array of different possibilities have been put forward over the years to explain not only how these various people were related one to another, but where they were all geographically located. Of crucial importance is the relationship between the people commonly identified as the original recipients of Paul's letter.

1. The Addressees—Philemon, Apphia and Archippus

What are we to make of the three named addressees of the letter, Philemon, Apphia and Archippus? Based on the close association of these three names in vv. 1–2, it has most often been suggested that the letter was directed to Philemon himself (as v. 1 implies), and that Apphia was Philemon's wife and Archippus their son. (Gorday 2000: 311 gives some examples from patristic writers, including Chrysostom, Pelagius, and Theodore of Mopsuestia.) Moreover, it is generally assumed that a Christian church met in their home in Colossae; v. 2, when linked to Col. 4.9, hints in this direction (see M.R. Vincent (1897: 176) and G.B. Caird (1976: 219) for remarks along these lines). This is perhaps the simplest reading of the text, and as a line of interpretation it has a long history behind it. Theodore of Mopsuestia (c. 350–428) was among the first to suggest that Archippus was Philemon's son, for example. Jerome (c. 342–420) concurred, although he believed that Archippus, not Philemon, was the leader of the church at Colossae. Numerous variations to this 'straightforward' reading exist, however. It seems that ingenuity reigns among scholars eager to establish alternative scenarios.

The relationship between Philemon and Apphia is a case in point. W.G. Kümmel (1975: 348) accepted that the Christians of Colossae met in Philemon's house, but thought that Apphia was his sister, not his wife. Carolyn Osiek (2000: 134) noted that Apphia *could* have been the wife of Archippus, although it would be rather unusual for the wife to be named before her husband.

C.H. Dodd (1929: 1292), on the other hand, pointed out that Archippus could have been *either* the son of Philemon and Apphia, *or* even the brother of one or the other of them. In short, the opening verses of the letter open up a number of possibilities as to the precise familial relationships between the three named recipients, Philemon, Apphia and Archippus. That is not the end of the matter, however.

A complementary range of possibilities arises when it comes to trying to determine where the Christian community to which they all belong was located Can we assume that it was the church at Colossae, or do other possibilities exist? What about the nearby towns of Laodicea, or even Hierapolis, as alternative places? There was, after all, a great deal of co-operation and contact between the churches of the Lycus valley, as Paul's exhortation in Col. 4.16 to read each other's letters confirms. We casually assume that Philemon's church was based in Colossae, but is this correct? Serious doubts have been raised about this, and alternative scenarios proposed over the years. Some of these have focused on the location of the church, and others have focused on its leader(s).

A good example of this is Martin Luther, who in 1528 argued that the congregation mentioned in Philemon 2 met in the house of Archippus, not Philemon (see Luther 1973: 271). John Calvin thought that Apphia was the wife of Philemon and that the church in Colossae met in their house, but conjectured that Archippus served as a co-pastor of the congregation (see Calvin 1964: 393). Another case in point is E.J. Goodspeed, who thought that Apphia was probably Philemon's wife, but similarly suggested that Archippus was actually the leader of the church that met in Philemon's house (E.F. Scott 1930: 98 similarly suggested that Archippus was more prominent within the life of the church than was Philemon). Moreover, in Goodspeed's opinion this church was in the city of Laodicea, not Colossae (see Goodspeed 1933: 6–8; 1937: 112; 1947: 208 for more on this point). Similarly, Alexander Maclaren (1887: 276–77) suggested that Archippus was the son of Philemon and Apphia, and that he lived with them in Colossae; he further suggested that Archippus worked over in Laodicea where he served as bishop of the church there. J.B. Lightfoot (1916: 307) also argued that Archippus was the son of Philemon and Apphia, and that his household was located not in Colossae (as is generally assumed), but in nearby Laodicea. A related suggestion was first made by John Knox, who pointed out that all the opening verses of the letter really tell us is that Paul addressed it to three individuals, and to the church that met in the house of *one* of them (the reference to '*your* house' in v. 2 is singular in Greek). Knox points out that it is only an assumption on our part that the *first* of those three people, namely Philemon, was the main recipient of the letter. Consequently, Knox proposed that *Archippus* was actually the person who owned Onesimus, and that this makes better sense of the complementary reference to Archippus in Col. 4.16–17 (more on this creative suggestion by Knox below). Similarly, Sara B.C. Winter (1984: 204; 1987: 2) argued that Onesimus had actually been sent to Paul by Philemon and the congregation which met in the house of Archippus in Colossae. She argued the slave was intended as a gift to Paul in order to assist him in his ministry, much as the church in Philippi sent Epaphroditus. Similarly, Wolfgang Schenk (1987: 3460–61), suggested that Onesimus was sent by Philemon to Paul, an idea that has been critiqued by a number of recent commentators (see Marshall 1993: 179; Dunn 1996: 331; Osiek 2000: 129; Arzt-Grabner 2001: 602–608, for more on this point). Schenk extended his argument in another contentious direction. He pressed the geographical distance involved in interpreting the letter to Philemon even further and maintained that Philemon, Apphia, and Archippus were based in Pergamum in western Asia Minor (see Schenk 1987: 3482–83). He does this by associating Philemon 22 with 2 Cor. 1.8 and 2.12, and suggesting that Pergamum was an established Hellenistic city where slave ownership played a significant role in civic life. This is an intriguing suggestion, but since it lacks a credible basis in the text of the letter, it is not one that has been well received.

2. The Supporting Cast: Epaphras and Nympha

Speculation about other people named within the letter to Philemon, and the closely related Colossians, has also been widespread. How do these various figures fit within the overall situation involving Philemon and Onesimus which lies at the heart of the letter to Philemon? What sort of alternative arrangements does this cast of supporting characters imply?

A case in point is the figure of Epaphras, who is named three times in the New Testament (Col. 1.7, 4.12; Philemon 23). On the strength of Col. 1.6–7, Epaphras is generally regarded as the person responsible for first bringing the Christian faith to

Colossae. Not surprisingly, Epaphras has featured regularly in attempts to reconstruct the historical situation involving Paul and Onesimus. Thus, A.N. Wilson suggested that Epaphras might have been the person responsible for bringing Onesimus to Paul in prison (controversially, Wilson pushed this idea a step further by suggesting that Paul's devotion to the young slave Onesimus was motivated by homosexual interests). Similarly, both Adolf Diessman (1926: 20) and Hans Binder (1990: 35) speculated that Onesimus had himself been arrested and was put in prison, which is where he first met Paul. Meanwhile, Henneke Gülzow (1969: 31) and Peter Stuhlmacher (1975: 49) thought that Onesimus may have even taken money from Philemon in order to finance his flight from Philemon, and G.B. Caird (1976: 223) similarly remarked about Onesimus, 'He must have helped himself to at least enough to pay his way to Rome.' On the other hand, Allen Dwight Callahan (1993: 357–76; 1997), in one of the most innovative interpretations of the letter to appear in recent years, argued that Onesimus was not the slave of Philemon at all, but rather his *blood brother* from whom he was estranged.

A.T. Robertson (1974: 279) once pondered whether the church that met in Philemon's house was in fact the same congregation that met in the house of Nympha in Laodicea (Col. 4.15). The mysterious reference to the church at Nympha's house raises another set of interesting possibilities pursued by commentators. Leslie Houlden (1970: 126), for example, speculated whether Nympha may have been the hostess in the church of which Philemon was the leader. On the other hand, W.G. Kümmel (1975: 337) suggested on the basis of Philemon 2 and Col. 4.15, 17 that there were *two* house churches in Colossae (a suggestion which means that he takes Nympha also to have been from Colossae).

3. The Principal Players: Paul, Philemon and Onesimus

As can readily be seen, much depends on the relationship that is imagined to gave existed between Paul and Philemon, and what role Onesimus had within it. So how close was the relationship between Paul and Philemon? Of what did it consist? Of course, the two men were brothers in the Christian faith, but was that the extent of their friendship? Several different ideas have been put forward which move beyond a mere 'spiritual' relationship between the two men.

For example, E.F. Scott (1930: 102) suggested that Paul and Philemon may have shared a business interest associated with the church in Ephesus (Houlden [1970: 228] and Dunn [1996: 301] concur). Scott (1930: 105–106) also conjectured on the meaning of the unspecified 'kindness' in v. 7, and suggested that it was an allusion to the fact that Philemon was responsible for 'the refreshing of the saints' following an earthquake which struck the Lycus valley in 60 CE (the region was notorious for seismic activity). Scott's point seems corroborated by the face that Tacitus, *Annals* 14.27, recorded a major earthquake which leveled the city of Laodicea in 60 CE. The fact that Paul does not specifically mention this disaster *may* indicate that Philemon was written prior to it, but there are some indications that the earthquake is alluded to in the Pauline letter (see Kreitzer 2004: 81–94, for further details). Wilfred Knox (1932: 136) also picked up on Philemon's assumed benefaction to the church at Colossae, describing him as 'a wealthy magnate of a small provincial town'. F.B. Meyer (1953: 187) wrote that Paul had a business account with Philemon, while E.H. Plumptre (1875: 262–63) went so far as to suggest that the reference to 'partner' (*koinonos*) in v. 17 may be a reflection of the fact that Paul and Philemon were business partners, with either Philemon or Archippus taking the place of Aquila and Priscilla in their tent-making enterprise (he also suggested that Onesimus served as the amanuensis when Paul dictated the letter to Philemon). However, Stephen Motyer (1986: 3) suggested that there may have been tensions between Philemon and Paul, pointing out that v. 13 hints that Paul might be fearful of Philemon's complacency in the service of the gospel, and that Onesimus was in this respect serving *on behalf of Philemon*. The trajectory of this 'business-partner' line of thought has been taken even further by others. On the basis of papyrological evidence, Peter Arzt-Grabner recently interpreted 'partner' (*koinonos*) in v. 17 to infer that Paul wanted Philemon to make a business partner of Onesimus (see Arzt-Graber 2001: 608–14; 2003: 226–29).

The big questions that remain, of course, are inextricably bound up with the mystery that lies at the heart of the letter. What was Paul's relationship with Onesimus? And even more importantly, what was his purpose in writing the letter to Philemon? It is common to interpret the paternal language in v. 10 as inferring that Onesimus was brought to Christian faith through Paul. Indeed, Chrysostom (1889: 545) went so far as to suggest on the basis of his verse that Paul may have also baptized him. As already noted, some commentators argue that Onesimus was actually commissioned by the church in Colossae to Paul in prison, just as the church in Philippi sent along Epaphroditus (see Phil. 2.25).

However, until rather recently the vast majority of interpreters have assumed that the relationship between Philemon and Paul was inextricably bound up with the person of Onesimus. Clearly, for some reason Paul wrote to Philemon with Onesimus in mind, but what precisely was the relationship between Onesimus and Philemon? Unfortunately, the text of Paul's letter to Philemon is anything but clear on this particular point. The traditional way of understanding the letter is to take Onesimus to be Philemon's runaway slave, a *fugitivus*, whose actions in escaping brought the force of the Roman law dealing with such cases upon him. It is to this traditional interpretation that we now turn.

3. The Traditional Interpretation: The Case of the Runaway Slave

In some respects the letter to Philemon is one of the most human stories in the Bible, for it concerns two flesh-and-blood individuals trying to find their relative places in the world and learning to live together under challenging circumstances. Arguably it is the most personal incident involving the apostle Paul that has been recorded within his letters. Here we see him getting personally involved with Philemon and Onesimus in a way that is uncharacteristic; here he lays himself on the line, not only theologically, but also socially and financially. Or so it appears. However, the precise circumstances of the relationship between the two central characters, Philemon and Onesimus, is by no means clear within the letter. Indeed, the circumstances surrounding Onesimus's flight from Philemon, and his (presumed) theft from his master, remain frustratingly obscure. In an attempt to shed light on the subject some scholars have turned to the Roman laws governing the penalties for harbouring runaway slaves (P. R. Coleman-Norton (1951: 172–77) offers a good introduction to the matter). It is, or course, impossible to know if these laws were applicable to the case of Onesimus given that we do not know the legal status of his owner (presumably Philemon). However, it is clear that slaves running away from their masters was one of the ways in which slavery was actively resisted within antiquity (Callahan and Horsley 1998: 139–43, discuss this). It is just possible that Onesimus falls within this category of resistance.

By reading between the lines of the text of Philemon a tantaylzing glimpse of Paul's involvement in the struggle between its two estranged figures is possible. Not surprisingly, there has been considerable debate amongst scholars as to the nature of the letter and the story contained within it. Clearly, at the simplest level, it is a missive from the apostle Paul to a Christian believer named Philemon; of that there is little doubt. But was it a *personal* letter from Paul to him about a private matter, with no intention of it ever being a matter of public discussion? This approach was adopted by J.B. Lightfoot (1916: 301) who once famously described Philemon as 'a strictly private letter'. Or was it a *public* letter, one really written with a larger group in mind, the church at Colossae perhaps, and was it merely directed to Philemon as a key figure involved within that congregation? A number of interpreters follow this way of interpreting the letter (see Ollrog 1979: 104; Winter 1987: 1–2; Dunn 1996: 301). Both readings of Philemon ('public' letter and 'private' letter) have been put forward by scholars over the years. Common to both is the idea that Paul wrote to Philemon in Colossae about the position of Onesimus, the slave of Philemon, whom Paul had somehow befriended. But beyond that there are several crucial questions that need to be addressed. Just what was the relationship between Onesimus and Philemon, and how and why did Paul presume to address it? An even more open-ended question is what happened to Onesimus and Philemon after Paul's letter was received in Colossae?

Exploration of these questions can here be handled under four headings, the first concentrating on the career of Philemon, notably his position as a slave-owner, and the other three addressing roles commonly assigned to Onesimus (fugitive, convert, and bishop). Taken together these four headings help set the parameters of what has been described as the 'traditional' interpretation of the epistle. They help affirm the suggestion that Onesimus was a slave who ran away from his master Philemon, and that he was converted to Christian faith by Paul the apostle. They also invite a brief exploration of the tradition surrounding the subsequent career of Onesimus as the bishop of Ephesus, and the legends surrounding the martyrdom of both Philemon and Onesimus, the former under Nero in 64 CE, and the latter in Rome during the reign of Domitian in c. 96 CE.

I turn now to consider these four headings in turn. At the same time, I want to call attention to some of the ways in which both Philemon and Onesimus have been interpreted in art through the centuries. Given the dramatic nature of Onesimus's life-story, it is perhaps not surprising that all three stages of his life (from fugitive, to convert, to martyred bishop) have become focal points in their own right for Christian art through the centuries. At one level this may seem somewhat unjust, for there has not been quite the same fascination for Philemon, the slave-owner from Colossae. Ironically, there is a sense in which it is true to say that Philemon, the master, has been eclipsed by Onesimus, the slave. There has been more artistic interest in the fate of the person who occasioned the production of the letter, than there has been in the original recipient of that epistle.

1. Philemon: The Slave-Owner from Colossae

Generally it is agreed that Philemon was a wealthy Gentile Christian from Colossae who had been brought to Christian faith through Paul's ministry. The language of obligation employed in Philemon 19 is usually taken to point in this direction: 'you owe me your very self (REB)'. It is an open question about when and where Philemon was brought to faith by Paul, although the most likely possibility is that it was during the apostle's extended stay in Ephesus (as suggested in Acts 18–19). The relationship between Paul and Philemon appears to have been a good one, if Paul's description of Philemon as a 'dear friend and fellow-worker' in v. 1 is anything to go by. Philemon's commitment to the church in Colossae is also warmly commended by Paul. In v. 5 he notes Philemon's 'love and faith towards the Lord Jesus Christ and for all God's people'. It is with this understanding of Philemon's dedication to the faith in view that Paul makes his bold request concerning Onesimus, generally understood to be one of Philemon' slaves.

It seems clear that Paul's writing to Philemon was intimately connected with a breakdown in his relationship with Onesimus. However, the letter to Philemon is frustratingly imprecise about further details of Philemon's life in this regard. How and where Philemon came to be the master of Onesimus is unknown, although Paul's letter has been taken to imply that at some stage in the recent past Onesimus had betrayed his master and run away from him. Although the letter seeks to effect a reconciliation between the two, it is necessarily silent about whether or not that reconciliation ever took place. It would be fair to say, however, that the consensus of scholarly opinion is that Philemon responded to Paul's plea, and Onesimus was welcomed back 'as a beloved brother'. Presumably Philemon continued to live and work as a Christian leader in Colossae following his reconciliation with Onesimus. Indeed, most of the traditions about Philemon stress his activities within the church in the city, and assume a family connection with Apphia and Archippus in this regard.

Occasionally Philemon, Apphia, and Archippus have been depicted together in Christian art. A good example of this is found in an illuminated manuscript in New College, Oxford,

The Traditional Interpretation 41

dated to c. 1220 (MS 7). There is a small drawing at the beginning of the text of Philemon (folio 278 verso) which shows Paul seated in prison the left, offering a written epistle to three figures to the right, one of whom is kneeling before him (Figure 1). These three figures represent the three recipients of the letter— Philemon, Apphia and Archippus. Luba Eleen (1982: 63–65) discusses the drawing, noting that the manuscript follows a pattern commonly adopted in the Middle Ages of using clues within the text of the epistle to provide inspiration for the illustrations of its recipients (interest in Pauline iconography rapidly developed in the 12th–13th century). Scenes from Paul's life, or those suggested from the epistles themselves, were inserted to illustrate the text of his letters, and the marginal drawing of Philemon, Apphia and Archippus at the beginning of the text of the letter to Philemon is a prime example.

Two more recent artistic examples of the recipients of Paul's letter to Philemon are icons produced by the Orthodox Church in America. The first shows the trio decked in fine clothes, the men wearing robes and carrying Bibles (Figure 2).

Interestingly, in this particular icon Apphia is placed centrally between Archippus and Philemon. The two men are similar in appearance, although Archippus has noticeably more hair and thus looks younger, which supports the tradition that he was the son of Apphia and Philemon. This may also explain why Apphia is shown within the icon as looking demurely at Archippus, perhaps filled with motherly affection and admiration.

The second icon (Figure 3) is very similar in terms of its arrangement of the trio, with Apphia centrally positioned, although Philemon is on the left of the picture and Archippus on the right. The relative ages of Philemon and Archippus is more clearly defined in this case, with the elder Philemon sporting a beard and the youthful Archippis appearing cleanshaven. Philemon cradles a Bible in his arms, while Archippus clutches a scroll in his left hand.

What happened to Philemon after he received Paul's letter is impossible to know for certain. Most commonly it is assumed that that Philemon remained in the city of Colossae throughout his life. Indeed, according to Theodoret, a bishop of Syria in the 5th century, Philemon's house in Colossae still survived in his time (see Godet 1887: 140; Bruce 1984: 222, on this point; Lightfoot 1916: 303, is sceptical about the matter, remarking that 'traditions of this kind have seldom any historical worth').

42   *The Traditional Interpretation*

Figure 1: 13th-century drawing of Paul in prison addressing Philemon, Apphia and Archippus (New College MS 7, folio 278 verso)

Moreover, there are some indications that Philemon became a church leader in the city of Gaza for a period, although how long is uncertain. Clearly Philemon was remembered by subsequent generations of Christians in the area, and it is no surprise to discover that legends surrounding his ultimate fate are also extant.

The martyrdom of Philemon is recorded in several early traditions. *The Roman Martyrology* offers an eulogy for Philemon,

The Traditional Interpretation 43

Figure 2: Icon of Archippus, Apphia and Philemon from the Orthodox Church in America

and his wife Apphia, on 22 November. The association of both with the city of Colossae is preserved within this tradition, as are some of the circumstances of their deaths during the reign of Nero (54–68 CE).

> At Colossae in Phrygia, SS Philemon and Apphias, disciples of St Paul; in the reign of the Emperor Nero, when the heathen burst into the church on the feast of Diana and others fled, they were captured. By order of the governor Artocle they were scourged and then buried up

44 *The Traditional Interpretation*

Figure 3: Icon of Philemon, Apphia and Archippus from the Orthodox Church in America

to their waists in a pit and crushed with stones (cited in J.B. O'Connell 1962: 254).

Interestingly, Archippus is similarly eulogized in *The Roman Martyrology* on 20 March; he is described as being from 'Asia'.

Although the traditions surrounding Philemon are universally complimentary and present him as a faithful witness to the Christian faith, the slave-owner from Colossae was eclipsed by his slave Onesimus. It is to him that we now turn.

2. Onesimus as *Fugitivus*: The Runaway Slave of Philemon?

Since at least the time of John Chrysostom (c. 347–407 CE) it has been traditional to interpret the letter of Philemon as the story of a *fugitivus*—the letter is taken to be about a runaway slave named Onesimus, who was estranged from his master, Philemon. As Chrysostom (1889: 545) says: 'This excellent man had a certain slave named Onesimus. This Onesmus, having stolen something from his master, had run away.' *Why* Onesimus stole from his master, and *where* he ran away to, are matters unknown; at one level these are secondary questions which do not greatly affect the essential point of Onesimus being understood as a *fugitivus*. However, the status of Onesimus as a runaway slave *does* have an important role to play in the traditional interpretation of the letter. This is so because the traditional interpretation of the letter asserts that the reason why Paul writes to Philemon in the first place arises directly out of his (Onesimus's) status as a runaway slave. In this scenario Paul's letter to Philemon is seen as an attempt to effect a reconciliation between Philemon and Onesimus, the agrieved master and the runaway slave. Paul is generally understood to seek to forge a new relationship between the two men, one which takes into account their common commitment to Christ.

Specific points of geography are brought in to support the traditional reconstruction of the original occasion and setting of the letter. The assumed close connection with the letter to the Colossians has often been invoked in this regard. For example, the fact that the letter to the Colossians contains reference to Onesimus (4.9), to Archippus (4.17), and above all to Epaphras (4.12), has been taken by many as confirmation that Philemon was indeed from the city of Colossae. This is significant, because nowhere within the letter of Philemon itself is there any explicit reference to Colossae or a clear statement that infers that Philemon was from the city.

Similarly, the fact that Paul describes himself as 'a prisoner' (vv. 1, 9) and speaks of his 'imprisonment' (vv. 10, 13), has prompted much discussion by scholars over the years as to the place of that detention. The place of imprisonment has implications for the reconstruction of Onesimus's life as a runaway slave. Traditionally Rome has been regarded as the place where Paul was imprisoned; this was the opinion of John Chrysostom and it probably remains the majority view among New Testament scholars even to this day. However, others suggest that it is more likely that Onesimus made his way to Ephesus or Caesarea, rather than Rome, which was much further away. On the other hand, others maintain that Rome was just the sort of place a runaway might go to get lost in the crowds and live in obscurity.

This leads us to consider how and under what circumstances Paul may have befriended Onesimus.

3. Onesimus as *Christianos*: The Convert of Paul

The traditional interpretation of the letter of Philemon takes Onesimus to have been a convert of the apostle Paul. It infers that the young runaway slave came into contact with Paul during the apostle's imprisonment, probably in Rome sometime between 58 and 64 CE. The textual basis for this interpretation rests upon several key phrases within the letter. Verse 10 is of special importance in this regard for in it Paul uses family language about the father-son relationship to address Philemon about Onesimus: 'I, Paul, appeal to you about my child, whose father I have become in this prison (REB)'. According to J.D.G. Dunn (1996: 327) Paul was probably between 50 and 60 years old when he wrote Philemon, if the term *presbutes* in v. 9 is any indication. Similarly, Philip Dodderidge (1756: 593) suggested Paul was about 53; F. Godet (1887: 145), gave his age as about 55; and Joachim Gnilka (1982: 43), suggested Paul was slightly older than 55. Onesimus, on the other hand, was probably in his early twenties, well before the emancipation threshold of 30, the age at which many slaves were manumitted by their masters.

Once Onesimus was converted to the faith he seems to have proved himself to be of great assistance to the apostle in his imprisonment. Indeed, traditionally the epistle has been seen as Paul's petition that Onesimus be released from his slavery to Philemon so that he might be sent back to him (Paul) as a freed man, in order to continue this service to the cause of Christ. The conversion of Onesimus to faith underlies the epistle as a whole, and there are several phrases within the letter to Philemon hint at this way of reading the text. Most importantly, in v. 11 Paul makes a pun on the meaning of his name ('Onesimus' = 'useful'), emphasizing that the slave has undergone a change of character which has altered him from being formerly 'useless' to now being 'useful'. In v. 13 Paul says that he would be 'glad to keep him with me' for the service of the gospel, and in v. 20 Paul addresses Philemon as a Christian brother and boldly states that 'I want some benefit from you in the Lord'.

The Traditional Interpretation   47

Occasionally the figure of Onesimus the Christian convert of the imprisoned Paul has been the subject of artistic interest. Yet, it is quite rare to find celebrated artists who have executed oil paintings which depict Onesimus as a figure in his own right. A notable exception is the French painter Georges Rouault (1871–1958), who painted a small head-portrait entitled *Onesimus* in 1952; the signed painting measures 15 1/4 × 9 1/4 inches and is in a private collection in Paris (see Pierre Courthion 1962: 349, for a colour photograph of it). Unfortunately, there is nothing within the painting which suggests either the subject's status as a runaway slave or his relationship with Paul the apostle. However, other images of Onesimus as a convert to Christianity are extant which do pick up these themes. This is expecially true in woodcuts and engravings illustrating versions of the runaway's story during the eighteenth and nineteenth centuries. Generally these images depict Onesimus with the apostle Paul during his imprisonment. A good example is the tract *Onesimus; or the Run-Away Servant Converted* which was first published in 1796. The youthful Onesimus stands before Paul, who is seated, the bars in the window behind him indicating that they are in Paul's prison cell. The apostle hands Onesimus a letter, presumably the epistle to Philemon, which he is to deliver to his master in Colossae. Interestingly, subsequent editions of the tract from 1798 and 1800 show Paul standing outside his prison cell, sending Onesimus on his way, his hand raised in what could be construed as a gesture of commissioning. In this case Philemon holds the aforementioned letter to Philemon in his hand (see Figure 4).

Figure 4: Title page illustrations of *Onesimus; or, the Run-away Servant Converted* (1796, 1798)

4. Onesimus as *Episkopos*: The Bishop of Ephesus

Assuming for a moment that Paul's letter to Philemon affected a reconciliation between the slave and his master, what happened to Onesimus afterwards? Did he carry on his ministry as a Christian leader? Certainly Col. 4.9 has been interpreted by some scholars to indicate that Onesimus was released by Philemon in order to assist Paul in his apostolic ministry (this assumes that Colossians was written *after* Philemon, an opinion adopted by those who take Colossians to be a Deutero-Pauline document). Not surprisingly, the traditional interpretation of the epistle of Philemon has often incorporated the legends and stories about Onesimus becoming an important leader within the early church. Several different locations are included within these traditions.

For example, there is some evidence to suggest that following his release Onesimus went on to become the bishop of Ephesus, perhaps even succeeding Paul's co-worker Timothy in the post. Thus, Ignatius of Antioch, writing from Smyrna in c. 110 CE, acknowledged a certain Onesimus to be a model of Christian behaviour within the church at Ephesus. He described him in *Ephesians* 1.3 as a man 'of inexpressible love and your bishop (*en agape adiegeto humon de episkopo*)'. Other early sources associate him with Beroea in Macedonia. According to *Apostolic Constitutions* 7.46.1, 3–5, Onesimus served as bishop of the city:

> Now concerning those bishops which have have been ordained in our lifetime, we let you know thatthey are these ... Of Laodicea in Phrygia, Archippus. Of Colossae, Philemon. Of Borea in Macedonia, Onesimus, once the servant of Philemon.

Some images of Onesimus as a bishop also have survived in Christian art. One of the most intriguing examples is found in the city of Göreme in Cappadocia in eastern Turkey. The eleventh-century Yilanli (Snake) church, a part of the Göreme Open Air Museum contains a fresco of Onesimus on the eastern wall of its central vault (see Figure 5). The painting is somewhat damaged, but the saint's name in capital Greek letters can be still made out on the right side of the work, as can his youthful features and his splendid red robe of his office.

What about the ultimate fate of Onesimus? According to some western traditions Onesimus died as a martyr in Rome, and his body later being transferred to Ephesus where he had been bishop. Thus, *The Roman Martyrology* offers the following eulogy for Onesimus on 16 February:

> At Rome, blessed Onesimus, of whom St Paul the Apostle writes to Philemon, and whom he ordained Bishop of Ephesus after St Timothy, and committed to him the work of preaching. He was brought bound to Rome and stoned for Christ's faith, and was first of all buried there; later his body was removed to the place where he had been ordained bishop (cited in J.B. O'Connell 1962: 34).

Other ancient traditions similarly describe Onesimus's death. For example, one Greek eleventh-century miniscule (designated 42) contains a subscription to its text of Philemon which describes Onesimus's martyrdom in Rome at the hands of Tertullus, the provincial administrator. In addition, another eleventh-century manuscript contained in the Österreichische

Figure 5: Eleventh-Century Frescoe of Onesimus in Yilanli Church, Göreme in Cappadocia, Turkey

50 *The Traditional Interpretation*

Figure 6: Jacques Callot's etching of the martyrdom of Onesimus (1636)

Nationalbibliothek in Vienna (designated *Codex Vindolonensis hist. gr. 3*) also records the death of Onesimus in Rome at the hands of Tertullus. However, it appears that the anonymous hagiographer of this manuscript has conflated features of the story of the biblical Onesimus with that of a namesake Onesimus Leontinus, who suffered martyrdom during the persecutions of the Emperor Valerian (257–260 CE) (Craig L. Hanson 1977: 319–39, discusses this Greek account of Onesimus's martyrdom).

Figure 7: Icon of Onesimus from the Orthodox Church in America

Yet, what is perhaps most interesting about this particular version of the martyrdom of Onesimus is the fact that vv. 10–16 of Paul's letter to Philemon are cited in full within the text (lines 56–67).

Other traditions record that the biblical Onesimus was martyred by stoning not in Rome, but in Ephesus where he had served as bishop. Thus, the French artist Jacques Callot (1592–1635) depicted his stoning in a fine etching which was published in 1636 in *Les Images de Tous Le Saincts et Saintes de L'Année* (see Figure 6). As this etching illustrates, Onesimus's feast day is celebrated within the Roman Catholic Church on 16 February.

On the other hand, within the Orthodox Church the death of Onesimus is celebrated on 15 February. As a martyr Onesimus is usually included within the Orthodox Church's so-called 'List of

The Traditional Interpretation

the Seventy', a catalogue of the names of the early saints who were appointed by the Lord Jesus Christ and sent out into the world (see Luke 10.1). The icon image of Onesimus produced by the Orthodox Church in America presents him as a younger man, dressed in a modest red robe and clutching a scroll in his left hand, an obvious symbol of Paul's letter to his master Philemon (Figure 7).

4. Traditions Re-thought: The Goodspeed and Knox Hypotheses

The basic lines of interpretation of Philemon as set out by John Chrysostom held sway for over 1500 years. Following Chrysostom's lead it was commonly agreed that Onesimus was a 'fugitive slave' who was being sent back to his estranged master Philemon in Colossae by the apostle Paul. Indeed, it was not until the twentieth century that fresh interpretations were offered which substantially altered this basic reading of the text. The first of these challenges to the conventional reading of the text came in the early part of the century and was intimately connected with a reassessment of the Pauline corpus as a whole, and the prison epistles in particular.

The names of two American New Testament scholars came to be associated with this challenge to the status quo: E.J. Goodspeed (1871–1962) from the University of Chicago, and John Knox (1900–1990), a student of Goodspeed's who later became the Baldwin Professor of Sacred Literature at Union Theological Seminary in New York. Each shall be examined in turn, although there was much interaction between the two scholars, and mutually reinforcing ideas within their thought can readily be identified.

1. E.J. Goodspeed: Ephesians as a Covering-Letter to the Pauline Corpus

Discussion of the so-called prison epistles of Paul was given a fresh impetus by the work of E.J. Goodspeed on the letter to the Ephesians in 1933. His well-known theory was that Ephesians was published as a covering letter to the Pauline corpus (C.L. Mitton 1955: 45-54, offers a good discussion of Goodspeed's contribution to New Testament studies). According to Goodspeed, the formation of the so-called Pauline corpus was prompted by the publication of the Acts of the Apostles in about 85 CE; this generated interest in the apostle Paul and his role in the spreading of the Christian faith. Goodspeed's suggestion that the writer of the letter to the Ephesians was the person responsible for the composition of the Pauline corpus was closely connected by him to a theory about Colossians and Philemon. He assumed on the basis of the textual similarities between Ephesians and Colossians that the latter was 'the germ of the collection' (Goodspeed 1933: 6), and that the lost letter to the Laodiceans (mentioned in Col. 4.16) was in fact the epistle to Philemon. Furthermore, on the basis of Col. 4.17, Goodspeed argued that Archippus was probably a Laodicean, charged with the responsiblity of ensuring that Philemon treated his slave Onesimus humanely.

More important was Goodspeed's theory about the author of the letter to the Ephesians (to the Laodiceans!). He suggested that the author of Ephesians was the person who collected together the Pauline corpus, a suggestion that cried out for further explanation. Who was this shadowy, unnamed figure, and how is it that he became responsible for the formation of the Pauline canon? Initially Goodspeed did not identify the person by name. However, a proposed answer was to come through the innovative ideas of a fellow New Testament scholar who was heavily influenced by Goodspeed's ideas—his student John Knox (Knox 1968: 279–80 acknowledges the importance of Goodspeed upon his thinking). Knox picked up where Goodspeed left off and pushed the ideas one step further. He offered a re-interpretation of Philemon that was truly original, one that challenged conventional wisdom and turned some long-cherished scholarly assumptions on their head.

2. John Knox: Re-thinking Onesimus and his Situation

John Knox's *Philemon among the Letters of Paul* first appeared in 1935, and it opened a new chapter in the history of the interpretation of the epistle. Simply put, his interpretation of Philemon proceeded along two crucial fronts: it challenged the traditional understanding of the relationship between Philemon and Onesimus, and it identified Onesimus as the creative genius behind the formation of the Pauline corpus. To achieve the first point Knox introduced the idea that *Archippus*, not Philemon, was in fact the owner of the runaway slave Onesimus. To support the second point, Knox identified this slave who had been converted by Paul with the Onesimus described by Ignatius as the bishop of Ephesus (see *Ephesians* 1.3). In effect, Knox created a new, two-pronged interpretative scenario in which the identity of Onesimus was re-worked, and this paved the way for a new stage in the study of Philemon. This solution fit well with Goodspeed's original suggestion about the circumstances surrounding the formation of the Pauline canon, and, not surprisingly, Goodspeed eventually threw his weight behind Knox's suggestion (Goodspeed 1956: 15; also see Knox 1959: 10). Knox's ideas about Onesimus were supported by several other interconnecting arguments, many based on exegetical points arising from the text of Philemon and Colossians. Four of these are worth noting briefly.

a. *Archippus as the Owner of Onesimus*
The elevation of the character Archippus to a place of prominence could be regarded as the trigger for Knox's re-assessment of the epistle of Philemon. Yet, even here Knox was reliant upon Goodspeed in one crucial respect in this regard. As noted above, Goodspeed had argued that Paul in Col. 4.17 directed his command at Archippus in order to ensure that Onesimus was well-treated by Philemon. Knox, on the other hand, read this as an exhortation *to Archippus himself* that he release Onesimus. One of the reasons Knox felt able to do this was his reading of Philemon 1–2, where Philemon, Apphia and Archippus were all included in the greetings offered by Paul. This, coupled with the fact that the mention of 'the church which meets in *your* house' is in the singular in Greek, and the nearest antecedent noun is Archippus (not Philemon!), clinches the point as far as Knox is concerned. In short, Knox modified the suggestion made by Goodspeed about the opening verses (Philemon 1–2) and argued that Archippus was being asked to perform his Christian 'duty' (the *diakonian* mentioned in Col. 4.17). This Christian obligation consisted of giving up his slave Onesimus for Christian service, and allowing him to return to Paul so that he might assist the apostle in his ministry amongst the churches. (Goodspeed 1937: 118). Knox's interpretation proved to be very influential and the basic argument of it has continued to be advocated by several recent commentators, including L. Cope (1985: 45–50) and Sara B.C. Winter (1987: 1–15). However, others, such as Donald Guthrie (1990: 661–64), dispute Knox's central reconstruction of the relationships of the various characters and do *not* agree that Archippus was the owner of Onesimus.

Furthermore, Knox also suggested that Philemon was known to Paul as a 'beloved fellow-worker' in the cause of the gospel (as the affectionate terms *agapetos* and *sunergos* in v. 1 indicate). This is why (Knox contended) Paul named Philemon as the first addressee within the letter. He noted that Philemon, whom he suggested lived in Laodicea, was a prominent church leader within the Lycus valley, and was therefore in a position to ensure that Paul's message about Onesimus would be given serious attention. Indeed, Knox suggested (1960: 49–61) Philemon might well have been the overseer of the churches in the Lycus valley, succeeding Paul's own colleague and associate Epaphras in this regard. Other commentators make similar suggestions. For example, Helmut Koester (1982: 134) suggested that the church at Colossae was even founded not be Epaphras, but by Philemon, whom Paul had converted in Ephesus. Meanwhile, G.B. Caird (1976: 214) suggested that Archippus may have served as the replacement for Epaphras during his absence in Rome (also see F. Godet 1887: 141; E.F. Scott 1930: 102; R.P. Martin 1974: 159; and F. Hahn 1977: 183, on this as a possibility).

It is uncertain whether Paul and Philemon ever met in person, but it does not matter very much since Knox's theory about the letter to Philemon is not dependent upon such contact. In any event, such a meeting may be deemed improbable, given the fact that it is unlikely that Paul had ever visited Colossae himself. However, one alternative would be to propose that Philemon had traveled to visit Paul, perhaps in Rome, or Ephesus, where he was in prison James Alex Robertson 1920: 35, suggested a visit to Ephesus; E.F. Scott 1930: 98, hypothesized a visit to Rome).

b. *The Nature of the Request Concerning Archippus*
A related point concerns the request that Paul made concerning Onesimus, a request that lies at the heart of the letter and was the reason for its composition in the first place. A phrase within v. 10 was the textual focal point in this regard: 'I appeal to you concerning my son *(parakalo se peri tou emou teknou)*'. Knox concentrated on the meaning of the preposition *peri* in the verse and suggested that Paul was making a petition not only 'on behalf of' Onesimus, but 'for' Onesimus himself (Winter 1987: 6 and Osiek 2000: 136 disagree, and argue that Paul's petition was intercessory in nature). In other words, Paul wanted Onesimus returned to him so that he could be of service to him in his ministry (many agree on this basic point, including Calvin 1964: 397; Harrison 1950: 275–276; Wiles 1974: 216, 223; Bruce 1977: 403, 406; Stuhlmacher 1975: 40; O'Brien 1977: 56; Ollrog

1979: 103–106. However, Caird (1976: 222) doubted this on the grounds that it is difficult to reconcile with what Paul appears to say in v. 15, and Houlden (1970: 226) says that in v. 19 Paul is involved in 'a piece of sheer arm-twisting'. To support this interpretation, Knox takes the verb translated as 'I send back' in v. 12 (*anepempsa*) to mean 'I send up (for a legal decision by Philemon)'. As Knox (1960: 21) states:

> In the New Testament period it was commonly employed to indicate the reference of a case from a lower to a higher court. It is used four other times in the New Testament and always with this meaning, three times in the Luke-Acts account of Jesus' trial and once in the same work's narrative of Paul's appeal to Rome. That the term has the same legal connotation in the Philemon passage there is not the slightest reason to doubt, Paul is referring Onesimus case to his legal owner for decision.

c. *Onesimus the Runaway Slave is Identified with the Bishop of Ephesus*

One of Knox's most contentious suggestions concerned the idea that the freed slave Onesimus went on to become the bishop of Ephesus (see Knox 1955: 557–60). Knox further argued that because of his position in the church Onesimus was able to secure a place for the epistle to Philemon within the early collection of the Pauline corpus. Knox bases this idea on the fact that Ignatius's *Letter to the Ephesians* 1.3; 2.1; 6.2 (written in the early second century) makes reference to a person named Onesimus and describes him as the city's episcopal representative (interestingly, Onesimus figures as a character in John Gambol's play *The Martyrdom of Ignatius*, written in 1740, although he appears as one of the 'Messengers of the Churches', and *not* as a bishop). This suggestion assumes that Onesimus was a very young man at the time that of his encounter with Paul, perhaps not more than seventeen or eighteen years of age. We can assuming that the encounter with Paul took place sometime during the mid-late 60s CE. This means that when Onesimus came to meet Ignatius as he was on his way to martyrdom in Rome in c. 117 CE he (Onesimus) was probably about 75 years old or so. Certainly this is within the bounds of mathematical possibility; there are many other examples of people living into their seventies and eighties during this period. It should be remembered that Polycarp, the bishop of Smyrna, was well into his eighties when he was matryred in c. 155 CE.

However, the suggestion, although intriguing, has not been widely accepted, either by New Testament commentators or by Ignatian scholars. William R. Schoedel, for example, pointed out that Onesimus was a very common name for slaves in the ancient world and states that there is 'little chance' that John Knox is right (Schoeder 1985: 43–44; Heinrich Greeven [1954: 378] and Joachim Gnilka [1982: 6] are also doubtful). Similarly, John W. Martens (1992: 73), although admitting that Knox's 'new view was rather breathtaking and brilliant', offered a withering attack on his claims that Ignatius was alluding to Philemon in the first six chapters of his letter to his letter to the Ephesians. Still, some commentators, notably P.N. Harrison, have accepted Knox's proposal as a real possibility (Harrison 1950: 268–94; also see Moule 1957: 21; Stuhlmacher 1975: 18–19, 54; Caird 1976: 217–18; Bruce 1977: 403–406; 1984: 200–202). Indeed, Harrison developed Knox's theory about Onesimus a further step by suggesting that Onesimus may have met Paul following his emancipation by Philemon. He based this idea upon the possibility that Onesimus was in fact the same person known as Onesiphorus, who is mentioned in 2 Tim. 1.16–18 (Harrison 1950: 288–89; he assumed Pauline authorship of the Pastorals in this scenario). Harrison speculated that Onesimus/Onesiphorus grew up in the faith, married and settled down to Christian ministry in Ephesus, until c. 63–64 CE when he departed to Rome in order to minister to Paul during the final years of his life. As a result, Harrison (1950: 289) argued for the identification of Onesimus with Onesiphorus:

> If these two are not the same, it seems a very curious coincidence that two different men with names so much alike were rendering the same kind of service to the Apostle at the same time and place.

d. *The Authenticity of Colossians*
The fact that Philemon has only rarely been questioned as a genuine epistle of the apostle Paul has had implications for scholarly discussions about other letters within the Pauline corpus. The perceived relationship with the letter to the Colossians was a crucial element in Knox's reinterpretation of the historical circumstances of Philemon. Knox argued that the historical circumstances of what we know (or can deduce) about Philemon can be

used to support the authenticity of the letter of Colossians (Knox 1937: 144–60; 1960: 29–47). Some of the unusual features of Colossians can be explained by assuming the same historical circumstances surrounding the writing and delivery of Philemon.

Knox's theory about Philemon only really works if Colossians is accepted as a genuine letter of Paul, particularly when key similarities of detail between the two are adjudged to indicate a common historical set of circumstances. Knox addressed precisely this topic in an article entitled 'Philemon and the Authenticity of Colossians' which was first published in 1937. He puts the central point thus:

> if Colossians is genuine, it will reflect not merely the language of Philemon but also, or rather, the concrete historical situation of Philemon (Knox 1937: 147).

Or again:

> If Colossians is genuine, there will be parts of it, otherwise obscure or not particularly significant, which will be illuminated by a realization of the concrete facts of Onesimus' situation (Knox 1937: 148).

One of the most obvious benefits of this way of approaching Colossians is that it offers an explanation for the so-called *Haustafeln* section of Col. 3.18–4.1. According to Knox, Paul borrowed a convention of the day and included this moral and ethical teaching in his letter to the church at Colossae precisely because the demand he was making about the release of Onesimus needed to be set against a recognition of the wider checks and balances required for society at large to continue to function. Moreover, this way of interpreting the rather uncharacteristic *Haustafeln* is supported by slight differences of tone and expression between Colossians and Ephesians (which Knox takes to be the product of a later writer who was well-acquainted with Colossians). For example, he noted that the phrase 'there is no partiality (*prosopolempsia*)' in Col. 3.25 argues for a new relationship to brought into effect between slaves and masters, a matter which pointed to the case of Onesimus which was being addressed at the time. Knox (1937: 159) says:

> The obvious way to interpret this strange sentence is by supposing that there was a slave, or that there were slaves, at Colossae who for some reason or other were in the position of appearing to receive partial treatment in spite of having injured someone.

Confirmation of this way of reading Colossians seems to come in the parallel passage in Eph. 6.9 where the reference to 'partiality' is moved to the end of the paragraph and functions more naturally as an exhortation to the slave masters. In other words (Knox suggested), the writer of Ephesians moves the 'partiality' phrase because the situation in which he was writing did not arise out of a debate about the fate of Onesimus—this was a historical context of a previous time which no longer pertained. In Knox's opinion (1960: 38):

> He altered it because apart from the concrete situation to which it originally referred, the verse is scarcely intelligible.

Other interpretations have also been suggested which raise questions about the validity of the 'runaway slave' hypothesis as the correct way of reading the letter to Philemon. Often these are based on key verses in the letter, or on the closely related letter to the Colossians. Thus, on the basis of Col. 4.7–9 some commentators suggest that Philemon did actually release Onesimus in order to allow him to serve Paul in helping to spread the gospel message (Stuhlmacher 1975: 18–19, 57). This points toward a reconciliation bertween Onesimus and his master.

In addition, the fact that the name of Demas appears without censure in Philemon 24 (and Col. 4.10) suggests that relations between him and Paul are good. But was that always the case? Indeed, if 2 Tim. 4.10 is anything to go by, the tension between Paul and Demas erupted into open censure, for Demas is spoken of in very harsh terms. There Demas is accused of 'having loved the world', and is said to have 'deserted me (Paul)'. However, at the time of the writing of Colossians and Philemon, Paul and Demas appear to be on good terms. This is so even though there may have been a history of tension between the two men, which erupted again later (as 2 Timothy suggests). Could the kind words about Demas in Philemon 24 be an indication of the kind of reconciliation that Paul is wanting to encourage take place between Philemon and Onesimus? Perhaps Paul's friendship with Demas was being paraded before Onesimus as an example of what can take place between two people, potentially at odds with one another, when they are both committed to the cause of the gospel.

5. New Challenges to the 'Runaway Slave' Hypothesis

Up until about twenty years ago there was something of a scholarly consensus about the status of Onesimus as a *fugitivus,* a runaway who had fled from his rightful owner Philemon. It was assumed that the canonical letter to Philemon revealed Onesimus to be a runaway slave, even though no specific mention of him having fled from Philemon is ever made within the epistle. It is true that many interpreters have taken the verb 'he was separated (*echoristhe*)' in v. 15 to imply that Onesimus had run away, although the expression is somewhat ambiguous and this need not necessarily be what happened. Indeed, there may be more to the meaning of the Greek verb *echoristhe* than is at first appreciated; it may have been deliberately used in order to convey a particular theological point. Thus, speaking of Paul's intention along these lines, M.R. Vincent, noted:

> The word is chosen with rare tact. He does not say 'he ran away,' which might excite Philemon's anger; but 'he was separated,' and by the use of the passive, he puts Onesimus' flight into relation with the ordering of Providence' (Vincent 1897: 188).

Other commentators have argued the same point. Sara B.C. Winter (1987: 10), silimarly stated that 'Since Chrysostom Paul's use of the passive voice has been understood to convey God's agency in this separation.' It seems clear that, as Marion L. Soards (1990: 216) has suggested, 'This aorist passive form of the verb *chorizo* (*echoristhe*) is the key to interpreting Paul's speculative statement.' All of which is to say, that the idea of Onesimus as a deliberate *fugitivus* is not one that arises unquestioningly from the text of Philemon itself. As Brook Pearson commented about reading Philemon as a reconstruced story of a 'runaway slave':

> This narrative derives from inferences drawn from certain of its elements, which are then read back into the text of Philemon itself, and used as an assumptive foundation

for both translation and interpretation. This, like many historical 'reconstructions', has led readers of the letter to think that more is known about the situation behind it than is actually the case (Pearson 1999: 254).

Little wonder then that in recent years there has been a reaction against this 'fugitive slave' hypothesis in favour of alternative reconstructions of events, and correspondingly different assessments of the role of Onesimus. In the past twenty years three main alternatives have come to the fore, each of which challenges the traditional interpretation of the letter of Philemon at one or more crucial points.

1. Onesimus as an Asylum-Seeker

The first of these challenges to the traditional interpretation of the letter sees Onesimus turning to Paul as an asylum-seeker taking advantage of the Roman law governing master-slave relations. It has long been recognized that within the ancient world religious sites and temples afforded sanctuary to certain categories of fugitives from justice (on this point see Preiss 1954: 35; Lohmeyer 1964: 172; Bruce 1977: 399–400; Schenk 1987: 3466–75). Similarly, there is some evidence from Ptolemaic Egypt that fugitives could seek asylum in private households, claiming the family hearth as a form of temple-sanctuary. E.R. Goodenough (1929: 181–83), argued this, citing Philo *De virtutibus* 124 as a case in point. Could Onesimus's flight to Paul be viewed as another example of a fugitive on the run from the law? Did Onesimus find his temple-sanctuary in the form of the prison cell of the apostle?

However, there are notable difficulties with seeing too close a parallel between a religious temple or household hearth and a prison cell. These led Brian M. Rapske (1991: 193–95), to question whether Paul's place of imprisonment would have qualified as an official place of asylum. In any case, the asylum-seeker hypothesis has opened up new ways of approaching the letter to Philemon. For example, the asylum-seeker motif was adopted and creatively re-developed in 1985 by Peter Lampe in an article in *Zeitschrift für die neutestamentliche Wissenschaft*. Lampe's main point was to suggest that according to Roman law a disaffected slave who approached a friend of his estranged master, in an attempt to achieve a reconciliation with that master, was not considered a *fugitivus*. This insight, when applied to the situation involving Philemon and Onesimus, offered a new way of interpreting the epistle as a whole, one that undermined the traditional way of understanding it as arising out of the needs and concerns of a runaway slave. Indeed, Lampe's theory even provides a fresh way of explaining Paul's promise (in Philemon 18–19) to make right the debts owed by Onesimus to Philemon. Far from assuming that this is money the Onesimus stole from Philemon to finance his flight away from his master, it is better (Lampe suggested) to view it as Onesimus stealing from him in order to make his way to Paul and try to effect a reconciliation with Philemon. Crucial to Lampe's proposal were the discussions of cases involving runaway slaves which are found in Roman legal texts.

A more developed version of the 'asylum-seeker' hypothesis was put forward by Rapske in his article published in *New Testament Studies* in 1991. In this case Onesimus is assumed deliberately to have approached the imprisoned apostle Paul and consulted him about how to overcome the strained relationship he had with his slave-master Philemon. Thus, Paul was approached by Onesimus as an *amicus domini* ('a friend of the master'). A number of recent commentators follow this as a basic approach (including Lampe 1985: 135–37; 1992: 21–22; Bartchy 1992: 307–308; Dunn 1996: 304–307; 1998: 700). The assumption is that Onesimus knew of the high regard that Philemon had for Paul; it is likely that he had heard Paul spoken about by Philemon and the church in Colossae. Rapske suggests that Onesimus purposefully went to Paul because he knew that the apostle was socially in a position to intervene positively on his behalf.

2. Onesimus as a Sent Slave from the Church in Colossae

In 1987 Sara B.C. Winter published an interesting article in *New Testament Studies* about the epistle to Philemon which also challenged the traditional interpretation of it as concerned with the runaway slave Onesimus. She also questioned whether the 'asylum–seeker' scenario really stands up to scrutiny, given the fact that Paul's prison cell would hardly have been recognized as a place of asylum. In a word, Winter vigorously disputed the idea that Onesimus was a *fugitivus* at all.

In one sense Winter's proposal was a direct development of the ground-breaking ideas put forward by John Knox a generation earlier. She built creatively upon the foundations laid by him, including Knox's dismissal of the idea that Onesimus met

Paul when he himself was imprisoned as a runaway. Winter suggested, rather, that another explanation for Onesimus's encounter with Paul in prison needed to be sought. She argued that a credible alternative was available, providing that one took into account the nature of the letter of Philemon as an ecclesiastical document, a public letter to the church in Colossae. In this regard Winter followed up Knox's ideas about the role that Archippus had within the life of the congregation in Colossae, and went on to stress the nature of Paul's letter to the church in the city as a public, rather than a private, document. As she emphasized: 'The letter is addressed to three individuals and a house church' (Winter 1987: 1).

Much of Winter's case rests on a re-worked reading of the greetings contained in vv. 1–3 of the letter. Traditionally Philemon has been viewed as the intended recipient of the letter, mainly because he is the person first named in the greetings. Winter suggested, however, that the addressees are listed in what might be described as an ascending order of priority, at least as far as the appeal concerning the slave Onesimus is concerned. Archippus is listed *after* Philemon and Apphia, but this potentially misleads us as to his true role in the whole Onesimus affair. On the contrary, Winter argued that *Archippus* was the wealthy patron of the house church to which Paul's letter was directed; he was, she asserted, also the master-owner of the slave Onesimus.

Winter further suggested that this church which met in the house of Archippus was most likely based in the city of Colossae, and both Philemon and Apphia were members of it. Most significantly, she asserted that the church in Colossae sent Onesimus to Paul in prison in Ephesus, just as Epaphroditus had been sent to him by the church in Philippi (see Phil. 2.25). Interestingly, Winter (1987: 2), notes in this regard that the description in Philemon 2 of Archippus as a *sustratiotes* ('fellow-soldier') in Philemon 2 is significant and that the term only appears elsewhere in the New Testament in Phil. 2.25, where it is applied to Epaphroditus (Wansink 2001: 1233, follows Winter's lead on this particular point). Therefore, when Paul made his legal petition about Onesimus in vv. 8–14 of Philemon, he was asking Archippus to manumit his slave so that he might remain with Paul and fulfill his higher calling to Christian service.

The crucial point here is that Winter offered an alternative reading of the traditional relationship thought to exist between

Philemon and Archippus, one which created space for a different understanding of the letter as a whole (although R. McL. Wilson [2005: 322–23] criticizes her arguments about the public nature of the letter). The result was that Onesimus needed no longer to be seen as a slave on the run from his estranged master, but as a servant who had been sent to Paul in prison. In short, Onesimus was an assistant from the church which was based in his master's house. Finally, it is worth noting that Winter also challenged the idea that Paul sent Onesimus back to Colossae with the letter we now know as Philemon. Rather, she suggested, Onesimus remained with Paul in prison in Ephesus and through the letter, which was delivered by Tychicus to the church in Colossae, made his petition to Archippus about the useful slave Onesimus.

3. Onesimus as the Physical Brother of Philemon

Perhaps the most controversial recent interpretation of the letter is that of Allen Dwight Callahan which contends that Onesimus was not a slave at all, let alone a *fugitivus*. Rather, Callahan contends, Onesimus is to be viewed as a physical brother of Philemon, as a literal reading of v. 16a potentially suggests. Callahan's ideas were first published in the *Harvard Theological Review* in 1993, but they have been refined and expanded in a short commentary published in 1997 entitled *Embassy of Onesimus* within the innovative series *The New Testament in Context*. His interpretation is not entirely an original one, but is in fact a revival of a particular line of interpretation used by pro-slavery campaigners in the Antebellum South in the United States. Callahan (1993: 363–65) cites several examples from Antebellum writers, including a Virginian named George Bourne who published a pamphlet entitled *A Condensed Anti-Slavery Bible Argument* (1845), and a clergyman from Kentucky named John Gregg Fee who published *An Anti-Slavery Manual* (1848) in which the argument that Philemon and Onesimus were natural brothers was strongly put forward (more on this below in Chapter 6).

Callahan's argument is in large measure an attempt to pull the exegetical rug out from under the feet of those who follow the 'traditional' reading of the letter without giving due care and attention to the presuppositions which he feels such an interpretation brings to the text. Three interpreters of Philemon, representing three distinct periods of church history, are fastened upon by Callahan within his book from 1997. The three are: John

Chrysostom, a voice from patristic antiquity, Martin Luther, a voice from the late Middle Ages, and J.B. Lightfoot, a voice from industrial modernity. In Callahan's words, all three of these representatives 'had read the epistle as a letter of introduction for a slave who was both a criminal and a fugitive' (Callahan 1997: 4). This is an illegitimate starting point, he contends.

In particular, Callahan argued that the traditional interpretation of Onesimus as a runaway slave needs to be laid at the feet of John Chrysostom (c. 347–407 CE). He also asserted that it must be recognised that Chrysostom was fighting his own fourth-century battles about social class and hierarchy. Not surprisingly, it was the description of Onesimus as 'a beloved brother' in v. 16 which was identified as a crucial interpretative focal point in Callahan's critique. An extended excursus (pp. 51–55) is given over to discussing it, including passages about fraternal relations in such texts as Plutarch's 'On Brotherly Love', Hierocles' 'On Fraternal Love', and Philostratus's *The Life of Apollonius of Tyana*. These are presented as offering parallels from the ancient world about the importance of good relations and love between physical brothers.

Callahan's controversial interpretation of Philemon sparked off a vigorous debate about the extent of the biblical evidence concerning the 'slave-master' hypothesis, and the nature of the patristic interpretations which mention Onesimus and Philemon in these terms (see the exchange between Mitchell 1995: 135–48 and Callahan 1995: 149–56; also worth consulting is the discussion in Harrill 1998: 757–59; Horsley 1998: 178–82; Osiek 2000: 129–31). Other facets of Callahan's interpretation are also worth noting briefly, such as the idea that Paul sent Onesimus to Philemon (and the church that met in his house) as his apostolic representative (he is here applying the insights of Funk 1967: 249–68, about the 'apostolic *parousia*' to his interpretation of the letter of Philemon). Thus, Callahan contends, Paul's exhortation to Philemon in v. 17, that he should 'accept him (Onesimus) as you would accept me', is the language of diplomatic representation. However, perhaps the most contentious dimension of Callahan's interpretation of Philemon arises out of his reading of a phrase in v. 19 ('I will repay'). Once again, an extended excursus is given to the phrase (pp. 56–62). Callahan tied the phrase to the idea that reparations should be paid to African-Americans whose ancestors were slaves, a call for justice which had a history going as far back as the Radical Restoration in the immediate aftermath of the American Civil War. How and why Paul's promise to repay Onesimus's debts can be be linked to reparations paid to those who ancestors suffered under slavery is never made clear. Indeed, there is something of a fault in logic here, given the fact that Callahan's main contention is that Onesimus was never a slave, let alone a runaway slave, at all. In short, if the Onesimus—Philemon relationship was really a fraternal one (i.e. that the two men were physical brothers), then it is difficult to see why their story can legitimately be invoked as a platform for a contemporary call for reparations to be paid for the abuses of slavery.

Nevertheless, not all are convinced that any of the three hypotheses here discussed represents a credible alternative to, or is enough to overturn, the traditional way of interpreting the letter. In fact, a number of commentators have continued to adhere to the traditional suggestion about Onesimus being a *fugitivus*. The 'runaway slave hypothesis' has continued to be a potent force in scholarly discussion of Philemon. Indeed, J.D.M. Derrett once suggested in 1979 that Philemon was written precisely in order to forestall any investigation by authorities that the Christians associated with Philemon were harbouring runaway slaves (Derrett 1979: 65; for a critique of Derrett's ideas, see Elliott 1995: 43–44). On the basis of Col. 4.7–9, Robertson (1920: 39), suggested that Paul sent Onesimus back to Philemon *under the guard of Tychicus*. If correct, this too might be an indication of a sensitivity to public perception about Christian attitudes to runaway slaves. It is worth noting that Norman Petersen's imaginatively conceived and provocatively argued study *Rediscovering Paul: Philemon and the Sociology of Paul's Narrative World* (1985) assumed throughout that Onesimus was a runaway slave of Philemon. In 1986 David Daube, while arguing that radical ideas about the meaning of Christian conversion were responsible for Paul omitting any mention of Onesimus's manumission in his letter to Philemon, admitted the underlying validity of the runaway slave hypothesis. For Daube the crucial point was that 'the man baptized by Paul is no longer the man that was owned by Philemon' (Daube 1986: 40).

More recently, in 1991 John Nordling and John M.G. Barclay both published studies of Philemon which affirmed the traditional view of Onesimus as a fugitive slave (Nordling 1991; Barclay 1991). Also see Nordling (2004: 3–19). Both writers rehearsed many of the standard arguments of the traditional interpretation, while also offering some new angles on the old questions. Nordling's study in *Journal for the Study of the New Testament* concentrated on a number of extra-biblical texts from the ancient world that help shed light on relationships between runaway slaves and estranged masters. In addition to the oft-cited letter of Pliny to Sabinianus (*Epistle* 9.21), he discussed several of the Oxyrhynchus papyri which give details of how some slave-catchers carried on a lucrative trade in capturing and returning fugitives. There was, he suggested, a 'runaway slave racket' within the ancient world which has often been overlooked by interpreters of Philemon. Nordling also noted several neck-collar inscriptions which give details of how some runaway slaves were identified and rewards offered for their capture and return. Such parallels helped confirm the validity of the traditional reading of Philemon as a letter ultimately concerned with the case of the fugitive slave Onesimus, or so Nordling argues. It is true that Onesimus is nowhere unambiguously described as a runaway slave in the letter, but this is due to Paul's sensitive handling of a delicate situation. As Nordling concludes:

> the real-life circumstances whuch prompted the letter in the first place prevented Paul from explicitly mentioning *Onesimus fugitivus* (Nordling 1991: 119).

John Barclay's article in *New Testament Studies* is often cited and it also makes a significant fresh contribution to the interpretation of Paul's letter. After reviewing the challenges to the traditional interpretation of the epistle, his conclusion was that 'the runaway slave hypothesis is still the most likely explanation of the facts' (Barclay 1991: 164). Two factors in particular moved Barclay to affirm the traditional interpretation. The first concerned the tactful way in which Paul hinted at the strained relationship between Onesimus and Philemon, never referring directly to Onesimus's status as a runaway. It is likely, Barclay suggested, that Paul realized that he was dealing with a delicate situation, one to which Philemon could react very badly. The second concerned the character of Onesimus as hinted at by two phrases in the letter: the description of him in v. 11 as formerly 'useless' to Philemon, and the suggestion in v. 18 that Onesimus had somehow wronged Philemon or owed him something, a debt which Paul willingly took on himself.

Together these considerations make it highly unlikely, in Barclay's opinion, that Onesimus would have been trusted enough either to be sent to Paul by Philemon (or the church at Colossae), or commissioned with special duties and responsibilities in assisting Paul during his imprisonment. In this respect, Barclay was unconvinced by the general approach to the letter suggested by Sara B.C. Winter (as discussed above). He asserted that the 'runaway slave hypothesis' offered the simplest and most straightforward reading of the text, even though it is by no means clear what Paul desired or expected to happen when he sent the letter to Philemon. Paul's epistle is sufficiently vague so as to leave us in doubt about what was being asked for in the matter of the *fugitivus* Onesimus. This last point is perhaps the most distinctive contribution that Barclay made to the interpretation of Philemon. Indeed, he went so far as to suggest that Paul himself '*did not know what to recommend*' to his friend Philemon about his runaway slave Onesimus (Barclay 1991: 175).

The studies of both John G. Nordling and John M.G. Barclay clearly demonstrate that serious scholarship still finds much within Philemon that supports the traditional reading of the letter as one preoccupied with the case of a runaway slave named Onesimus. Yet, nagging questions remain, notably about whether the traditional reading is simply a scholarly assumption that is brought to the text (see Pearson 1999: 253–80, and Byron 2004: 127–31, for more along these lines). Yet whatever decision one reaches about this particular point, it is fair to say that the runaway slave hypothesis is a given when it comes to what is arguably the most significant use made of the letter of Philemon over the years. We turn now to consider how the epistle figured in the heated abolitionist debates of the eighteenth and nineteenth centuries.

6. Philemon as a Morality Lesson: Christian Ethics and the Fight for Abolition

The letter to Philemon has long been an important source for Christian sermons and teaching on ethical and moral issues. The central image of a runaway slave being brought to face the consequences of his actions readily lent itself to such adaptation. For some interpreters the character Onesimus became a universal representative of humanity, a person who was sinful and in need of redemption. Thus in his *Preface to the Epistle of St Paul to Philemon,* first published in 1522, Martin Luther famously spiritualized the slavery of Onesimus and transformed it into a metaphor of the Christian's spiritual life. Paul identified himself with Onesimus, Luther argued, and insofar as Christ has redeemed us from the slavery of sin which held us fast, 'we too are all His Onesimi' (Luther 1960: 390).

Building upon this way of reading Philemon as a morality lesson, and recognizing that the letter has sometimes been described as a document without any theological substance, Marion L. Soards remarks:

> From the time of Chrysostom, Theodore, and Jerome to and through the Reformation, the interpretation of Philemon was done on almost exclusively *moral or hagiographically moral lines*, not in theological terms (Soards 1990: 209–20).

A number of English writers from the seventeenth and eighteenth centuries turned to the letter of Philemon for inspiration along these lines. An interesting case in point was William Attersoll (d. 1640), an Anglican clergyman who matriculated at Peterhouse, Cambridge in 1579. He became rector of Isfield, near Lewes in Sussex, and served there faithfully for many years. Attersoll was a prolific writer and published a number of lengthy commentaries on biblical texts which were designed for godly gentry living in rural areas. One of his largest works, stretching to over 500 pages, was *A Commentarie upon the Epistle of Paule* to *Philemon* (1612). The commentary was very popular and went through several editions during Attersoll's lifetime. It outlined 'oeconomicall, politicall and ecclesiasticall' duties for the devout Christian, basing them mainly on the interactions between the characters Philemon and Onesimus.

Other writers of the period concentrated on specialized themes or texts from Paul's letter to Philemon. One of the best examples of this was John Goodwin's *The Returne of Mercies:, Or, the Saints Advantage by Losses* (1641). Goodwin was an important Independent minister who served the congregation of St Stephens in Coleman Street, London and made a practice of preaching sermons which applied the biblical texts to the Christian's moral life. This book, which extends to 383 pages, contained a variety of sermons, all of them based on v. 15 of Philemon. Goodwin left no stone unturned as the moral and theological significance of the verse was expounded and applied to the moral questions of his day.

Another interesting example worth noting briefly was Richard Steele's *A Discourse concerning Old-Age* (1688). Steele (1629–1692) was a nonconformist minister who supported the Parliamentarian cause during the Civil War. He was appointed the chaplain of Corpus Christi College in Oxford, but resigned his post in 1662 in the face of a resurgent Anglicanism. His *Discourse concerning Old-Age* was written to those coming toward the end of their lives and was designed to give them comfort in their Christian faith. In it Steele delineated the various 'Graces proper for Old Age', specifically identifying 'Charity or Love' as the 'Seventh Grace'. Paul the Apostle, Steele argued, was an example of someone who exhibited this supreme grace: 'how pathetical was *Paul the Aged* in his tender charity to *Onesimus*, Philem[on] 9, *Being such a one as Paul the Aged, for loves sake I beseech thee for my son Onesimus.*' The moral lesson of Charity was to be applied to other Christians, for 'in this *Grace* doth every *good Old* Man and Woman excell' (Steele 1668: 121).

Another good case of the moralizing use of Philemon is the anonymous tract entitled *Onesimus; or, the Runaway Servant Converted*, first published in c. 1796 by the Cheap Repository for Moral & Religious Tracts in Cheapside, London. After relating the biblical story of the runaway Onesimus, who goes to Rome and is converted by Paul, the writer of the 16-page, one-penny tract then applies the story to unhappy *women* who have fallen into a life of open and allowed sin, and are perishing both as to body and soul, either in our great town, or among the dregs of the people of our metropolis (1796: 11).

A similar example was Jonas Hanaway's *Virtue in Humble Life, containing Reflections on relative duties, particularly those of masters and servants* (1777). The book contained various stories and anecdotes of people, living and dead, and was set out in 209 conversations between a father and his daughter aimed ar achieving 'domestic peace and Christian piety'. Conversation 5 was explicitly based on Paul's letter to Philemon and promoted a healthy respect for law-keeping and the need for legal punishment of wrong-doing as an essential ingredient for a healthy society. Within this diatribe the case of Onesimus is appealed to as an example of the Christian virtue of forgiveness on the part of Philemon. Hanway suggested Paul's letter to Philemon carried the sentiment that 'An opportunity of forgiveness is an opportunity to exercise the noblest power of the human soul', and that within the letter:

> The apostle treats his friend with the politeness of a *gentleman*, as well as the sincerity of a *christian*, and the authority of an *apostle*; for though he reminds him that he owes his own salvation, under God, to the instruction which he had given him, yet he writes in the stile of a petitioner in favour of *Onesimus*, whom he well knew *Philemon* might naturally entertain a jealousy of. However, in confidence that he would act like a christian, St *Paul* ventures to send *Onesimus* a long and tedious journey, from *Rome* to *Colosse*, with his commendatory letter (Hanway 1777: 18).

However, it was not always been slavery, nor the runaway male slave Onesimus, that has served as the focal point of such moralizing. Occasionally other characters in the epistle come to the fore in this regard. For example, an anonymous tract published in 1643 during the early days of the English Civil War, presented a dialogue between Archippus, a Minister, and Philemon, a godly Christian. The tract is entitled *An Alarme for London: To awake and mourne for sin, before God make her weepe for judgements*. The conversation between Archippus and Philemon centred on their moral agonizing about human sinfulness and how they might avoid breaking any of the Ten Commandments so as to avoid God's wrath. Clearly the two dialogue partners were given the names Archippus and Philemon because of their association in the epistle of Philemon. The fact that the two men were traditionally viewed as members of the same congregation in Colossae was taken to indicate the congregational nature of life in the capital city of London (in this respect Colossae served as a cipher for London within the tract). What is perhaps most intriguing here is the fact that slavery as such, was not the focal point of ethical concerns (the words 'slave' and 'slavery' do not appear once in the work).

Another interesting example is *A Call to Archippus; or, An Humble and Earnest Motion to some Ejected Ministers* (1664) (see Figure 8). This pamphlet is generally thought to be from the pen of Joseph Alleine (1634–1668), a nonconformist minister

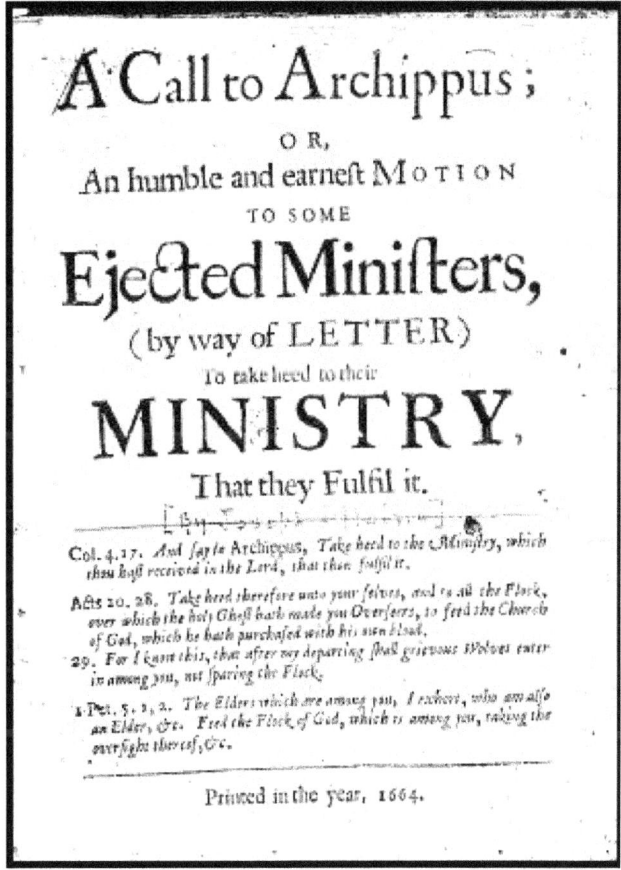

Figure 8: Title page of *A Call to Archippus; or, An Humble and Earnest Motion to some Ejected Ministers* (1664)

from Taunton in Somerset who was ejected from his church in 1662. The pamphlet used the figure of Archippus, notably the exhortation in Col. 4.17, as the basis for its exhoration that ministers fulfil their responsibilities to their congregations to which they have been called, even if they had been officially relieved from their posts.

Works such as these clearly illustrate that the human side of the story of Philemon and Onesimus captured the imagination of subsequent generations of readers. The importance of the letter of Philemon as a document with a rich moral heritage has been well established by such publications from the seventeenth-eighteenth centuries. Even more importantly, Paul's teaching about the relationships between slaves and masters became a debating point as the controversial matter of slavery rose to the top of the political agenda during the nineteenth century. Indeed, William Wilberforce invoked the Pauline ideal of the equality of masters and slaves in Christ in his influential work *A Letter on the Abolition of the Slave Trade* (1807), quoting the text of Col. 3.11–12 on the title page of his work (see Figure 9).

When considering the importance of Paul's teaching on master—slave relations, Adolf Deissmann (1926: 19) long ago warned against losing the human dimension of Paul's letters and turning the people addressed within them into ideas, so that the 'slavery' question becomes more important than the individual slaves such as Onesimus. Nevertheless, it remains the case that Paul's letter to Philemon has had its greatest impact in connection with the debate over slavery. It is not surprising that Philemon became a crucial Biblical text in the ensuing abolitionist debate, particularly within the United States.

1. Paul: Slave Collaborator or Apostle of Emancipation?

The task of interpreting Paul's attitude to slavery is like the proverbial attempt to sail between Scylla and Charybdis familiar in ancient Greek myth. On the one hand, one needs to steer clear of the temptation to conclude that Paul had nothing to say about slavery and that his silence on the matter simply supported the institution. On the other hand, one needs to avoid crashing on the interpretative rocks which assert that he is an out-and-out abolitionist. Most books on New Testament ethics contain a section on the question of slavery, and most point out the highly ambiguous nature of Paul's teaching on the subject

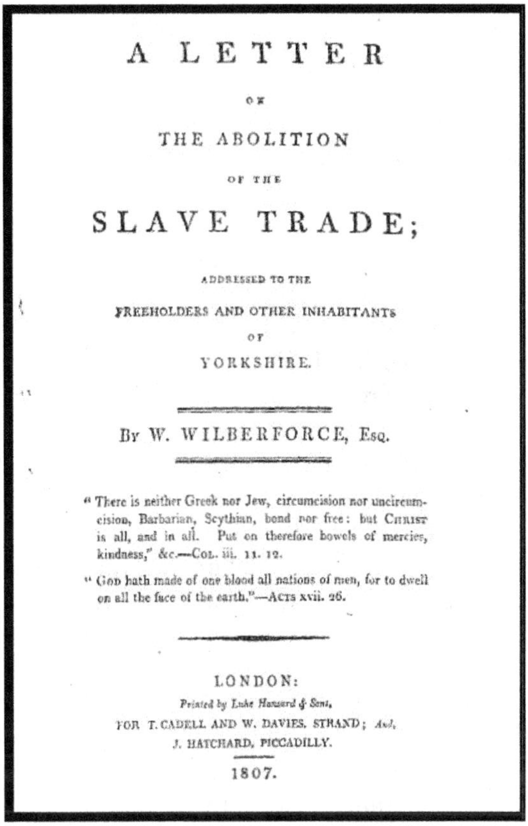

> A LETTER
>
> ON
>
> THE ABOLITION
>
> OF THE
>
> SLAVE TRADE;
>
> ADDRESSED TO THE
>
> FREEHOLDERS AND OTHER INHABITANTS
>
> OF
>
> YORKSHIRE.
>
> By W. WILBERFORCE, Esq.
>
> "There is neither Greek nor Jew, circumcision nor uncircumcision, Barbarian, Scythian, bond nor free: but CHRIST is all, and in all. Put on therefore bowels of mercies, kindness," &c.—COL. iii. 11. 12.
>
> "GOD hath made of one blood all nations of men, for to dwell on all the face of the earth."—ACTS xvii. 26.
>
> LONDON:
> Printed by Luke Hansard & Sons,
> FOR T. CADELL AND W. DAVIES, STRAND; AND
> J. HATCHARD, PICCADILLY.
>
> 1807.

Figure 9: Title page of William Wilberforce's *A Letter on the Abolition of the Slave Trade* (1807)

(for more on the tension within Paul's ethical teaching over the slavery question, see Schrage 1988: 232–35; McDonald 1998: 169–75). Inevitably the letter to Philemon figures within these discussions, particularly when it comes to exploring the Christian teaching about the thorny issue of emancipation from slavery.

It is quite difficult to determine precisely what the early Christians' attitude was to slavery as an institution, let alone their practices when it came to the manumission of slaves. There is some evidence to suggest that some early Christian communities pooled together the resources of their members and purchased the freedom of slaves. It is difficult to know for sure if this meant that only *Christian* slaves were being so manumitted, or if the practice was part of a larger evangelistic strategy on the part of the churches concerned. In any event, several Christian writings mention the liberation of slaves by Christian communities, including Ignatius, *Letter to Polycarp* 4.3; *Shepherd of Hermas* 8.10; *Apostolic Constitutions* 4.9.2; Justin Martyr, *Apology* 67.6; and several letters of Augustine (see Osiek 1981: 373–74; Chadwick 1983: 432–33; Harrill 1993: 18–132; Combes 1998: 56–63; Braxton 2000: 215–20, for more details). The liberation of slaves by Christian communities has been taken to offer an important backdrop against which to view the suggestion that at the heart of the epistle of Philemon was Paul's appeal that Onesimus be set free from his slavery.

Not surprisingly, many interpreters over the years have identified the letter of Philemon as an important scriptural text in the debate over slavery, and its author Paul has correspondingly been viewed both as a supporter of the institution of slavery and as a champion of its abolition. Over the years the apostle has been invoked by Catholics and Protestants alike in this regard. Pope Leo XIII cited Paul's dealing with Onesimus approvingly in his declaration of 5 May 1888 entitled 'In plurimis'. This edict was aimed at the bishops of Brazil and called for them to act with integrity in the face of political developments calling for the abolition of slavery in the country. In 1887 F. Godet could go so far as to base the emancipation movement at Philemon's door and say that 'Wilberforce was but a follower of St Paul' (1887: 154). E.F. Scott (1930: 100) commented that the letter is to be regarded as 'one of the landmarks in the history of emancipation.' A.T. Robertson similarly remarked:

> It seems a long step and a long time from Paul's gracious words to Philemon to Lincoln's blunt assertion that the Union cannot continue half-slave and half-free. But it is safe to affirm that Paul made possible Lincoln's emancipation proclamation (Robertson 1920: 45).

George A. Buttrick (1955: 561) once described the letter of Philemon as 'a seed that finally split the rock of slavery.' This kind of assessment may sound quite contemporary, but it was not unusual to find even nineteenth-century advocates of slavery who recognized that the institution was not going to last forever. Even Professor Moses Stuart (1780–1852), who was often cited as being one of the most celebrated spokesmen for the anti-abolitionist movement in the Antebellum North recognized the force of the gradualist position (John Giltner 1961: 27–40, discusses Stuart's anti-abolitionist stance). Stuart was committed to the ultimate emancipation of slaves and their and resettlement in Africa, once remarked:

> Paul knew well that Christianity would ultimately destroy slavery, as it certainly will. He knew too, that it would destroy monarchy and aristocracy from the earth; for it is fundamentally a doctrine of true liberty and equality. Yet Paul did not expect slavery or anarchy to be ousted in a day; and gave precepts to Christians respecting their demeanor *ad interim* (Green 1839: 8).

The debate over what the Bible has to say about slavery needs to be viewed against the rise of biblical criticism as an academic discipline during the nineteenth century. Few at the time, on either side of the debate, would have disputed that the Bible had an important role to play in determining what was morally and ethically demanded of them. However, determining *what* that Biblical teaching consisted of was much more difficult task. Hermeneutical questions soon predominated, although it is now clear with hindsight that a paradigm shift away from a strictly literal reading of the text was taking place (Harrill 2000 offers an engaging study of this). This was particularly true among anti-slavery campaigners and abolitionists, who found that their cause was not supported by a literalistic reading of the Bible. The traditional historical readings of the text soon gave way to interpretations which focused on moral arguments based on conscience and moral principles. In any event, the letter of Philemon was catapulted into the front line of the interpretative debate. As J. Albert Harrill noted:

> Antislavery and abolitionist authors tried to force exegetical control over this letter because it was potentially the most dangerous book in the entire Bible (Harrill 2000: 151).

2. Philemon and Onesimus in the Abolitionist Debate: Some Examples

Some commentators have argued that Paul expected Philemon to liberate Onesimus from his slavery, some even suggesting that such an act was part of his Christian duty to a fellow believer (including Godet 1887: 150; Jülicher 1904: 125; Lohmeyer 1930: 191; Knox 1960: 23–26; Koester 1982: 135; Petersen 1985: 290;

Bartchy 1992: 70–71, 308–309; Elliott 1995: 47–48; Russell 1998: 20; Polaski 1999: 65–72). Others, however, think this is unlikely (including Kümmel 1975: 349, and Vos 2001: 101). Still others deny that Paul had manumission in mind at all (including Maclaren 1887: 185; Lohse 1971: 203; O'Brien 1982: 297–98; Dunn 1996: 334–35; Barth and Blanke 2000: 415–17; and Frilingos 2000: 99–101). John M.G. Barclay (1991: 171–77) suggests that Paul was being deliberately ambiguous over the question of manumission given the complexities of the situation. Craig S. Vos (2001: 100) questions whether Onesimus's manumission would have made any substantial difference in his relationship with his master, given the strong authoritarian and patriarchal nature of society at the time. Such an act of manumission would not have been at all unusual within Roman society, provided that there were no extenuating circumstances. On the other hand, many interpreters comment on the abiding memory of Spartacus's slave revolt (73–71 BCE) as something which would have made Christians cautious about suggesting, or even *appearing* to suggest, that slaves should be encouraged to rise up against their masters (see Caird 1976: 215 on this point).

Occasionally, commentators have suggested that *Jewish* traditions about the treatment of slaves, notably Deut. 23.15–16, were governing Paul's expectations concerning Philemon's release of Onesimus from slavery (see Oesterley 1974: 207–209; Motyer 1986: 4). On the other hand, Davies (1995: 341) suggests that Paul and the church in Colossae may have been deliberately ignoring, or treating as irrelevant, the injunction found in Deut. 23:15–16 regarding the return of runaway slaves. In any event, the prohibition in Deut. 23.15–16 against returning a runaway to his master was frequently adduced by abolitionists as evidence of the biblical basis upon which Paul's actions should be judged. The controversial and outspoken Angelina B. Grimke is a case in point. In her 'Appeal to the Christian Women of the South', first published in 1836 in the *Anti-Slavery Examiner*, the organ of the New York-based American Anti-Slavery Society, she inferred that Paul was bound by the prohibition from Deuteronomy, and that this determined his actions. Aiming her thoughts directly at the Southern readers, Grimke provocatively asserts:

> Onesimus was not thrown into prison and then sent back in chains to his master, as your runaway slaves often

are—this could not possibly have been the case, because you know Paul as a Jew, was bound to protect the runaway, he had no right to send any fugitive back to his master (Grimke 1836: 14).

Clearly Deut. 23.15–16 was seen by many to be a key biblical text in the struggle against slavery. In addition, the stipulations contained in Exod. 21.2 and Deut. 15.12, which state that servitude should last a maximum of six years, were also invoked as significant. Similarly, the declaration made in Exod. 21.5–6 and Deut. 15.16–17 may well gave been in the back of Paul's mind when he wrote in Philemon 15 of Onesimus's voluntary return to Philemon in order to serve him for life.

Perhaps more than any other New Testament texts, Paul's letters were at the centre of the interpretative debate over slavery. Indeed, H. Sheldon Smith once remarked that pro-slavery forces in the pre-Civil War south felt much more at home in the letters of Paul than they did in the teachings of Jesus, because those documents contained specific instructions on the duties of masters and slaves. In fact, virtually every proslavery tract of any consequence explored the Pauline epistles far more exhaustively than any other portion of the New Testament (Smith 1972: 134).

The hermeneutical arguments raised by the pro-slavery lobbyists were powerful, and the reactions to them, understandably, were passionately held. Some helpful discussions of this have been produced over the years, including H. Sheldon Smith (1972: 129–65), who offered an excellent introduction on the use of the Bible by Southern religious leaders to defend slavery, and Allen Dwight Callahan (1998: 235–49), who discusses how African Americans responded to the ambivalent teaching of Paul on the question of slavery. Also worth consulting is J. Albert Harrill (1998: 759), who contains an important note on abolitionist interpretations of Onesimus.

Paul's letter to Philemon was one of the most important biblical texts employed by the pro-slavery lobby within the American Antebellum South. In the words of Larry R. Morrison:

> As far as the New Testament was concerned, the major passage Southerners found which accepted, indeed justified slavery, as the Epistle of St Paul to Philemon, sometimes referred to as the Pauline Mandate (Morrison 1980–81: 19).

Many published reactions to such arguments are to be found in the printed literature of the day. A host of books, pamphlets, newspaper articles, and sermons are available which address the point, most produced by established publishing houses in the cities of the North and South. Even British writers joined in the debate, usually on the side of the abolitionists. For example, the pro-slavery interpretation of Paul's letter of Philemon was parodied in a anonymously-written poem entitled 'The Land of the Free; or, A Rod for Republican Slave-Holders and their Abettors'. This appeared in a pamphlet entitled *America and her Slave-System*; it was published in London in 1845 and reflects a British perspective on the American struggle with slavery (the poem itself was re-published in *The Liberator* on 17 July 1846). It concentrated on how far supporters of the institution of slavery went to justify their position. According to the poem, their interpretation of the New Testament included the belief:

That the holy apostles—especially Paul—
Thought compulsory bondage no evil at all;
Nay, that Paul sent Onesimus back in a huff,
For daring to think he'd been slave long enough;
But wrote to his master a letter entreating
To spare the "ungrateful" deserter a beating!

Of course, this is not to say that in the USA all Southerners adopted the pro-slavery position without reservation. There were many reservations expressed from a number of quarters. This was certainly the case when it came to the issue of runaway slaves being returned to their masters, a point which arose directly from a particular reading of the letter to Philemon. There are some very interesting examples of how Christian denominations qualified their supposedly pro-slavery positions. Christopher H. Owen, for example, pointed out one way in which Methodists in the south took a stand about the return of fugitive slaves to their masters, noting that it was common for advertisements about runaways to appear in newspapers, books and journals. However, Methodists took a stance *against* this practice. Owen says:

> Unlike secular papers, southern Methodist publications viewed notices for escaped slaves as excessively worldly and therefore excluded them from their publications.

St Paul advised the slave Onesimus to return to his master, the *Wesleyan Journal* asserted, but the apostle had "never advertised" the runaway (Owen 1998: 53).

One very interesting example of a minister preaching about Philemon to a group of Southern slaves in the 1840s has survived and is oft-cited. This concerns the Reverend Charles Colcock Jones (1804–1863), a Presbyterian missionary known as the 'Apostle to the Slaves', who tendered a report of his activity in the Tenth Annual Report of the Association for the Religious Instruction of the Negroes in Liberty County, Georgia. Jones had studied at Andover and Princeton Theological Seminaries before returning to his home church in Georgia to begin a ministry among the slaves in his native county. Although Jones was convinced that slavery was a violation of God's divine laws, he believed that the way to overcome it was to work for change within the existing system. As Jones tells the story:

> Allow me to relate a fact which occurred in the spring of this year, illustrative of the character and knowledge of the negroes at this time. I was preaching to a large congregation on the *Epistle to Philemon*; and when I insisted upon fidelity and obedience as Christian virtues in servants, and, upon the authority of Paul, condemned the practice of *running away*, one half of my audience deliberately rose up and walked off with themselves, and those that remained looked anything but satisfied, either with the preacher or his doctrine. After dismission, there was not small stir among them: some solemnly declared 'that there was no such epistle in the Bible;' others, 'that it was not the gospel;' others, 'that I preached to please masters'; others, 'that they did not care if they ever heard me preach again' (cited by Albert Barnes 1846: 319).

Occasionally slaves did voluntarily return to their masters after having run away. A celebrated case in point was Nat Turner, who led the bloody slave rebellion in Southampton County, Virginia in 1831 during which a number of black slaves and 55 whites were killed. Remarkably, Nat had run away from his master ten years earlier in 1821 and remained on the run in the woods for thirty days or so. He turned up at the Turner farm of his own free will, spouting Bible verses and filled with a sense of his own destiny as a prophet of God after a vision from the

Spirit directed him to "return to the service of my earthly master" (see Stephen B. Oates 1975: 31–32, for details).

There are other examples of slaves who ran away from their masters and did *not* return to their masters. One of the most celebrated is the case of Anthony Burns, a slave who escaped from his master in Virginia and made his way to Boston, Massachusetts. He became the subject of a bitter and highly public extradition battle in 1854, after he was arrested by a fugitive-slave catcher and moves were made to extradite him to Virginia. A legal battle ensued and Burns was forced to return to his master under armed guard (see Shapiro 1959: 34–51, for a good study of this important event).

However, Burns's freedom was eventually bought by supporters and he returned to Boston. At one point Burns had become a member of the Baptist Church in Union, Virginia and had requested that his membership be transferred to a different Baptist Church where he was worshipping. A church meeting was held on 20 October 1855 and the request for transferral was denied and Burns excommunicated from the fellowship. The reason given was that Burns had 'absconded from the service of his master, and refused to return voluntarily—thereby disobeying both the laws of God and man'. Burns replied to these charges in an articulate and empassioned letter, citing a number of biblical texts in support of his action, including 1 Cor. 7.21, Deut. 23.15–16, Exod. 21.16, and 1 Tim. 1.9–10. Most importantly, he invoked the story of Onesimus's return to Philemon and turns the tables on his accusers who suggested that he had acted in an un-Christian manner by refusing to return. Burns stated:

> The advice you volunteered to send me, along with this sentence of excommunication, exhorts me, when I shall come to preach like Paul, to send every runaway home to his master, as he did Onesimus to Philemon. Yes, indeed I would, *if you would let me*. I should love to send them back *as he did*, "NOT NOW AS A SERVANT, but above a servant:—A BROTHER—a brother beloved—both in the *flesh* and in the Lord;" both a brother-man, and a brother-Christian. Such a relation would be delightful—to be put on a level, in position, with Paul himself. "If thou count me, therefore a *partner*, receive him *as myself*." I would to God that every fugitive had

the privilege of returning to such a condition—to the embrace of *such* a *Christianity*- "not now as a servant, but above a servant,"—a "partner,"—even as Paul himself was to Philemon! (cited in Stevens 1856: 280–282).

Another celebrated case of a runaway slave who refused to return to his master is that of Moses Roper, who first published his life story in London as *A Narrative of the Adventures and Escape of Moses Roper from American Slavery* (1837). Roper's book was an important contribution to the developing anti-slavery campaign and was a prototype for the genre of slave-narratives which poured forth in the 1840s and 1850s. It recounted his life as a slave, from his birth in 1815 in North Carolina to a white slave-holding father and an enslaved mulatto mother, through years of abuse as a young slave at the hands of about fifteen different masters, to his flight to freedom in 1834 and his eventual arrival in England in 1835. The book was a best-seller, going through ten British and American editions by 1856 (Ian Frederick Finseth 2003: 23–34, discusses Roper's life).

Subsequent editions of Roper's *Narrative* were published with additional materials, including some letters addressed to the author. Interestingly, some of these were quite critical of the exploits of Roper, blaming him for bringing many of his difficulties upon himself by running away from his legal slave-masters. One in particular brought the incident of Onesimus and Philemon into the equation. This was a letter written by Edward Lingard from Manchester in England on 18 September 1837. Lingard had read Roper's account, and was impressed by what it exposed about slavery, but argued that 'his entire history is a series of fugitive conduct, which cannot be approved upon Christian principles'. Moreover, citing the example of Onesimus as a biblical example to follow, he argued:

> it is either his incumbent duty to return to his master, acknowledge his past unprofitable conduct, and for what he has wronged him make restitution, or if not, I think the money raised by the sale of his book should, *first of all,* be applied to the purchase of his freedom and paying compensation, which done he may, with a quiet conscience, go forward with the expense of his education, and expect God's blessing to crown the excellent work to which he purposes dedicating himself (Roper 1848: 54).

Lingard's letter also elicited an angry response from a Quaker named Joseph Eveleigh who supported Roper's actions in running away. Eveleigh's reply, which was written on 18 December 1837 and then published in the 1848 edition of Roper's *Narrative*, also invoked the case of Onesimus the runaway slave to make its central point. Eveleigh argued that the right of one human being to enslave another without consent as fundamentally wrong, and the flight of any slave from a master is justified. However, Eveleigh subtly changed the rules of the debate, for he asserted that Onesimus was only to be viewed as 'an individual who had bound himself as a servant by his own consent' (Roper 1848: 55).

What is most interesting about this argument is the fact that the Philemon—Onesimus relationship is not regarded as one of master-slave, but of servant or employer-hireling. This is a way of reading the text that gets explored more fully by other anti-slavery campaigners, including Albert Barnes, and John Greg Fee (see below). It was an argument no doubt prompted by the fact that the King James Version of the Bible happens never to use the word 'slave' as a translation for *ebed* in the Old Testament or for *doulos* in the New Testament. As one anti-slavery preacher, Jonathan Blanchard, the pastor of the Sixth Presbyterian Church in Cincinnati, put it in a public debate in 1846: '*If they were slaves, the translators of our Bible would have called them so*' (Blanchard and Rice 1846: 336). However, the point was challenged by his debating opponent, the Reverend N.L. Rice, the pastor of the Central Presbyterian Church in Cincinnati. Rice replied:

> But the argument which he seems to think conclusive on this subject, is this: If the word *eved* meant *slave*, the translators of our English Bible would have so rendered it. This is indeed a miserable evasion. They translate it *servant* and *bond-servant*. Does not Mr. B. know that the Latin word *servus*, from which the English word *servant* is derived, signifies *slave*, and that the word servant, when our translation was made, had its literal and proper meaning. But if the word *servant* does not mean *slave*, will he tell us the meaning of *bond-servant*, by which the word *eved* is translated? Does it not mean *slave*? (Blanchard and Rice 1846: 344).

Exegetically, however, it is an extremely weak argument and was severely criticised by many competent Biblical scholars, notably Moses Stuart of Andover Theological Seminary near Boston, who became a major figure in the ensuing debate (Goodspeed 1943: 169–70, discusses this point, as does Meeks 1996: 233; Harrill 2000: 151, describes it as 'semantic subterfuge of the biblical text in English').

There are a number of important writers, both pro-slavery and abolitionist in sentiment, who refer to the letter of Philemon within their publications and public addresses in the 1830–1860s. Some of the more important examples are discussed briefly here; they are, broadly speaking, chronologically arranged according to the publication date of their work concerned.

a. Thomas Parry's Paul, Philemon, and Onesimus, or, Christian Brotherhood; Being a Practical Exposition of St Paul's Epistle to Philemon, Applicable to the Present Crisis of West Indian Affairs *(1834)*

In 1834 the Reverend Thomas Parry, the Archdeacon of Antigua in the Diocese of Barbados and the Leeward Islands, published a little booklet entitled *Paul, Philemon, and Onesimus, or, Christian Brotherhood; Being a Practical Exposition of St Paul's Epistle to Philemon, Applicable to the Present Crisis of West Indian Affairs*. Parry was formerly a Fellow at Balliol Collee, Oxford before finding his ministerial calling led him to the West Indies. Originally the substance of the book was preached as a sermon by Parry in St John's Church in Antigua on 29 December 1833. Within the sermon Parry sought to apply what he thought to be the spiritual and moral lessons gleaned from Philemon to the concrete setting in which he was ministering. In particular, two matters were focused upon: the need for education of the poor, and the relief of the destitute; both issues were addressed within an Appendix.

In part, the matter of emancipation had been brought to a head by the Legislation of Antigua, which had in November of 1833 submitted to the Government a proposal for immediate emancipation. The crisis facing Antigua in the face of this proposal was considerable—the demographics alone were frightening. According to Parry, 'the population of the island altogether being about thirty-six thousand, of whom nearly thirty thousand are slaves' (Parry 1834: 41).

Parry's exposition of the story of Paul, Philemon and Onesimus was a noble attempt to apply the truths contained within the epistle to his situation. He captured well the bridge needed between the first-century story and the nineteenth-century application. Note how Parry attempted to read between the lines of the biblical text (including 1 Cor. 7.21) in order to extract the essence of spiritual truth:

> He [Paul] shows, indeed, the greatest respect for Philemon's feelings as a master, and the most scrupulous regard for his rights as a proprietor, undertaking himself to make compensation for any loss that he had sustained. At the same time, he evidently desired the freedom of Onesimus, and ventured to hint as much. And may we not be permitted to observe that Christianity has not, amongst us, rested at the conversion of the Slaves? that although their freedom is not an object which she *commands*, it is one she *desires*, one too, for the safe enjoyment of which she *fits* her votaries; and while she respects all civil rights of property, and does not even denounce slavery as incompatible with religion, yet if the slave "*may* be free" without danger or injustice, she should "use it rather," especially between those who are both, the master and the slave, brethren in Jesus Christ. This I conceive to be the real spirit of our religion in regard to slavery;—a spirit of sound philanthropy, looking chiefly, though not exclusively, to the eternal welfare of mankind, and in all its proceedings controlled by a strict sense of justice (Parry 1834: 28).

b. Albert Barnes's An Inquiry into the Scriptural Views of Slavery *(1846)*

Albert Barnes published *An Inquiry into the Scriptural Views of Slavery* in 1846. This was an ambitious project which offered extended discussions of many Old and New Testament texts, including an section on 'The case of Onesimus, the servant of Philemon' (pp. 318–40). Part of the charm of Barnes's book is that it was clearly written and passionately argued; understandably, it was widely read and quickly became recognized as one of the authoritative treatments of the subject.

Barnes was among the first to question one of the key presuppositions of the pro-slavery position. He declared, 'There is no positive or certain evidence that Onesimus was a slave at all.' Barnes pointed out that the 'proof' of Onesimus's slavery rested entirely upon v. 16 of the epistle, but this was, in Barnes's opinion, inconclusive for the word 'servant' did not necessarily mean 'slave'. Moreover, insofar as the epistle adding anything to the political debate about the rights and wrongs of slavery, Barnes (1846: 321) stated, 'It is clear that the epistle can, under any circumstances, be adduced in favour of slavery only *so far* as it is certain that Onesimus had been a slave.' This essential point of the pro-slavery position Barnes sought to undermine within his work.

Not even the traditional view that Onesimus had run away from his master, or that Paul had returned him, could be adduced as proof that he was in fact a slave of Philemon. Barnes argued that indentured servants or apprentices could also run away from their responsibilities and be forced to return, but this did not make them slaves. In short, the text of Philemon just does not give us enough information to determine whether or not Onesimus was a voluntary, or an involuntary, servant. As Barnes noted:

> All that is said of him in ver. 16 of the epistle, or in any other part of the epistle, would be met by the supposition that he was a voluntary servant, and that he had been in fact intrusted with important business by Philemon (Barnes 1846: 322).

As far as the suggestion that Paul somehow forced or compelled Onesimus to return to Philemon is concerned, again Barnes is sceptical of how sure we can be about this. Speaking of v. 12 of the epistle, Barnes (1846: 323) says, 'There is nothing in the statement which forbids us to suppose that Onesimus was *disposed* to return to Philemon, and that Paul sent him back at his own request.' Indeed Barnes questions whether Paul ever had the right to send Onesimus back if he wanted to; there is no proof that he had the civic authority to do so. Thus, 'it should not be *assumed* that Paul sent him against his will, and thence *inferred* that he was in favour of sending back runaway slaves *against their* will' (Barnes 1846: 325). Moreover, Barnes (1846: 326) continued, 'There is no evidence that Paul meant that Onesimus should return *as* a slave, or with a view to his being retained and treated *as* a slave.' Indeed, in his opinion, v. 16 is best read as a declaration that Paul meant Onesimus was *not* to be regarded and treated as a slave upon his return. The contentious matter of returning fugitive slaves to their masters was by no means a merely theoretical discussion for Barnes. In the course of his discussion of the epistle of Philemon he revealed that he once had a personal experience of trying to persuade a runaway slave to return to his master, citing the biblical text as his warrant. Barnes failed, and the slave did not return, and later repented for having tried to persuade the unfortunate fugitive to do so (see Barnes 1846: 324). Yet, Barnes remained optimistic about the ultimate triumph of the abolitionist cause, and the importance of the story of Onesimus as someone who was accepted as a brother was affirmed. He stated:

> The principles laid down in this epistle of Philemon, therefore, would lead to the universal abolition of slavery. If all those who are now slaves were to become Christians, and their masters were to treat them 'not as slaves, but as brethren beloved,' the period would not be far distant when slavery would cease (Barnes 1846: 330).

c. *Augustus Baldwin Longstreet's* Letters on the Epistle of Paul to Philemon *(1845)*

A good example of a pro-slavery interpretation of Philemon is that offered by Augustus Baldwin Longstreet (1790–1870), a distinguished Methodist preacher and educationalist from Georgia. Longstreet's major work on the subject was *Letters on the Epistle of Paul to Philemon* which was published in 1845. The 47-page book contains five short chapters which Longstreet wrote following the General Conference of Methodists held in 1844. At the Conference tensions between pro-slavery and abolitionist factions had reached boiling point and bitter and acrimonious dispute followed (Christopher H. Owen 1998: 60–65 discusses this). In *Letters on the Epistle of Paul to Philemon* Longstreet took up the cause of the Southern Methodists to great affect, writing in a fluid and readable style which won many admirers. In the face of abolitionist arguments to the contrary, he asserted that it was possible for a Christian to be a slaveholder, and that Philemon was, indeed, both a respected Christian leader and a slaveholder. In this respect Philemon served as a model for Christian slaveholders in the South.

Baldwin challenged the suggestion (made by Barnes, among others) that Onesimus was not in fact Philemon's slave, but merely his hired servant. Baldwin counters this argument with biting sarcasm:

> *I assert confidently that he was a slave.* To have adduced proof of this position fifty years ago would have been considered an insult to the person to whom it was addressed. But in this age of theological illumination nothing is to be considered as settled which conflicts with the views and feelings of moral or political reformers. So we must go gravely to work to prove what, for seventeen hundred years, was never disputed, to wit *that Onesimus was a slave* (Baldwin 1845: 15).

Baldwin was keenly aware of the use made of the Bible within the abolitionist debate, particularly the importance of Philemon and the vagaries contained in v. 16 of the epistle. He was dismissive of interpretations of this verse which argued that the phrases 'brother beloved' and 'in the flesh' meant that Onesimus was the physical brother of Philemon. Baldwin responds to this line of argumentation:

> But some man may say—"What do you do with the 16th verse," where Paul says of Onesimus, "a brother beloved, especially to me, but how much more unto thee, both *in the flesh* and in the Lord?" I answer, do any thing with it rather than turn the whole epistle into nonsense, by supposing it to mean that Philemon and Onesimus were children of the same parents (Baldwin 1845: 21).

d. *Frederick Douglass's* Various Speeches and Addresses *(1845, 1846, 1852, 1859)*

The ex-slave Frederick Douglass (1818–1895) was one of the most important abolitionists of the Antebellum period. He travelled widely throughout the United States and Europe and was much sought-after as a public speaker. Many of his sermons, speeches and public lectures were published during his lifetime and received wide circulation. Several of these demonstrate that the letter of Philemon was a text well known to Douglass, particularly as the sending of Onesimus to Philemon was cited by pro-slavery advocates as proof of the sanctioning of slavery by Paul. In an address delivered at Freemasons' Hall in London on 18 May 1846 before the annual meeting of the British and Foreign Anti-Slavery Society, Douglass stated his position boldly. He declared, 'I do not agree with the opinion that the apostle Paul recognized Onesimus as the property of Philemon' (Blassingame 1979: 260).

In an address delivered in Cincinnati, Ohio on 27 April 1852 Frederick Douglass was again scathing in his condemnation of the use of Philemon in order to justify slavery. He railed against the fact that, within fifteen Confederate States, ministers and clergy 'declare the Fugitive Slave Law to be a second edition of the apostle Paul's epistle to Philemon' (Blassingame 1982: 343). The Fugitive Slave Law was also mentioned in a eulogy for the prominent abolitionist William Jay which Douglass gave on 12 May 1859. Within this address, which was delivered at the Shiloh Presbyterian Church in New York City, Douglass spoke eloquently about his dream of a time in the future when Doctors of Divinity shall find a better use for the Bible than in using it to prop up slavery, and a better employment of their time and talents than in finding analogies between Paul's Epistle to Philemon and the slave-catching bill of Millard Fillmore (Blassingame 1985: 258; Millard Fillmore was the President of the United States when the Fugitive Slave Act became law on 12 September 1850).

Perhaps the best known example of the use of the story of Onesimus by Douglass appears in a speech he delivered to a women's anti-slavery meeting held in Corinthian Hall, Rochester, New York on 5 July 1852. The speech was entitled 'What to the Slave is the Fourth of July?' and between 500 and 600 people were in attendance. Once again Douglass took the theological leaders and teachers of the American church to task for the way in which they misused the Bible to support the institution of slavery:

> But the church of this country is not only indifferent to the wrongs of the slave, it actually takes sides with the oppressors. It has made itself the bulwark of American slavery, and the shield of American slave-hunters. Many of its most eloquent Divines, who stand as the very lights of the church, have shamelessly given the sanction of religion and the Bible to the whole slave-system. They have taught that man may, properly, be a slave; that the relation of master and slave is ordained of God; that to send back an escaped bondsman to his master is clearly the duty of all the followers of the Lord Jesus Christ, and this horrible blasphemy is palmed off upon the world for Christianity (Blassingame 1982: 377).

Another good example of Douglass's use of the biblical story of Onesimus was an address entitled 'Baptists, Congregationalists, the Free Church and Slavery'; the lecture was delivered in Belfast, Ireland on 23 December 1845 (it was published in the *Belfast News Letter* on 26 December 1845). Within it he related the well-known incident of an encounter between a Professor Moses Stuart (whom Douglass calls Stewart) of Andover Theological Seminary, who had argued that slaveholding was not sinful in itself, and a Methodist minister from Vermont, the Reverend Wilbur Fisk (1792–1839), who wished to be better informed about the rights and wrongs of slavery as an institution. Stuart had been ordained as pastor of a Congregational church in New Haven in 1806, but gave up pastoral work in 1810, when he was elected to the professorship of sacred literature at Andover. Fisk, a professor at Wesleyan University at Middleton, Connecticut, had first approached Professor Stuart for advice on the matter early in 1837, and received a reply from him in Andover which was dated 10 April 1837. The explanation by Stuart was published by Fisk in William Lloyd Garrison's Boston-based abolitionist organ *The Liberator* on 9 June 1837 and by this means it quickly entered the public domain (Fisk 1837: 1; also see Wright 1837: 106, where the letter is discussed. The full text of Stuart's letter to Fisk was also published in Green 1839: 7–8, and discussed by Foster (1843: 47. Giltner 1996: 125, notes the publication in *The Liberator*, but gives the wrong date for it.). Stuart's justification of the institution of slavery reply became something of a *cause célèbre*, and even resulted in some colleagues and students leaving Andover in protest. A case in point was a Dr Blanchard, later a President of a Congregational college in Illinois. Payne (1888: 56) says that he 'abandoned Andover because Prof. Stewart had given such an exegesis of St Paul's letter to Philemon concerning Onesimus as to justify slavery.' Stuart's arguments were cited, or alluded to, by a number of abolitionists, including Frederick Douglass. The crucial paragraph, wherein Stuart mentioned the story of Philemon and Onesimus as a proof-text for his contention that slavery was not sinful in itself, reads:

> If any one doubts, let him take the case of Paul's sending Onesimus back to Philemon, with an apology for his running away, and sending him back to be his servant for life (Fisk 1837: 1).

Douglass picked up the story of Onesimus, injecting himself within its narration as a third party, and stated:

> Doctor Stewart sent him [Fisk] a reply, in which he referred to the case of Onesimus, whom he stated Paul had sent back to Philemon for life.
>
> He [Douglass] would be glad to know where Dr Stewart learned that Onesimus was sent back into slavery for life; was it, he would ask, from the law? If it was, he [Douglass] would tell him, that Jewish slavery was not for life; there was no such thing known among the Jews as slavery for life, except it was desired on the part of the servant himself. What did the Apostle say himself? He said, he sent back Onesimus greater than a servant; and told Philemon to receive him as he would receive him, Paul; not as a slave who could be sold in the market, but as a brother beloved (Blassingame 1979: 115–16).

Stuart's point about Onesimus being sent back to Philemon 'for life' was based on a phrase from Philemon 15 ('that you might receive him back *forever*'). His interpretation of the phrase became a matter of sharp criticism by several other abolitionist writers. Picking up on the fact that Paul sent Onesimus back not as a slave but as a brother beloved, H.C. Wright sarcastically chided, 'Why did the Professor suppress the truth here? ... Is this the way Professor Stuart instructs young men to interpret the Bible?' (Wright 1837: 106).

The fact that so eminent a Biblical scholar as Professor Stuart put forward such a specious argument on the meaning of Philemon 15 ('that you might receive him back *forever*') roused Douglass to rail against such 'Doctors of Divinity' on a number of occasions thereafter, particularly in the acrimonious debates surrounding the passage of *The Fugitive Slave Law* (1850). A key event in the political proceedings was Daniel Webster's speech before the US Senate on 7 March 1850, an address entitled 'The Constitution and the Union'. It was an empassioned speech which not only argued for the preservation of the Union at all costs, but put forward the idea that the southerners who demanded the return of runaway slaves had the Constitution on their side. The clearest declaration of Stuart's support of Webster's ideas was contained in his influential *Conscience and the Constitution* (1850). Here Stuart argued that Christians were obliged to obey the legal demands of the Fugitive Slave Act and show themselves to be good and loyal citizens, as indeed had Paul in similar circumstances his own day.

What did Paul do at Rome? A slave of Philemon, at Colossae, ran away and came to Rome. There he was converted to Christianity under Paul's preaching. The apostle was so pleased with him, that he was desirous to retain him as a friend and a helper. Did he tell the slave that he had a right, nay that it was his duty, to keep away from his master, and stay with him? Not at all. He sent back Onesimus, the slave, to his master (Phil. v. 12), and he tells the master, that he could not venture to retain Onesimus without knowing whether he would consent, v. 14. "Perhaps," says the apostle, "he departed for a season, that thou shouldst receive him forever."- He then expresses his ardent desire, that Onesimus may be treated with great kindness, and as a Christian ought to be treated (Stuart 1850: 61).

Stuart appealed to Philemon as a biblical model for the returning of slaves to their masters (see Mitchell 1998: 145–49, for more on this).

In contrast, abolitionists argued that Christians were called to obey a higher law of conscience when it came to returning slaves to their masters. Some more radical elements went so far as to counsel that the Christian was to disobey the law and defy the Constitution insofar as it was being used to justify the forced return of runaway slaves. In Stuart's opinion, this was going too far. His pamphlet put forth a defense of the Constitution and argued for obedience to it as a legalistic framework necessary for the preservation of the Union (as noted in Mitchell 1998: 139–45). Not surprisingly, the support that Stuart's interpretation of the epistle to Philemon gave to the pro-slavery camp meant that Stuart himself became the subject of sharp criticism by abolitionists. One notable example was Rufus W. Clark (1813–1886), like Stuart a graduate of Yale, who had himself attended Andover Theological Seminary. Clark's *A Review of the Rev. Moses Stuart's Pamphlet on Slavery* (1850) helped establish his reputation as a staunch abolitionist who was not afraid to speak out from the pulpit about his convictions in the matter. Unfortunately, Stuart's interpretation of the epistle of Philemon did not figure within Clark's refutation, although its influence is clear.

Occasionally Stuart himself was ridiculed and his ideas made the object of anti-slavery rhetoric. A case in point was the Quaker poet John Greenleaf Whittier (1807–1892), one of the leading activists in the abolitionist movement.

e. John Greenleaf Whittier's A Sabbath Scene *(1850)*

John Greenleaf Whittier's poem entitled 'A Sabbath Scene' was first published in the *National Era* on 27 June 1850; it also was published as a broadsheet in June of 1850 (Currier 1937: 69, 335–36; and Peterson 2000: 187–90, discuss the textual history of the poem). The *National Era* was arguably the most influential of all the abolitionist papers of the time, and Whittier served as its corresponding editor from 1847 to 1859. The poem was a direct response to the proposed Fugitive Slave Law, and effectively laid a charge against Northern clergymen who urged that the Christian's duty was to fall into line with the provisions of the Act and return fugitive slaves against their will to their masters (See Peterson 2000: 184–99, for a full discussion of the poetry of Whittier and Harriet Beecher Stowe which was written in response to the Fugitive Slave Law; Smith 1999: 303–304, also discusses the use of the Bible in Stowe's novel *Dred* published in 1856). The overly sentimental poem contains 27 four-line stanzas and is set as a dream in which a Northern Christian witnesses a young female runaway find her way to a church on a Sunday morning, hotly pursued by her angry master. The slave woman interrupts the church service, precipitating an exchange between her whip-brandishing master and the minister of the church. Interestingly, the provocative image of Paul returning the runaway Onesimus to his estranged master Philemon is invoked within the poem. Note the following seven stanzas of the poem, which begin with an heated exchange between the pastor of the church and the slave-owner, and conclude with a reference to Paul sending Onesimus back to his master:

> "Who dares profane this house and day?"
> Cried out the angry pastor.
> "Why, bless your soul, the wench's a slave,
> And I'm her lord and master!
>
> "I've law and gospel on my side,
> And who shall dare refuse me?"
> Down came the parson, bowing low,
> "My good sir, pray excuse me!
>
> "Of course I know your right divine
> To own and work and whip her;
> Quick, deacon, throw that Polyglott
> Before the wench, and trip her!"

Plump dropped the holy tome, and o'er
Its sacred pages stumbling,
Bound hand and foot, a slave once more,
The hapless wretch lay trembling.

I saw the parson tie the knots,
The while his flock addressing,
The Scriptural claims of slavery
With text on text impressing.

"Although," said he, "on Sabbath day
All secular occupations
Are deadly sins, we must fulfil
Our moral obligations:

"And this commends itself as one
To every conscience tender;
As Paul sent back Onesimus,
My Christian friends, we send her!"

The image of the runaway slave being tripped up by a 'Polyglott' Bible, strategically thrown at her feet by a deacon of the church is a powerful indictment of the ecclesiastical establishment using the Bible to support of the pro-slavery cause. A later edition of the poem, issued in 1854, contained a number of etchings depicting dramatic scenes from the poem (the illustrations were done by Baker, Smith and Andrew). One of these illustrations shows the slave woman tripped up by the stumbling-block of scripture, with the pastor of the church reaching out to capture her (Figure 10).

Whittier's poem also made specific mention of the scriptural arguments of Moses Stuart to support the return of runaway slaves as a Christian moral duty. In the early versions of the poem, explicit mention was made to Stuart and his support for Daniel Webster and his arguments in support of the Constitution. The relevant stanza of Whittier's poem (stanza 22) had the narrator awaken from his dream and question rhetorically:

Shriek rose on shriek,—the Sabbath air
Her wild cries tore asunder;
I listened, with hushed breath, to hear
God answering with his thunder!

96   *Philemon as a Morality Lesson*

Figure 10: A runaway slave is tripped up by the stumbling block of Scripture and caught by a Christian minister.
An etching from John Greenleaf Whittier's
A Sabbath Scene (1854 edition)

> All still! the very altar's cloth
> Had smothered down her shrieking,
> And, dumb, she turned from face to face,
> For human pity seeking!
>
> I saw her dragged along the aisle,
> Her shackles harshly clanking;
> I heard the parson, over all,
> The Lord devoutly thanking!
>
> My brain took fire: "Is this," I cried,
> "The end of prayer and preaching?
> Then down with pulpit, down with priest,
> And give us Nature's teaching!
>
> I woke, and lo! the fitting cause
> Of all my dream's vagaries—

Two bulky pamphlets, Webster's text,
With Stuart's commentaries! (Whittier 1850: 102).

Clearly the interpretation that Moses Stuart gave to the letter to Philemon became closely bound up with bitter political debates surrounding the Fugitive Slave Law of 1850. As John B. Pickard (1961: 33) stated in his assessment of the poem, 'its portrayal of the terrible results of the new law accurately foreshadowed occurrences every bit as unbelievable as the one presented in the poem.' Whittier's poem is a prime example of the impact that Stuart's writings had on the issue of returning slaves, but there are several other interesting instances in which Stuart's reading of Philemon came under scrutiny.

f. Stephen Foster's The Brotherhood of Thieves, or, A True Picture of the American Church and Clergy *(1843)*

Another good example of an anti-slavery interpretation of the epistle to Philemon was the Reverend Stephen S. Foster's *The Brotherhood of Thieves, or, A True Picture of the American Church and Clergy* (1843). Attempting to justify the institution of slavery as something compatible with the Christian faith is, Foster maintained, 'a gross and palpable falsehood'. Foster asserted that Paul's teaching on the matter cannot be misunderstood in this way, because:

> He calls Onesimus his *son*;
> and tells Philemon to receive him as his *"own bowels,"* that is, as his own offspring.
> He tells him expressly to receive him *"not now as a servant, bu above a servant, a brother beloved, both in the flesh and in the Lord."*
> He tells him still further, *"receive him as myself;"* that is, as you would the great Apostle to the Gentiles;
> and he adds, *"if he oweth thee aught, oput that on my account; I will repay it."*
>
> And he [Paul] remarks in apology for sending back Onesimus, that he had perfect confidence in Philemon, that he would do even more for him than he had asked. And yet with this plain and unequivocal statement before them, these distinguished biblical scholars have the audacity to tell us that Paul sent Onesimus back "to be a *servant* for life!" (Foster 1839: 48–49).

g. *James G. Birney's* Sinfulness of Slaveholding in All Circumstances; Tested by Reason and Scripture *(1846)*

James G. Birney published his *Sinfulness of Slaveholding in All Circumstances; Tested by Reason and Scripture* in 1846. The book emphasized how much of our attempt to reconstruct the historical circumstances of Onesimus and Philemon was mere conjecture, and that much was reliant 'in the imagination of the commentators' (Birney 1846: 50; Shanks 1931: 148-51 discusses Birney's interpretation of Paul's epistles). Not even the features of the traditional reconstruction should be regarded as certainties. Birney accepted the idea that Onesimus had wronged Philemon in some way, but precisely *how* was difficult to determine on the basis of the text if the letter alone. Birney (1846: 50) said, 'Onesimus was guilty of some great crime, known *probably* only to him, Philemon and Paul—for we suppose to the latter he unbosomed himself fully. In all likelihood, it was *purloining* from Philemon.'

Although he did not make a great point of it, Birney (1846: 49) tended to doubt that Onesimus was in fact the slave of Philemon: 'If Philemon had held Onesimus, as a slave, there are some strange things connected with it.' More significantly, Birney focused his discussion on the role that Onesimus would have played within the churches which Paul had helped to establish, and upon the need for Onesimus to return to the area. He noted that Paul commanded in Col. 4.7-9 that his letter, which was presumably delivered by Tychicus, be publicly read to the church. Birney (1846: 50) concluded that this probably also involved Onesimus making a public declaration about his life: 'So it appears, that Paul imposes on Onesimus, "as one of them," cojointly with Tychicus, a report of his own doings. Would the people of Colosse,—would Philemon and his family—have listened to this patiently from a returned slave? I suppose not.'

h. *Silas McKeen's* A Scriptural Argument in Favor of Withdrawing Fellowship From Churches and Ecclesiastical Bodies Tolerating Slaveholding among Them *(1848)*

Silas McKeen published *A Scriptural Argument in Favor of Withdrawing Fellowship From Churches and Ecclesiastical Bodies Tolerating Slaveholding among Them* in 1848. In it he argued that slaveholding was not permitted by apostles of the early church; the case of Onesimus and Philemon served as one of the scriptural texts used to support this contention. McKeen's essential point was that Paul sent the fugitive slave Onesimus back to his master Philemon, but with the expectation that he would be accepted as a Christian brother and that his slavery would cease. McKeen acknowledged Paul's instrumentality in affecting the reconciliation between Onesimus and Philemon, and went on to speculate:

> But did Paul expect that he was going back into a state of slavery—to be held and treated as a brute animal—to be, perhaps seized and punished as an example of warning to others? Did he expect that by sending him back, he and his posterity, if he should have any, would be doomed to hopeless bondage? By no means (McKeen 1848: 28).

Perhaps even more importantly, McKeen insisted that the challenge to slaveholders in the American South was clear, particularly if they laid claim to any Christian faith and wished to follow in the traditions of Paul and the other early Christian apostles. Addressing Christian slaveholders, McKeen said:

> Let their fugitive slaves firmly believe that they will be received and treated as Onesimus was, not as slaves, but as brethren; with all the cordiality which a truly Christian man would show towards the chief of apostles; and there will be no need of the hunters with their dogs and deadly weapons, to seize them and force them back. (McKeen 1848: 28–29).

i. George B. Cheever's God Against Slavery and the Freedom and Duty of the Pulpit to Rebuke It as a Sin against God *(1857)*

A similar point was made by the Reverend George B. Cheever in his *God Against Slavery and the Freedom and Duty of the Pulpit to Rebuke It as a Sin against God* (1857). He concentrated on the phrase 'not now as a servant' in v. 16a and argued that Paul's returning of Onesimus must be viewed against the backdrop of the Old Testament prohibition *not* to return slaves to their masters (Deut. 23.15–16), and the fact that Paul avoided using the word 'owner' when describing Philemon within the letter. Cheever said:

Paul would not, and could not, have returned Onesimus at all except to a man who, as a Christian, well knew God's judgment against slavery; nor to him, unless he had perfect confidence in his Christian integrity, that he would receive him as no longer a servant, a slave, even if he had been one before. Paul would never have sent back Onesimus to any doctors of divinity who proclaim slavery a divine institution, nor to any one who could have stood up and said, as doctors of theology since his day have done: We accept the system of human slavery, and conscientiously abide by it (Cheever 1857: 144).

j. George Bourne's A Condensed Anti-Slavery Bible Argument *(1845)*

One of the most interesting refutations of the pro-slavery interpretation of the epistle of Philemon was George Bourne's *A Condensed Anti-Slavery Bible Argument* (1845). Bourne (1780–1845), an ardent anti-slavery campaigner, was born in Westbury, England. He was a Presbyterian minister who went to America in 1814 to pastor a church in South River, Virginia. Bourne was so appalled by first-hand experience of slavery that he wrote *The Book and Slavery Irreconcilable* (1816) which asserted in no uncertain terms that slavery was sin, described as 'manstealing'. This book, his first of several against slavery, got him in trouble with his church superiors, particularly as it called for immediate emancipation of all slaves. Not surprisingly, he was charged with heresy and condemned by the Presbyterian Council of Virginia. Bourne was undaunted in his resolve and moved to Germantown, Pennsylvania, where he joined the Dutch Reformed Church and continued his campaigning against slavery by writing several books, including *A Condensed Anti-Slavery Bible Argument* (1845).

Bourne discussed Paul's letter to Philemon in chapter 19 of this book, a chapter entitled 'Pro-Slavery Interpretations of the New Testament'. He noted how the epistle had been taken to provide evidence that Philemon was both a slaveholder and a member of the Christian church, thereby justifying both the institution of slavery and the right of Christians to be slaveholders. Bourne affirms that Philemon was a member of Christian church, but he denies that this means that Philemon was necessarily a slaveholder and Onesimus his slave. Bourne focused his argument about this on the meaning of the terms *doulos* (in v. 16) and *oiketes* (in the subscription of some manuscripts), suggesting that they mean nothing more than a simple 'servant'. He says:

> we have no means of determining whether the persons designated in the New Testament by these words were free servants or slaves, except by the subject matter, by the context, and by the general description in the whole narrative. In this short epistle Onesimus is in the 16th verse called a "*doulos*" or man-servant simply, while in the postscript at the end of the epistle, which is supposed to have been the ancient superscription or direction to it, he is called an "*oiketes*," or house, or domestic servant, nothing more being indicated by either word to show the special nature of his servitude or service, to ascertain which, with any degree of reasonable probability, we are compelled to resort to the subject matter contained in the context, or rather to the whole epistle, which, so far as it goes, is clearly indicative, or descriptive, not of slavish, but of free service, and leaves no reasonable doubt of the fact that Onesimus was a free and voluntary servant of some kind (Bourne 1845: 83–84).

Bourne (1845: 85) linked this interpretative possibility to the reference in v. 18 to Onesimus 'owing' Philemon something, 'which was impossible if he were a slave, but not only possible but very probable, if he were a free servant.' Interestingly, a similar point was made a decade before by Angelina B. Grimke (1836: 14).

More significantly, Bourne briefly explored the possibility that the description of Onesimus as Philemon's brother 'in the flesh' (v. 16) indicated that the two men were natural brothers. This suggestion was also made in a letter written by an anonymous subscriber in the *Christian Reflector* (17 April 1845: 63). It was countered in an article by a writer describing himself as 'Alpha' in the *Christian Reflector* (1 May 1845: 8). Bourne did not necessarily agree that this was the case, but merely noted that some have entertained it as a possible way of interpreting the verse. If correct (Bourne suggested), it is taken to be yet another indication that Onesimus could not have been a slave, for natural brothers would never have treated each other in this way. Bourne also appealed to two other Biblical texts in support of his argument that Onesimus was not the slave of Philemon. First, he said that if Onesimus was a slave Paul would have followed the injunction of Deut. 23.15–16 and never have blamed Onesimus for not wanting to return to his master. Secondly, he noted 1 Cor. 7.21, 23, which he took to be an apostolic injunction for slaves to take their freedom if they could possibly do so. Occasionally it is argued by New Testament scholars, generally in connection with the interpretation of 1 Cor. 7:21, that it was not possible for a slave to refuse manumission from his or her owner (so Bartchy 1973: 97–98 asserts; Harris 1999: 60 agrees). However, this does not appear to be the case, at least in the opinion of some scholars (see Harrill 1993: 135; Braxton 2000: 203–204; also see Dames 1990: 681–97; Deming 1995: 130–37). In any event, the crucial point about manumission was engagingly pursued by Bourne when he says (1845: 84), 'Ought we for a moment to believe that the Apostle who gave such directions, would have voluntarily assisted in restoring Onesimus to the same unhappy condition he had just escaped from?' Obviously not!

All of which, Bourne argued, supported his interpretation of Philemon, one that flew in the face of the pro-slavery position (Callahan 1993: 363–364, discusses Bourne's ideas). Bourne summarized his central point:

> From the foregoing facts, taken in connection with the whole spirit and tenor of the epistle, there is not the slightest probability that Onesimus was a slave, or that Philemon was a slaveholder. The supposition that either were such is a libel on the Christian office and character of the Apostle Paul, and a wicked imputation on the special grace which gave him that office and character' (1845: 85).

k. Joseph Ruggles Wilson's Mutual Relations of Masters and Slaves as Taught in the Bible: A Discourse *(1861)*

Another good example of someone who turned to Paul's epistle to Philemon as a scriptural justification for the institution of slavery is Joseph R. Wilson (1835–1903), a Presbyterian minister from Augusta, Georgia. Wilson is perhaps best known as the father of Woodrow Wilson, the 28th US President (1913–1921). Joseph Wilson became pastor of the First Presbyterian Church in Augusta, Georgia in 1857. He published a booklet entitled *Mutual Relations of Masters and Slaves as Taught in the Bible:*

A Discourse (1861). This 21-page booklet was based on a sermon Wilson preached on Eph. 6.5-9 at his church on Sunday, 6 January 1861. Where the sermon was preached was an important factor in its own right—the church was used as a Confederate hospital during the Civil War.

One of the first things that Wilson did within the sermon is to challenge the lexical argument that the Greek word *doulos* meant 'servant' and not 'slave'. The Greek term, Wilson declared, 'refers us to a man who is in the relation of permanent and legal bondage to another: this other having in him and his labor the strictest rights of *property*.' The lexical arguments which sought to force a distinction between a 'servant' and a 'slave' were dismissed by Wilson as erroneous.

Following the traditional interpretation of the letter, Wilson went on to argue that Onesimus, a runaway slave of Philemon, was converted to faith under Paul's guiding hand. His conversion necessarily brought with it a change of understanding about his responsibilities to Philemon. Note how Wilson went on to justify the institution of slavery based on his hypothetical reconstruction of Onesimus's reasoning about his return to Philemon:

> Being converted, what was his duty to his defrauded master? The spirit of christianity, which now resided in his heart, informed his conscience of the fact that he was the *property* of Philemon, and that while he remained away from his owner's home and authority, he was committing the sin of robbery. He consulted the Apostle. What was *his* advice? He did not hesitate to urge Onesimus to go at once to his master, confess at his feet the grevious fault he had committed, and beg to be received once more among the number of his slaves. And that the reconciliation between master and servant might be hastened, Paul wrote, (and wrote under the inspiration of God,) a letter of beseeching tenderness to the offended owner, asking him to pardon the faithful fugitive and give him a place in his confidence, and telling him that he would now, with grace in his heart, be a far better servant than ever.
>
>   Such reasoning, from the implied allowance of slavery by inspired Scripture, is, my friends, conclusive enough upon the point in question. Let neither master nor servant dispute the righteousness, doubt the wisdom, or fear the

reproach of the relation which they sustain towards each other. It is not sinful. It is not inexpedient. It is not degradatory (Wilson 1861: 15).

In short, Wilson contended that slavery as an institution was not fundamentally incompatible with the Christian faith. His reading of Paul's letter was that Philemon and Onesimus were able to carry on the master-slave relation successfully once the runaway returned home and resumed his rightful place.

l. John Greg Fee's An Anti-Slavery Manual, or, The Wrongs of American Slavery Exposed by the Light of the Bible and of Facts *(1848)*

Another refutation of the pro-slavery reading of Phileman was John Greg Fee's *An Anti-Slavery Manual, or, The Wrongs of American Slavery Exposed by the Light of the Bible and of Facts* (first published in 1848 with a second edition appearing in 1851). Fee (1816–1901) was a devoted abolitionist educator who in 1858–59 helped establish Berea College in Kentucky, a school committed to racial integration. Fee's arguments were bold and innovative, for he, like George Bourne, challenged one of the assumptions of the pro-slavery movement and criticized the idea that Onesimus was himself a slave at all. Fee's argument centred on four interlocking points of deduction drawn from a close reading of the text of Philemon itself, notably vv. 14 and 18:

1. No man can prove that he was a slave, and not simply either a bound person or a hireling, indebted to Philemon.
2. The benefit spoken of in v. 14 can be accounted for as readily on the ground that Onesimus was simply a bound person, as that he was a slave.
3. The fact that the apostle expresses a doubt (v. 18) as to whether Onesimus owed Philemon any thing, is proof that he was not a slave. Had the apostle recognized Onesimus as the rightful property, the slave of Philemon, then there could have been no doubt as in the apostle's mind as to whether he owed him any thing. Also, slaves do not become indebted to their masters.
4. There is no evidence in the epistle that Onesimus was not a natural brother to Philemon—a younger brother, bound to the elder. This was very common in that age. Paul calls him "a brother beloved, especially to me, but how much

more unto thee, both IN THE FLESH, and in the Lord." ... To Paul, Onesimus was a brother, especially or peculiarly beloved in the Lord,—as a Christian,—in a spiritual sense. To Philemon he was not only a brother especially beloved in the Lord, but also a brother specially beloved in the flesh (Fee 1851: 109).

m. Harriet Beecher Stowe's Uncle Tom's Cabin *(1851)*

The passing of the *Fugitive Slave Law* in 1850 was an important factor in the decision by Harriet Beecher Stowe to write her influential novel *Uncle Tom's Cabin*. The book was first published between June of 1851 and April of 1852 as a serial within the weekly *The National Era* based in Washington, DC. The story was told in forty instalments of this influential anti-slavery newspaper. It was then issued in 1852 in two volumes by the Boston-based publisher John P. Jewett and Company. Many abolitionists from the North viewed *Uncle Tom's Cabin* as a valuable contribution in their struggle against slavery and hailed it as a great literary achievement.

The novel made specific mention of the story of the runaway Onesimus at one key point. This occured in a chapter entitled '11: In Which Property Gets into an Improper State of Mind', in the midst of a conversation between a disaffected slave George Harris and Mr. Wilson (a white businessman not unsympathetic to the plight of slaves). Paul's advice to Philemon concerning the runaway slave Onesimus (Philemon 10–19), together with the controversial admonition about 'remaining in the state in which you were called' (1 Cor. 7.21) are worked into the discussion between the two men:

> "Well, George, I s'pose you're running away—leaving your lawful master, George—(I don't wonder at it)—at the same time, I'm sorry, George,—yes, decidedly—I think I must say that, George—it's my duty to tell you so."
>
> "Why are you sorry, sir?" said George, calmly.
>
> "Why, to see you, as it were, setting yourself in opposition to the laws of your country."
>
> "*My* country!" said George, with a strong and bitter emphasis; "what country have I, but the grave,—and I wish to God that I was laid there!"
>
> "Why, George, no—no—it won't do; this way of talking is wicked—unscriptural. George, you've got a hard

master—in fact, he is—well he conducts himself reprehensibly—I can't pretend to defend him. But you know how the angel commanded Hagar to return to her mistress, and submit herself under the hand; and the apostle sent back Onesimus to his master."

"Don't quote Bible at me that way, Mr. Wilson," said George, with a flashing eye, "don't! for my wife is a Christian, and I mean to be, if ever I get to where I can; but to quote Bible to a fellow in my circumstances, is enough to make him give it up altogether. I appeal to God Almighty;—I'm willing to go with the case to Him, and ask Him if I do wrong to seek my freedom."

"These feelings are quite natural, George," said the good-natured man, blowing his nose. "Yes, they're natural, but it is my duty not to encourage 'em in you. Yes, my boy, I'm sorry for you, now; it's a bad case—very bad; but the apostle says, 'Let everyone abide in the condition in which he is called' (Stowe 1982: 183–84).

7. Pauline Biographies, Fictional Histories, and Contemporary Conversations

The letter to Philemon has continued to be an important source for the exploration of Pauline themes on a number of fronts. One of the most interesting of these has been in the area of what might be broadly described as *biographical studies* of Paul himself, particularly when the category is expanded to include fictional assessments of his life. Thus, not only has the epistle played a role in attempts by New Testament scholars to construct historical biographies of the apostle, but it also has been a key text for novelists and playwrites composing fictional accounts of his life, as well as some highly creative attempts to initiate some fictional contemporary conversations with Paul and his associates from Colossae. We shall proceed to examine these three areas in turn.

1. Pauline Biographies

Not everyone agrees that the letter to Philemon has something significant to contribute when it comes to a study of the life and thought of Paul. Some New Testament scholars who have written biographies on Paul or introductions to his theology pay scant attention to the Onesimus-Philemon incident, and are even dismissive of its contribution to a study of Pauline thought. C.K. Barrett's *Paul: An Introduction to His Thought* (1994) is a case in point when he remarks:

> In fact we have all that we need for an understanding of Paul's thought in Romans, 1 and 2 Cor., Galatians, Philippians, and 1 Thessalonians. The short personal letter to Philemon adds little of theological substance (Barrett 1994: 7–8).

Other standard introductions to the apostle follow suit in this regard. E.P. Sanders's *Paul* (1991) mentions the letter to

Philemon at only one point, referring to the injunction in v. 22 that Philemon prepare a room for him as an illustration of the fact that the normally austere Paul occasionally lived in comfort. Some assessments are slightly more attentive to the Onesimus–Philemon story, although direct references to it are often few and far between. For example, Martin Dibelius's *Paul* (1953) makes only two passing references to the letter to Philemon itself. These occur in connection with his suggestion that the letter was written between 55 and 60 CE while Paul was imprisoned in Caesarea for two years (Acts 24.27). Dibelius also suggests that it was directed to the Colossian slaveowner Philemon and that the letter to the Colossians was also written at the same time. Thus both letters are a reflection of the seriousness with which Paul regarded the church situation in the Lycus valley and indicate his intention to go there following his release from prison. Somewhat remarkably, nothing of the nature of the awkward human predicament involving Onesimus is ever mentioned by Dibelius in his reconstruction of Paul's life-story.

A slightly different scenario is presented by Günther Bornkamm's *Paul* (1971), although once again the Onesimus–Philemon incident plays only a marginal role in the reconstruction of Paul's life and thought. Bornkamm thought that the letter to Philemon was written by Paul during his imprisonment in Ephesus, perhaps about 54 or 55 CE. At the same time, he regarded Colossians as non-Pauline and did not attempt to unravel the complexities of how Colossians and Philemon fit together. However, he suggested that Philemon does reveal something of the apostle's personality:

> [T]he letter's ingenuousness affords a unique glimpse into Paul's warmth of heart, his ability to identify himself to the full with others, his skill as a pastor, yes, and his sense of humor, which did not desert him even in prison (Bornkamm 1971: 84).

E.J. Goodspeed's *Paul* (1947) was written in retirement and served as something of a culmination of his ideas about Paul and the nature of the documents of early Christianity (he vigorously disputed the idea that Aramaic sources underlie the gospels, for example). Not surprisingly, Goodspeed's novel stressed the Hellenistic dimensions of Paul's life, while downplaying its Jewish dimensions. The novel gave a different geographical scenario to the Paul—Onesimus—Philemon relationship, one that was in keeping with Goodspeed's overall theory concerning the origin of the letter to the Ephesians and the production of the Pauline canon (Goodspeed 1947: 215 suggested that Onesimus himself was responsible for the first publication of Paul's letters in Ephesus, where he was the bishop). Goodspeed set the relationship within the time-frame of Paul's imprisonment in Rome, and, as most biographers do, gave due attention to the role of Epaphras in alerting the apostle to difficulties that the church in Colossae was experiencing (on the basis of Col. 4.13 Epaphras is viewed as responsible for all of the churches in the Lycus valley). However, Goodspeed suggested that Onesimus was a runaway slave who had robbed his master Philemon, *who lived in Laodicea*. When Paul wrote his letter to Philemon and broached the subject of Onesimus, he as careful to address the letter to Archippus as well. Archippus was (according to Goodspeed's reconstruction) the leader of the church that met in Philemon's house and by including Archippus in the letter's addressees Paul was ensuring that the Onesimus—Philemon matter would be dealt with publicly by the church. In addition, to ensure that this happened, Paul also took pains to include within the letter he sent to Colossae via Tychicus instructions concerning the letter that he wrote to the Laodiceans (that is to say, Philemon). Thus, Goodspeed was able to incorporate Paul's exhortation to Archippus recorded in Col. 4.17 ('See that you fulfill the ministry that you have received in the Lord') within his scenario. Speaking of Archippus, Goodspeed suggested that:

> His Christian service evidently is to see that Philemon treats Onesimus at least humanely and, if possible, accedes fully to Paul's wishes (Goodspeed 1947: 209).

The intention of Paul, according to Goodspeed, was that Onesimus be released from his slavery by Philemon, and that he be sent back to him (Paul) in Rome so that he can be of service to him in his ministry for the cause of the Christian gospel.

Jerome Murphy-O'Connor's *Paul: A Critical Life* (1996) accepted the idea that Paul's prison epistles, including Philemon, were written during the apostle's captivity in Ephesus. According to Murphy-O'Connor, the Ephesian captivity makes much more sense of the geographical circumstances implied by both Colossians and Philemon than does a Roman captivity of Paul. However, he followed the suggestion of Peter Lampe (1985) that Onesimus was not, strictly speaking, a runaway, but a slave in danger of punishment who had sought out a friend of his master in order to effect a reconciliation. Onesimus deliberately went to Ephesus, probably at the instigation of Epaphras, to find Paul because he knew that Paul would have influence over his Christian master Philemon back in Colossae (Murphy-O'Connor 1996: 177, 235). It is possible, Murphy-O'Connor admits, that Philemon was converted to Christianity directly by Paul himself. However, it is much more likely that Philemon and Paul had never met and that Philemon was converted to the faith through Paul's envoy to the Lycus valley, Epaphras (E.F. Scott 1930: 112 also argued this point). Then Philemon, his wife Apphia and Archippus became the nucleus of a house-church in Colossae. Interestingly, Murphy-O'Connor goes on to hypothesize that later, after Onesimus himself is converted to Christianity, Archippus left the church community in Colossae and became caught up with the false teachers in Colossae. Once Epaphras arrived in Ephesus and informed Paul of this, the apostle wrote the urgent letter we now know as Colossians. The difficulty with this scenario is the time-lag it implies between the writing of Philemon and Colossians, and the fact that it rests on a very contrived interpretation of the opening phrase in Col. 4.17 ('Tell Archippus [*kai eipate Archippo*]'), which Murphy-O'Connor takes to mean that Archippus has to be 'told' because he was no longer an active worshipper in the church and would not have heard the letter from Paul being publicly read (Murphy-O'Connor 1996: 236–237). He is dependent upon Goodspeed (1937: 112), for the germ of this idea.

James D.G. Dunn's *The Theology of Paul the Apostle* (1998) is similarly persuaded by the suggestion by Lampe (1985) that Onesimus may not have been a runaway slave. Dunn's discussion of the letter to Philemon is minimal (only two paragraphs in a volume of over 700 pages), although the complexity of the interpretative issues it raises are well noted. He describes the letter as 'the best example of Paul's sensitivity and skill as a mediator between individuals of different social status' (Dunn 1998: 576). More substantial is Dunn's use of Philemon as an example of 'Ethics in Practice', where a paragraph on Philemon is attached to a discussion of slavery and 1 Cor. 7.20–23 (Dunn 1998: 700). Dunn notes that Paul's main concern in the letter to Philemon was to bring about a positive reconciliation between Philemon and Onesimus, without necessaily being overly directive about how their relationship was to be worked out.

The tendency to overlook or downplay the contribution that Philemon has to make in a reconstruction of Paul's life is more than met by the approach of Gerd Lüdemann in his *Paul: The Founder of Christianity* (2002). Whereas others had argued that Philemon was relatively unimportant, Lüdemann made Philemon the epistolary starting point for his study of Paul, saying that 'anyone interested in Paul's religion must regard Philemon as a pearl among his letters' (Lüdemann 2002: 65; he is here consciously following the lead of Adolf Deissmann 1926: 18–19). Lüdemann accepted that Paul probably wrote the letter from his imprisonment in Ephesus, and suggested that it was composed between the writing of 1 Corinthians and the various letter fragments now known as 2 Corinthians. As will become clear below, for Lüdemann this is significant for the eschatological concerns and preoccupations of 1 Corinthians form an immediate prelude to the ideas contained in the letter to Philemon.

Lüdemann acknowledged that the tide had turned away from those who view Onesimus as the fugitive slave of Onesimus, and in favour of those who see Paul as someone who had been approached by Onesimus to mediate between master and slave. However, he does not feel that Paul ever addressed the question of Philemon giving Onesimus his freedom within the letter; far higher concerns were on the apostle's mind within the epistle.

In the end, Lüdemann argued that it was possible to find all of the key paradigmatic elements of Paul's theology and practice within the epistle to Philemon, although some lie just beneath the surface and are not as boldly declared as we might like. This enabled Lüdemann to suggest that it is possible to turn the tables on negative assessments of Philemon as a letter of theological substance, and instead view it as the place where we get closest to the heart and soul of Paul's own religious beliefs. What counted above all in the apostle Paul's thinking was the 'new reality' which was to be found in Christ; this perception was to govern the actions of Philemon and Onesimus, since they shared a common life as Christian believers. This 'new reality' was to transcend socio-economic boundaries, and to redefine slavery and freedom to the extent that the debates about the Christian's role in the debate over the abolition of slavery become irrelevant. Ultimately, Lüdemann asserted, concentration on what the epistle of Philemon has to say about the slavery issue misses the point, and fails to take into account the eschatological perspective of Paul:

Much to the chagrin of many modern exegetes, Paul displays a consistently conservative attitude towards issues of socioeconomic status, including slavery. The chief reason for this is his imminent expectation of the end. Paul thought that this world was about to come to an end. Why bother about the preliminary things? He relativizes slavery and freedom because what counts is freedom in Christ (Lüdemann 2002: 79).

2. Fictional Histories

Another angle on the Philemon—Onesimus story focuses on the narrative dimensions of it, developing these into full-bodied works of historical fiction. This approach has a long history behind it, and is driven in part by the fact that Paul's letter leaves the relationships between characters open-ended and undefined. F.C. Baur once likened the letter to Philemon to a Christian romance, saying that he detected within it 'the embryo of a similar Christian fiction' (cited in Godet 1887: 152). This insight has certainly proven to be true, as this embryonic story of Philemon and Onesimus has been developed in works of many popular novelists over the years. Occasionally critically acclaimed writers of creative fiction have turned to the biblical story of Paul the apostle for their basic story-line and included the Philemon and Onesimus episode as a constituent feature. Some writers do not refer to either Philemon or Onesimus at all in their work. A good example is Taylor Caldwell's *Great Lion of God* (1970); another case in point is the recent fictional biography by Walter Wangerin entitled *Paul: A Novel* (2000).

At the same time, other writers whose work has not been so critically acclaimed, have also re-worked the story of Paul's encounter with Philemon and Onesimus to good effect. Frequently such books have been written by Christians for Christians, and they books tend to be pietistic in their approach and assume a conservative attitude toward the biblical text. Historical-critical insights into the New Testament documents are eschewed and there is an often unspoken value placed on 'reading the Bible stories as they stand'. There is often no recognition of theological developments within the Pauline corpus, no appreciation of the deutero-Pauline nature of some of the epistles, and a tendency to weave together material from the letters with stories and insights gleaned from other sections of the New Testament, notably the Acts of the Apostles, with little or no recognition of

Biographies, Histories, Conversations   113

the methodological difficulties involved. We turn now to consider briefly twelve examples of such works of historical fiction.

a. *Scholem Asch's* The Apostle *(1943)*

Scholem Asch's *The Apostle* was published in 1943. Asch was born in Kutno, Poland in 1880, but moved to the city of Warsaw in 1899 and began his writing career there, publishing stories, poems, novels and plays in both Yiddish and Hebrew. In 1909 he emigrated to New York City where he wrote mainly for Yiddish newspapers. He had some success as a playwright, but really came into his own as a prolific writer of historical fiction, with many of his novels concentrating on Jewish and Christian subjects. His novel about Paul entitled *The Apostle* was part of a trilogy dedicated to exploring New Testament characters; the other two parts were entitled *The Nazarene* (1939) and *Mary* (1949). The intention was that the novels portrayed Jesus, Paul and Mary in such a way as to bridge the gap between Jewish and Christian readers. However, Asch was not really successful in this endeavour. In fact, the novels antagonized some of Jewish readers in America to such a degree that Asch was driven to move to Israel in 1956 and remained there until his death a year later.

Asch offered one or two interesting angles on the reconstruction of Paul's life, despite the fact that the story of Philemon and Onesimus played a minor, but memorable, part within *The Apostle*. For one thing, Asch has *two* characters in the novel named Onesimus; one who accompanies Tychicus to Ephesus and then goes on to Colossae to deliver Paul's letter to the church there, and the other who is the runaway slave of Philemon of Colossae. At first glance this seems a bit confusing, but it does serve to separate the reference to Onesimus which is contained in Col. 4.9 from those which appear in the letter to Philemon (some scholars argue that Col. 4:9 refers to a *second* visit of Onesimus to Colossae, one that was probably later than the visit which he made to deliver the Letter of Philemon to the congregation there (see Winter 1987: 2 for more on this point). Indeed, it is worth pointing out that Asch thereby resolves a difficulty which has perplexed some scholars concerning the runaway slave's mysterious freedom of movement (how *can* a slave in prison be sent on a mission such as Paul suggests, and does Philemon release Onesimus for this purpose?) The answer is simple: it is *another* Onesimus who was sent with Tychicus to

Colossae in order to deliver the letter there, a letter which, incidentally, was completed several days *before* the letter to Philemon was written and sent to Colossae with Onesimus the runaway slave. In short, the creation of *two* characters named Onesimus is quite a clever idea, and it is not unreasonable given the fact that Onesimus was quite a common name for slaves in the first-century world (a point well documented by Connolly 1987: 179–81; Arzt-Grabner 2001: 596; 2003: 86–87).

Asch solved the mystery over who introduced Onesimus to Paul by creating an extra-biblical character who steps into the scenario of Paul's Roman imprisonment. In the novel Paul is shackled to a Roman guard at his hired house on the Aventine hill, with Timothy and Aquila and Priscilla serving as faithful attendants and colleagues. Onesimus himself is brought to Paul by another runaway slave named Antonius, who is a Christian, having been brought to faith through the ministry of Paul, Aquila and Priscilla some days before. Since that time Antonius has gone on the run, having disobeyed his master by refusing to throw an unwanted child sired by the master into the Tiber river. The two runaways meet in a secret cellar in a run-down area of the city which is home to many slaves in their predicament. Antonius tries to persuade Onesimus to return to Philemon and be forgiven, but Onesimus refuses to believe that any slave-owners, even Christian ones, would be so forgiving. So Antonius decides to take him to God's messenger, Paul the Apostle. Both runaways confess their situation to Paul, and Onesimus is amazed to discover that Paul knows his master Philemon, as well as his wife Apphia who had at one time visited Paul in Ephesus. Paul accepts Onesimus, and then sends him with Timothy to Priscilla where he is cared for. We then read:

> When two weeks had passed, Onesimus appeared again before Paul, a new man inwardly and outwardly. His hair was cut and combed, his chin shaven, his body decently covered. In the two weeks of his stay with Aquila and Priscilla he had given himself to the Messiah and had been received into the brotherhood of the Christians.
>
> Paul called for papyrus and writing implements, and with his free right hand—the other being chained to his guard—he wrote a letter to the master of Onesimus, Philemon of Colossae ...

A slave had fled from Philemon; Paul returned him, a brother (Asch 1943: 652).

One other brief point worth mentioning within the story is the way in which Asch highlights the demand that Paul places upon runaway slaves to return to their earthly masters. This occurs as Paul also requires Antonius to return to his master, who happens to be Tigellinus, the commandant of Nero's Praetorian Guard and a person very much to be feared. Antonius does as Paul requires of him, is flagellated for his crime, and learns a valuable lesson about true freedom in Christ despite earthly enslavement.

b. John Pollock's The Apostle *(1969)*

John Pollock's *The Apostle* (1969) attempts a popular biography of Paul. The story of Philemon and Onesimus figures at two points within the story of Paul's life as Pollock relates it. The first of these (pp. 141–42) involves the introduction of Philemon into Paul's life during his ministry in Ephesus. Philemon is presented as a slaveholder and landowner from Colossae who comes to Ephesus to superintend the sale of his wool. While in the city he befriends Paul, is converted to Christianity and then returns to Colossae where he lives with his wife Apphia and their son Archippus. Paul sends to them Epaphras, a native of Colossae but a member of the Ephesian church., and a house-church soon develops within Philemon's home. The second more extensive scene (pp. 223–30) is set during Paul's Roman imprisonment and is dated by Pollock to AD 62. Onesimus is abruptly introduced into the story as a runaway slave who had drifted to Rome after leaving his master Philemon. Paul converts the slave to the Christian faith and then involves him in his ministry. Epaphras arrives from Colossae with news of the church there and Paul decides to write a letter to them and send it via Tychicus. He also writes a letter to the church in Ephesus (our Ephesians) and a third, private letter to Philemon in Colossae which addresses the question of Onesimus's manumission (the letter was probably penned by Timothy). Paul sends Onesimus back to Philemon, and the runaway slave is to hand Paul's note to his master. Concerning Paul's views on slavery, Pollock states:

> By implication the letter to Philemon displays Paul's total rejection of slavery as a state compatible with the gospel in a Christian society. Paul was no Spartacus

calling slaves to revolt: a sudden end of slavery would reduce the Roman Empire to chaos and he was a realist enough to recognize that to agitate for abolition in his lifetime would be senseless, merely provoking the crushing of Christians as a menace to law and order (Pollock 1969: 227).

So Onesimus is sent back to Philemon, who is to treat him not as a returned piece of lost property, but as a brother Christian. Interestingly, Pollock does not pick up on the idea that Paul wants to have Onesimus released from his slavery in order that he might be returned to Paul and be of assistance to him in the spreading of the gospel message. Rather, according to Pollock's reconstruction, Onesimus finishes out his days back in Colossae. The last fleeting glimpse we get of Onesimus in the book is the possibility of Paul, having been released from his imprisonment in Rome, contemplating a trip to the churches in the Lycus valley 'to enjoy Philemon's guest room at Colossae, served by a delighted Onesimus' (Pollock 1969: 230).

Pollock's *The Apostle* is a good example of how the larger-than-life figure of Paul has attracted the lion's share of interest among writers of popular historical fiction. However, the story of Philemon and Onesimus has itself also generated quite a number of substantial works of historical fiction in its own right.

c. *Edwin A. Abbott's* Onesimus: Memoirs of a Disciple of St Paul *(1882)*

Perhaps one of the most interesting examples of this is Edwin A. Abbott's *Onesimus: Memoirs of a Disciple of St Paul* (1882), which was originally published anonymously. Abbott (1838–1926) was an English schoolmaster and theologian who attended St John's College, Cambridge before being ordained in 1862. In 1865 he became headmaster of the City of London School, a post he held until his retirement in 1889. In retirement he devoted himself to his literary and theological interests, including the writing of religious romances. In addition to *Onesimus: Memoirs of a Disciple of St Paul*, Abbott wrote two other works of narrative fiction, *Philochristus: Memoirs of a Disciple of the Lord* (1878) and *Silanus the Christian* (1906).

Onesimus: Memoirs of a Disciple of St Paul is a full-bodied effort (311 pages), one that attempts to integrate the insights of

Biographies, Histories, Conversations 117

historical-critical research with a fine sensitivity to the techniques of good narrative fiction. Thus, the Preface to the work has Onesimus address the Reader directly:

> Art thou a slave, as I was? Or an orphan, as I was? Or wanderest thou still, as I long wandered, in the wilderness of doubt and sin? Then for thee is written this story of one made free in Christ, and adopted to be a child of God, and in the end brought safe out of the deep darkness of Satan into the Light of the Eternal Truth.

The story is divided into eight books, and is ostensibly written as the memoirs of Onesimus for his Christian colleague Epaphras. The story begins with Onesimus's birth in Pergamus during the reign of Tiberius. The child has a twin brother and both are abandoned by their parents at birth, and adopted by a woman from the town of Lystra. The ten-year old Onesimus meets Paul in c. 46 CE while the apostle is on his missionary journey through Iconium. His foster-mother dies when he is 16, and the twins are sold as slaves, Onesimus eventually being bought by the merchant Philemon. Philemon is from Colossae, where his lives with his wife Apphia and step-son Archippus. Onesimus is taken to Colossae where he befriends several other slaves, including Epictetus from the nearby town of Hierapolis and is introduced to philosophical and theological discussions by him. Soon Philemon takes Onesimus to Antioch to find out more about the Christian movement. The quest for more information then takes them to Jerusalem, and then on to Athens where Philemon and Onesimus separate, with Philemon returning to Colossae and Onesimus staying in Athens ostensibly to study and perfect his Attic dialect. Here Onesimus falls in love with a young woman named Eucharis, the daughter of Molon his rhetoric teacher. Onesimus writes to Philemon and asks that he might be given his emancipation, or at least a promise of it, so that he can marry Eucharis. Philemon writes back, asking that Onesimus return to Colossae immediately; Onesimus does so and is told by Philemon that he has been converted to Christian faith by Paul. He also informs Onesimus that he has arranged for him to marry the daughter of one of Colossae's most influential citizens, a girl named Prepousa. Part of the arrangement involves Onesimus being given his freedom and a small estate; the assumption is that Onesimus will become a Christian like his master. Onesimus defers, and goes to Hierapolis to seek the advice of his fellow-slave Epictetus. Meanwhile, Eucharis writes to him and confesses her love for him, as well as her growing interest in Christianity. Soon after this Onesimus is falsely accused by another of Philemon's slaves of stealing a scroll from the master's library. Another letter arrives from Molon which brings news of the death of Eucharis. Onesimus is grief-stricken, and attempts to hang himself, but is prevented from doing so by Philemon, who interprets the suicide attempt as proof of the theft of the library scroll. Incensed, Onesimus attacks Philemon and is only prevented from hilling him by the intervention of other slaves. It is then decided that Onesimus is to be sent to an *ergastulum* north of Laodicea in punishment.

Rather than face this prospect, Onesimus steals some money from Philemon and runs away to Pergamus where he meets a priest of the temple of Aesclepius who puts him on the trail of his mother, the woman who had abandoned him and his brother at birth. He flees to Corinth where he works as a scribe, and one day visits the tomb of Eucharis in Athens. Then he travels to Rome and finds employment as an actor in the Imperial palace, one night even coming across Paul in prison as he awaits his trial before Nero; Onesimus recognizes Paul from the chance encounter many years ago. Onesimus is frightened by Paul because the apostle knows his master Philemon, but he is attracted to the preacher nonetheless. He falls under the spell of Paul's teaching and preaching and is converted, confessing all his misdeeds to the apostle. Onesimus is baptised a week later, and decided himself that it is necessary for him to return to Colossae. Paul agrees and writes a letter to Philemon to take with him. The arrival in Colossae is a success; as Onesimus says, "I had not been an hour in Colossae before Philemon signified his desire to emancipate me without conditions' (1882: 211).

Philemon and Apphia treat Onesimus like a son and eventually he takes over Philemon's role as leader of the church in Colossae. Philemon himself dies shortly afterwards, just as the great fire in Rome breaks out and Christians are beginning to be persecuted. The apostle Peter is killed and Paul is again imprisoned, so Philemon goes to Rome to see him before he is executed. Paul relates his life-story to Onesimus, who dutifully writes it down. The time comes for Paul's execution, and Onesimus stays with him until the end. He then returns to Colossae and continues to work in the church there. He lives through the period of the Jewish War and eventually befriends a Jewish Christian named

Philocrestus from Londinium who reveals details about his natural father and mother. Onesimus takes on more and more responsibility in the church, and travels to Rome where he learns more about the earthly life of Jesus and obtains copies of the first three gospels. His quest to learn more grows and he decides to go to Ephesus to meet the Lord's disciple John. However, he is caught up in a riot against the Christian movement in Smyrna, and is soon martyred there. Onesimus's story concludes with an appended note from the elders of the church in Smyrna which describes the martyrdom of Onesimus and his fellow Christian Trophimus.

The book contains brief notes in which Abbott admits that he has played somewhat fast and loose with the primary sources, freely re-working first- and second-century texts so as to create his story. For example, he uses the work of Epictetus to set up a dialogue between Christian and Stoic views of slavery, one that is conducted largely through letters that Onesimus and Epictetus write to each other. Similarly, the martyrdom of Onesimus and Trophimus toward the end of the novel is a free adaptation of the *Martyrdom of Saint Perpetua and Saint Felicitas*. Abbott admits that he is guilty of an anachronism in this sense, but states in his defence:

> the life of St Paul's convert is really better illustrated by this systematic anachronism than by the most felicitously invented dialogue of modern scholars (Abbott 1882: 307).

d. *Charles Edward Corwin's* Onesimus, Christ's Freedman: A Tale of the Pauline Epistles *(1901)*

A second example of romantic fiction is Charles Edward Corwin's *Onesimus, Christ's Freedman: A Tale of the Pauline Epistles* (1901). This is a slightly longer work (332 pages), which is divided into 24 chapters. In the preface to the novel the author takes a moment to point out his awareness of some of the contemporary results of scholarly investigation into the Pauline epistles which he uses to help set up the story. He notes, for example, that Ephesians was probably a circular letter written with a number of churches in mind, and that it might well be the letter to the Laodiceans mentioned in Col. 4.16. He also suggests that Archippus was bishop of Colosse and that the church of Laodicea met in the house of Nympha. Nevertheless, these ideas are mere prolegomena to the task of narrative fiction and Corwin (1901: 11) states that his hope in telling the story is that the 'little bird of imagination is allowed to escape from its cage'.

The story as a whole covers the period 54–63 CE, with the vast amount of it taking place in either Ephesus or Rome. In many ways, the central character of the novel is really Archippus, rather than Onesimus, although the last chapters dealing with Paul's Roman imprisonment do have the runaway slave taking a more prominent role in the story. One of the most unusual features of the characterization within the novel is the fact that Nymphas of Laodicea is presented as a man, rather than a woman, no doubt reflecting the assumptions of the AV/KJV that a male figure is meant. There is uncertainty as to the Greek expressions in Col. 4.15, which is why the RSV makes Nympha a woman. Philemon is a wool merchant from Colosse; his wife is Apphia and they have two children, a son named Archippus and a daughter named Menodora. Onesimus is the slave of Philemon but he is rather indolent and proud. As the story opens Archippus is a young man attending school at the house of Tyrannus in Ephesus. He has gone there with his friend Nymphas from nearby Laodicea. Philemon sends Onesimus to Athens so that he can attend to his son Archippus; Nymphas is also attended by his servant Manes, an older man who has been a slave for many years and does not want to be manumitted because he can see the advantages of his situation. The two young students are soon joined by Epaphras from Colosse, who also has a slave named Tychicus who is a Christian. The three students begin to attend the afternoon lectures offered by Paul and his followers, among whom are Timothy, Aquila and Priscilla, Luke the physician from Antioch. Philemon and his wife and daughter come to visit Archippus during the festival for Diana of Ephesus at which Apollonius of Tyana performs some magic tricks and impresses the pagan crowds. During the festivities Apphia and Menodora are attacked by a group of drunken men in the groves surrounding the temple of Diana; Nymphas tries to defend them and is injured. A group of Christians led by Luke, Timothy and Epaphras come to the rescue of the women. Onesimus is among the drunken revellers, but he manages to escape detection. His involvement in the incident means he is blackmailed into spying on the Christians, and even attempting to poison Paul, by the tradesmen of Ephesus, including Demetrius the silversmith, Alexander the coppersmith, a Jewish rabbi named Isaac. Eventually Philemon

Biographies, Histories, Conversations 121

returns to Colosse with his wife and daughter; while in Ephesus, under the influence of Paul, all three of the students are converted to Christian faith. Their conversion does not go down well with the folks back home and the three young men struggle, each in his own way. Archippus develops a serious fever and his family in Colosse is sent for; Paul, who has gone to Troas on a mission, is also asked to come and heal the dying convert. This Paul does, and the result of it is that Philemon and his family are also brought to faith. The Ephesian merchants organise a riot against the Christians in the city, and Onesimus disappears with stolen money in the melee that follows. Once order is restored, Paul marries Nymphas and Menodora before leaving on his Roman journey, travelling via Macedonia and Greece. Paul takes Tychicus with him, while Archippus and Epaphras are ordained to the ministry of the gospel. Nympha for his part pledges his house in Laodicea as a meeting place for Christians, with Epaphras of Colosse serving as their bishop. Similarly, Philemon gives his house in Colosse over to the Christian cause and Archippus is made bishop there.

Meanwhile, Onesimus sneaks away on a corn ship heading for Rome. Four years later, in 61 CE, Paul is also in Rome, a prisoner under house arrest. Onesimus is reduced to poverty, and barely scrapes a living selling cakes. He is framed for the theft of some jewellery and is cast into prison. Eventually he is auctioned off as a slave and sent to a gladiatorial school. Aristarchus and Epaphras are arrested for their faith and also end up in prison with Paul in Rome. Tychicus discovers the predicament of Onesimus and reports to Paul. The apostle and his Christian entourage pool together their money and buy Onesimus's freedom. He comes to live with Paul and the others and it is not long before he is converted to Christian faith. He is baptized and begins to develop as a believer, although Paul soon challenges him about his relationship with his master Philemon. Onesimus decides to return to Colosse and face the situation, and he packs his travelling case for the journey. Next there is an interesting passage which describes this case, one of the few places where Corwin steps outside of the narrative world he has created in the novel:

> In it lay three letters, unsealed, all written by the hand of Paul, one to the Church of Ephesus, one to the Church of Colosse, and one to Philemon. Paul had told Onesimus

he might read them if he wished. Now he picked up the letter to the Colossians. Could we hold those priceless autograph manuscripts in our hands, as Onesimus did that night, the universities of Europe and America would mortgage all their endowments to buy the treasure, but we cannot. We can, however, look over the shoulder of the slave and read with him (Corwin 1901: 317).

What follows, of course, is a large section of Colossians, followed by the whole of the letter to Philemon, both of which Onesimus reads. The story then attempts to tie up all the loose ends. Paul is acquitted and makes his promised visit to Laodicea and Colosse, accompanied by Epaphras, Luke, Timothy, Aristarchus and others. Eventually all of the characters converge on the house of Nymphas and Menodora in Colosse, where Paul catches his first glimpse of their young son, named Paul in his honour. In such a setting Onesimus is truly content, having realized his freedom in Christ.

e. Lauren M. Hoyt's Onesimus the Slave: A Romance of the Days of Nero *(1915)*

Another good example of a novel of narrative fiction is Lauren M. Hoyt's *Onesimus the Slave: A Romance of the Days of Nero* (1915). This again is a substantial work (324 pages), one that blends together romantic prose with a modicum of historical references and biblical information about Onesimus. In this story Onesimus, an Olympic award-winning athlete, is the son of a Roman senator and he lives in the city of Joppa in the Roman province of Syria. As the story opens tensions between Rome and the Jews are threatening to spill over into Joppa and Onesimus is in charge of a small militia which is preparing to defend Joppa against the invasion of Roman soldiers. The Roman soldiers conquer the city and Onesimus is taken prisoner. He is taken to Caesarea, where he is sold into slavery and purchased by Philemon, a wealthy merchant from Colossae. Philemon makes Onesimus serve as a galley slave aboard one of Philemon's ships, a situaton which is understandably regretted. Eventually the ship is in port in Alexandria where Onesimus manages to steal some money, jump ship and escape. He meets an old friend who helps him, and together they set off for the Upper Nile on an expedition for the Emperor Nero. Onesimus hatches a scheme whereby he can report to Nero the results of the Nile adventure and he returns to Alexandria where he boards a ship for Rome. On board he befriends a wealthy Roman businessman named Florus and his beautiful daughter Berenice. A storm damages the ship and it sinks, but not before Onesimus manages to save himself, Florus and Berenice on a raft he constructs. Another ship bound for Rome picks them up and the journey to Italy continues. Onesimus has his audience with Nero in Rome and he and Berenice begin to fall in love with each other. One evening Onesimus is strolling in the streets around the Praetorium and encounters the apostle Paul, bound to a Roman soldier. He recognizes Paul as the person who had converted Philemon to Christianity in Ephesus. Onesimus listens to Paul's testimony and is drawn to Christian faith, but he is worried about the implications that a step might have. He discusses this with Paul:

> "Is it necessary, then, that I go back and surrender myself to my old master, and again be made a galley slave?"
>
> "Yea, thou must return to they master if thou would of a truth become a Christian, for thou art the property of Philemon in the eyes of the law," said Paul (Hoyt 1915: 252).

Onesimus agonizes over his decision, and what it will mean to he relationship with Berenice. She begs him to forsake his Christian beliefs and not go to Philemon. However, Onesimus makes his decision to return and visits Paul to inform him. Paul writes the letter to Philemon (which is reproduced in full within the novel), and sends Onesimus on his way with Tychicus as a companion. Interestingly, when they arrive in Colossae, Philemon reads Paul's letter, comes to the conclusion that slave-owning is wrong, and decides to manumit all of his slaves. He also says:

> "Paul wants thy freedom, that thou mayest return to him, to comfort and assist him. He has not asked for thy manumission but I see that that is his wish, and it shall be done at once, so that thou mayest return soon to be with him" (Hoyt 1915: 282–283).

Onesimus returns to Rome and discovers that Paul has been acquitted and released. Paul is en route to Ephesus and left word that he wanted Onesimus to join him there so that the work of the gospel can continue. That night Onesimus attends an illegal meeting of Christians where he hears Timothy read from a letter he just received from Paul. Roman soldiers break up the meeting and Onesimus is arrested. Berenice hears of Onesimus' predicament and tries to assist him. Onesimus is taken to the amphitheatre where he is forced to fight with wild beasts in front of Nero, who is accompanied by Berenice. Onesimus is attacked by a tiger and presumed killed; Berenice claims his body and removes it to her house, where, miraculously, Onesimus revives. They swear their undying love to one another, Berenice converts to the Christian faith, and the pair are married. The Neronic persecutions commence again, and the happy couple flee Rome for Ephesus in order to continue the Christian work there with Paul.

Unfortunately, much of Hoyt's story meanders in and out of the problems and circumstances of secondary characters who have not the remotest connection to any of the details generally used to reconstruct Onesimus' story. Instead, Onesimus becomes something of an Indiana Jones-type character, enjoying dangerous and thrilling adventures in far-off exotic places. Nevertheless, there is some interesting use of primary sources here (Josephus's *Jewish War* 2.18.10 provides the backdrop for the Roman sacking of Joppa, for instance). Perhaps the most interesting feature, in any case, is the way that the subtlety of Paul's appeal to Philemon for the release of Onesimus is recognized and presented.

f. James Alex Robertson's **The Hidden Romance of the New Testament** *(1920)*

A slightly shorter example of narrative fiction is contained in James Alex Robertson's *The Hidden Romance of the New Testament* (1920), a work which, chapter-by-chapter, deals with a number of characters from the biblical text. Robertson turns to the story of Onesimus and Philemon within the final chapter of his work, the eleventh chapter entitled 'The Story of a Runaway Phrygian Slave' (pp. 245–61). Robertson's narrative style is somewhat unusual, weaving into his straightforward story-telling (in the best romantic tradition!), frequent asides consciously directed to the reader which are quite guarded and hesitant, or which inject information drawn from historical-critical study of the text (including verse references from the New Testament and details about variant readings from different biblical manuscripts). Unfortunately, this makes for disjointed reading. It also has the effect of making the reader feel that Robertson is not altogether comfortable with his own narrative enterprise.

Biographies, Histories, Conversations 125

However, he does attempt to create a fictional narrative world which offers some unusual ideas.

Robertson begins with the friendship of two young men from Colossae, the rich Philemon, and his less well-off friend Epaphras. The two make their way to the city of Ephesus where they attend the lectures of the Sophist teacher Tyrannus. In particular, they attend the public teaching offered by Paul at Tyrannus's school and both are brought to Christian faith by the preaching of the Apostle. Onesimus is also brought into the story line at this point, for he is is said to have accompanied Philemon on the visit to Ephesus as a body-servant. Indeed, the narrative relates:

> Perhaps this slave had even seen the Christ-intoxicated Jew, for the young men had become his friends and he may have visited them in their rooms. But the dull ears of the Phrygian slave could not comprehend (Robertson 1920: 247).

Philemon and Epaphras eventually return to Colossae (accompanied by Onesimus), where they become 'flaming propagandists of the new faith'. A Christian church was established which met in Philemon's house, and one of the believing women, named Apphia, was soon married to Philemon. Robertson also notes that Archippus was a member of the Christian community, and speculates that he may have been a brother (or a son) of Philemon. Epaphras and Philemon also help establish churches in nearby Laodicea and Hierapolis. Epaphras in particular, is said to have established ahiimself as a 'peripatetic evangelist' in the area, with Archippus looking after the congregation of Colossae whenever he happened to be away.

Philemon's Phrygian slave Onesimus wins his way into the confidence of his master, but absconds with some money when a responsible task was given to him which proved to be too great a temptation. Onesimus makes his way westward along the Meander river to Ephesus. From there he takes a boat to Cenchreae, where he walks across the isthymus to Corinth, and from there boards a ship bound to Italy and then on to Rome itself. While in Rome, amidst the teeming multitudes, Onesimus begins to suffer a crisis of conscience. Lonely, hungry and desolate, he befriends some other slaves who invite him to attend some of their meetings in the catacombs. Eventually he is brought to an encounter with Paul the Apostle, whom he had first met long before in Ephesus. Robertson imagines the encounter between Onesimus and Paul in his prison cell:

> In fancy we stand foir a moment in the cell, listening to the voice of Paul. "And so," we hear him say, "you were tired of slavery and you wanted freedom. And now you have found that being the slave of a good master is ten thousand times more to be desired than bad freedom. You are tired of freedom. Look at me; I am like you, a slave—the fettered slave of Jesus Christ ..." (Robertson 1920: 252).

The friendship between Onesimus and Paul grew with Paul sensing that the runaway slave's fate lie in his return to Colossae. One day two men from Colossae arrive at Paul's cell—Tychicus and and Epaphras, the greatest friend of Onesimus's' old master Philemon. They brought news of trouble within the Christian churches of the Lycus valley. False teachers had infiltrated the church and led many astray, including Archippus. Paul decides to write letters to both the church at Colossae and to Philemon, sending them with Tychicus who is accompanied on the journey by Onesimus himself. Robertson imagines an emotionally-charged scene as Philemon receives Paul's letter and learns what Paul desires of him with regard to Onesimus. He writes:

> Philemon read the letter, and a pleased look at once began to come into his face. By-and-by he broke out into laughter; and then he read on silently, but his lips trembled; he was moved. And when the reading was done, he sent for the fugitive and kissed him; and said: "Onesimus, you were my bondsman; you absconded and deserve to die. But you have died. You have escaped into another life, into another service—the service of Jesus. Henceforth you are free. You can stay if you like, but not as a slave any more. You must be one of ourselves" (Robertson 1920: 260–61).

g. Patricia St John's **Twice Freed** *(1970)*

More recent examples of romantic re-tellings of the story of Onesimus are also fairly easy to find. A good example is Patricia St John's *Twice Freed* (1970). Effectively this is a Christianized version of a Mills-and-Boon novel with the brave and handsome Onesimus falling in love with a frail but beautiful Eirene.

Unfortunately their love for each other faces an enormous challenge, for he is a slave of the Colossian farmer Philemon and she is a freeborn daughter of a wealthy Laodicean merchant named Polemon. The story presents Apphia the wife of Philemon and Archippus their son, and heightens the drama by having Archippus and Onesimus childhood playmates whose friendship is strained in later life by their respective roles as master and slave. The two young men vie for the affections of Eirene. The interweaving of this romantic story-line with other features of the New Testament continues throughout the novel. Onesimus's father, for example, is said to have visited Jerusalem shortly after Jesus's crucifixion and resurrection and to have witnessed the martyrdom of Stephen. Epaphras, a native of Colossae, is presented as responsible for bringing Christianity to the city of Hierapolis, following some tiime spent working with tent-makers in Ephesus. Epaphras persuades Philemon and his entourage to visit Ephesus where they meet the silversmith Demetrius and listen to Paul lecturing at the school of Tyrannus. Philemon and Onesimus visit Paul in the house that he shares with Aquila and Priscilla (Paul happens to be dictating 1 Corinthians to Achaicus, Stephanas and Fortunatus when they arrive!), and Philemon is converted. Soon Philemon and his entourage are caught up in the tumult of the riot of Demetrius and the silver-smiths, and Archippus comes to faith. Onesimus is resistant to Christianity and burns with a deep desire to be free. He is in Laodicea on his master's business when a great earthquake strikes and in the confusion that follows Onesimus steals Philemon's money and goes on the run. He goes to Ephesus, boards a ship to Athens where he is robbed of all his money. He then makes his way to Corinth where he is befriended by members of the church there. He then boards a ship bound for Ostia, the port city of Rome. Eventually, after scraping out a meager existence, he joins a gladiatorial school, exchanging one form of slavery for another entertaining the crowds of Nero's circuses. He earns his freedom from the arena and encounters Aquila, last seen in Ephesus, who takes him to his house where he meets Priscilla and has his wounds attended by Luke the physician. Eventually Luke takes Onesimus to Paul, where he is recognized by Epaphras who has recently arrived from Phrygia. Epaphras gives details of the situation in the Lycus valley, Paul writes Colossians to counter the heresy developing in the church there. Paul then turns his attention to Onesimus who

128 *Biographies, Histories, Conversations*

confesses all and is converted to faith in Christ. He decides to become a servant to help Paul, but, accompanied by Tychicus, is sent back to Philemon in Colossae where he confronts his past, is forgiven and granted his freedom in accordance with Paul's wishes and flies to the waiting arms of the girl of his dreams, Eirene of Laodicea.

h. Winthrop and Frances Neilson's Letter to Philemon *(1973)*

A second example is Winthrop and Frances Neilson's *Letter to Philemon* (1973). This book is presented in 23 chapters covering 222 pages and is set during the early days of the Emperor Nero's reign. The story is presented in the first person, with Onesimus retrospectively telling his story to the reader. It opens with the emancipated slave Onesimus on board a ship bound to Athens with his wife Aurelia, also a freed slave, at his side. Onesimus reveals how he was purchased at the age of six by Philemon of Colossae at a slave auction in Antioch, how he came to the household of Philemon and his wife Apphia, together with their son Archippus in Colossae. He also reveals that Philemon and Aurelia had another son named Persilio with whom Onesimus grew up and for whom he was a childhood companion and friend. Persilio and Onesimus are introduced to Mithraism as young boys, and both make moves to be initiated into the cult. Onesimus gets implicated in a sexual scandal involving another of the young slave boys and the virgins serving the Mithra temple in Colossae and is severely chastised. Soon afterwards Persilio is taken ill and dies, with the blame being laid by Archippus upon Onesimus for violating the rites of Mithra and bringing the anger of the god upon the house. Onesimus takes a trip to Ephesus with Philemon who goes there in order to trade goods and. While there Onesimus meets Vergilio Pontius from Rome and falls in love with Aurelia, one of Vergilio's slaves. Onesimus and Philemon also encounter the Christian who live in Ephesus, notably Paul, Epaphras, and Luke. Philemon joins the Christians and wants to have his household baptized, much to Onesimus' objection—he wants nothing to do with religion. Vergilio returns to Rome, while Onesimus and Philemon return to Colossae where Paul sends Epaphras to set up a church in Philemon's house. Philemon himself leads the church but neglects his business affairs somewhat and tensions eventually develop within the household. Archippus becomes a

Christian but adopts a severe, ascetic approach to his faith. Vergilio makes a visit to Colossae and Onesimus discovers that Aurelia has been sold to the household of Nero in Rome. Onesimus, who has been given responsibility for business affairs, is revealed to have been neglectful of his duties and is whipped and stripped of his position within the household. He decides to run away and manages to forge official papers, steals some jewels from Philemon and Apphia, and makes his way to Rome via Ephesus and Corinth. He arrives in Rome in AD 61, at the tender age of 21, sets himself up as a scribe, and begins to try and find Aurelia. As chance would have it he is sent to transcribe some letters for Paul who is under house arrest. At the household Epaphras recognizes him, but promises to keep his status as a fugitive secret. Onesimus is slowly drawn into the world of the Christians in Rome, and he does manage to have a meeting with Nero's wife Octavia where he sees Aurelia. He has several other adventures, including a late-night escape from the Praetorian guards who attempt to arrest him as a runaway and a shipwreck off the coast of Ostia, before he finds that he is back in the circle of Paul and his Christian companions. Onesimus confesses everything to Paul and decides to become a Christian; he also meets Aurelia again who challenges him about his earthly master and his responsibilities to Philemon. Paul decides to send Tychicus to Colossae with a letter to the church there and Onesimus himself decides that he must return to Philemon and set everything right. Onesimus returns to Philemon and is savagely beaten by his master; eventually Onesimus hands over Paul's letter to Philemon and reconciliation takes place. Philemon realizes his Christian responsibilities and releases Onesimus from his servitude, arranging for his Roman citizenship and sending him back to Paul in Rome. Onesimus returns just in time to find the city of Rome in the throes of an anti-Christian persecution with Paul in the Mamertine prison awaiting execution. Epaphras informs Onesimus that Aurelia has become a Christian but that she has been crippled by torture and sold into a house of prostitution. Onesimus finds her, buys her freedom and they are married. Onesimus takes her to Paul in prison where she is healed of her lameness. The pair exchange final greetings with Paul before he is martyred, and then embark on a ship to Athens (with which the story commenced) to begin their new lives together in the service of the gospel.

A couple of points are worth mentioning about the story of Onesimus here presented. First, there is an attempt to weave together the fictional story with the biblical story, especially as it is related in Acts. For example, during his first trip to Ephesus with Philemon Onesimus finds himself caught up in the riot led by Demetrius the silversmith recorded in Acts 19.23–41. Specific mention is made of Luke the physician writing his two-volume work, and most of the story-line fits comfortably within the general framework of Luke's writing particularly when integrated with isolated verses and suggestive hints contained within Paul's letters. Also, the whole text of Paul's letter to Philemon is included in the story-line as Onesimus hands Paul's letter to his earthly master. At the same time, there is an abiding interest in presenting the corruption and decadence of Nero's reign, particularly as it concerns Nero's infamous treatment of his wife Octavia and his affair with Poppaea. This shows that attention has been paid to some of the secular historians of the classical world, notably Suetonius and Tacitus (although neither is specifically mentioned). However, perhaps the most innovative contribution that the novel makes is its presentation of the clash between Mithraism and Christianity as opposing religions of the first-century world. This is carried through to such an extent that the (so-called) Colossian heresy might even be said to be identified with Mithraism, with the extreme asceticism hinted at in Col. 2.21–23 finding a suitable expression within the novel's story-line in the form of Philemon's son Archippus.

i. Lance Webb's **Onesimus** *(1980)*

Another example is Lance Webb's *Onesimus*, originally published in 1980, and re-issued in 1991 under the title of *Escape from Ephesus: A Novel of the First Century*. The story opens with an account of Aristarchus, the treasurer of the province of Asia, who falls foul of a political rival who manages to have him executed as a threat to the state, with his wife and three children being sold into slavery. The eldest son, whose original naame was Gaius, is bought at the Ephesus slave-market by Philemon, a wool and silk merchant from Colossae. Philemon renames the seventeen year-old slave Onesimus, anticipating that he will prove useful as a tutor to his daughter Helen. The newly-acquired slave returns to Colossae with Philemon and joins the household; Philemon's wife is named Apphia, and his son Archippus. Onesimus serves his master for seven years, although his relationship with Philemon becomes strained as Onesimus continues to long for his freedom, and begins to develop romantic feelings for his tutorial charge Helen. Onesimus accompanies Philemon on a business trip to Ephesus and befriends Paul the apostle preaching in the house of Tyrannus. Philemon and his family become Christians under Paul's ministry and establish a church in their home back in Colossae. Onesimus continues to long for his freedom, burning with resentment at what he perceives as hypocrisy among the Christians, proclaiming freedom in the name of their Lord and yet tacitly supporting injustice by keeping slaves. Eventually, after ten years or so of enslavement Onesimus decides to run away and makes his bid for freedom while on a business trip to Ephesus with Archippus. He steals some money from Archippus and books passage on a ship bound for Rome, the easiest place for a runaway slave to find anonymity and begin a new life. In Rome he falls on hard times, loses all his money, and nearly starves to death amongst the lowest classes of society where he is forced to hide as a runaway slave. In desparation he decides to seek help from Paul, who is in a prison under imperial guard awaiting his trial before the emperor Nero. Onesimus meets Paul and the two engage in an extended conversation about the nature of freedom, both spiritual and worldly. The runaway slave Onesimus agrees to serve as Paul's amanuensis, putting his skills and training to good use as the apostle continues his correspondence with the Christian churches he has established. He stays with Paul for several weeks, meeting a numver of Christians who come to Paul's aid in his house-imprisonment, including Timothy, Junia Tychicus, and the fellow Phrygian Epaphrus, from the city of Colossae. Throughout this time Onesimus is still struggling to understand the Christian faith and what his response to it should be. One day Paul announces that he will write a letter to the church at Philippi; he asks Timothy to help him compose the letter, and asks Onesimus to be the scribe. It is during the course of the dictation of this letter that Onesimus comes to understand the Christian faith and is converted, to the tear-filled joy of both Paul and Timothy. Onesimus is baptized the next day by Paul and plans are made to send him back to Colossae to face his estranged master Philemon. Paul writes a letter to the church at Colossae which is to accompany Tychichus and Onesimus. Interestingly, the admonition to Archippus contained in Col. 4.17 is given an explicit application, namely that Archippus intercede on behalf of Onesimus before his father Philemon:

> The letter to the church at Colossae was finished, including some personal greetings indicating that Tychicus would bring them Paul's own message of love and announcing that Onesimus would be coming with him. Onesimus was moved as Paul dictated the words describing Onesimus as "our trustworthy and dear brother, who is one of yourselves."
>
> Onesimus also appreciated the closing paragraph which included a special word to Archippus, "Attend to your duty in the Lord's service and discharge it to the full." Onesimus knew this meant in part that Paul was depending on Archippus to help soften the heart of his farher Philemon, and Onesimus knew this charge would be fulfilled. He fully trusted Archippus (Webb 1980: 164).

The struggle about the nature of Christian freedom and liberty in the face of the harsh realities of life under an imperial system built upon slavery is explicitly noted a number of times within the story-line. The words of Gal. 3.27–28 are an important proof-text in this regard; the text is cited by Paul, Philemon and Onesimus alike at various points.

Webb includes a chronological chart of the major events in Onesimus's life, projecting the against key events in Roman imperial history and the life of the Christian church. It is worth noting that the novel was so successful as a popular re-telling of the story of Onesimus that Webb published a follow-up entitled *Onesimus: Rebel and Saint* (1988). This sequel accepts the proposal made popular by John Knox that Onesimus became the bishop of Ephesus, and deliberately incorporated it within the story-line. In this regard Webb weaves together a narrative which extends the story to include Onesimus's association with John the Elder and the church in Ephesus. He even relates that John the Elder specifically appointed Onesimus as leader of the Ephesian church just before his (John's) death in 92 CE. The novel concludes with the death of Onesimus at the hands of his Roman persecutors in 110 CE.

j. Arthur Temple Cadoux's Onesimus *(1952)*
Finally, it is worth noting that Onesimus himself has been the focus of numerous plays, many consciously designed as religious

dramas with an overtly religious purpose in view and a Christian audience in mind. Rarely are these of great literary value, although occasionally some of the insights offered by New Testament scholarship are incorporated within them. This can sometimes serve as an indication of the extent to which critical ideas are filtering into the public domain.

A good example is Arthur Temple Cadoux's *Onesimus* (1952), published by the Religious Drama Society of Great Britain. The expressed aim of this Society was

> to foster the art of drama as a means of religious expression and to assist the production of plays which explore and interpret the Christian view of life (Cadoux 1952: 31).

Cadoux's *Onesimus* sets the whole story against a backdrop of Paul's imprisonment in Ephesus. Cadoux (1874–1948) wrote the play with a view to it being presented in his own church in Broomhill, Glasgow. Unfortunately Cadoux died before it was performed there, but it was given as a memorial service for him on 20 February 1949.

The play has twelve characters, only four of which are based on people named within the letter of Philemon itself:Paul, Philemon, Onesimus and Archippus. Interestingly, Cadoux's play takes the unusual step of making Archippus another of Philemon's slaves. I know of no other work which explains the mystery of the relationship between Archippus and Philemon in this way. Somewhat curiously, the play does not have a character named Apphia, who is traditionally assigned the role of Philemon's wife.

The play contains seven Scenes spread over three Acts, together with a Prologue and an Epilogue that together provide the setting for the story of the three main Acts which are told as a recollection of events that had happened some time before. The Prologue and Epilogue are both set in Colosse, in the home of the wealthy businessman Philemon; the action of the three Acts is spread geographically between the town of Colossae, the nearby town of Hierapolis (where Philemon's friend Zotion has a shop), and the city of Ephesus (where Paul is in prison, supported by a Christian deacon named Ampliatus).

As the play opens, the Prologue has Philemon in the living room of his house in Colosse, accompanied only by his servant Archippus. Philemon is in a state of despair, for he has just had news of the death of Paul the apostle. Archippus recognizes his master's anguish and engages him in conversation:

> Archippus: Master, you are sad to-day. There is darkness on your spirit.
> Philemon: Did you not hear the news from the Roman ship? They have killed Paul.
> Archippus: Paul of Tarsus? Even he?
> Philemon: He has indeed followed his Master. To death itself. But half of my very heart has gone with him.
> Archippus: It is in truth a heavy blow. What can I say or do to bring you comfort.
> Philemon: Fetch me Paul's letter. To read it again will help me to realize that death cannot separate us.
> *[Archippus brings letter from table backstage]*
> Archippus: Here it is. I beg you, read it aloud. For me too it is indeed precious. (Cadoux 1952: 1)

Philemon begins to read the text of Paul's letter to him, commencing at v. 1 and reading up to v. 19, where Paul's promise to reimburse Onesimus's debt is mentioned. At this point Archippus interrupts Philemon and the following exchange takes place:

> Archippus: But Onesimus did not steal from you did he? I never heard fully all that happened, beyond that he returned with Paul's letter. How did he come to know Paul?
> Philemon: Did he not speak of it to you?
> Archippus: Never without some disquiet, so that I forebore to ask, and now that he is working on your country estate, we seldom see him.
> Philemon: He is never to blame. Let me tell you how it all happened. It was here in this very room that the trouble started (Cadoux 1952: 2).

As the story then unfolds through the three Acts we discover that Onesimus was in conflict with another of Philemon's slaves, who is simply called the Steward, and that this steward was unscrupulous, dishonest, and cruel in his treatment of other slaves within the household. The Steward was also devious, to the extent that he befriended Philemon's adopted son, whose name was Phlegon, and exploited this friendship to cover his own indiscretions. It was this conflict with the Steward and Phlegon that eventually led to Onesimus running away to Ephesus. The Steward and Phlegon then made accusations against Onesimus, including the theft of some money that Philemon had left lying around, although it was in fact they who stole it.

Onesimus fled to Ephesus where he met with the kindly Ampliatus who begins to share with him the Christian message and eventually sets up a meeting with Paul. Paul tells Onesimus about Christ's suffering and death for the salvation of the world, and this soon leads to his becoming a follower. Paul is later told by Ampliatus of Onesimus's status as a runaway slave, and this prompts him to insist that he return to his master in Colossae. The conversation between the two is perhaps the most interesting section of the play, for it highlights not only that slavery was an accepted norm of society in the first-century world, but suggests that Philemon needed to be helped to mature in his understanding of his Christian responsibilities:

> Paul: I learn that you were slave to Philemon in Colossae and ran away. Did you ever think of going back to him?
> Onesimus: I have thought and spurned the thought. God created me free, and I owe it to God and myself to remain free.
> Paul: In the church here are many slaves. I have watched you treat them as free men.
> Onesimus: Yes, they are free in soul, God's freemen.
> Paul: And you?
> Onesimus: But by what right do men make property of men? You would not own a slave.
> Paul: No. But slavery is so old, so woven into life's fabric that not all the faithful see its wrong. Philemon is a good man but in many things still a child. He will grow, but if he heard I kept his slave from him, he would think it dishonest. If then I spoke of enfranchisement, he would think, "Charity is cheap when another pays."
> Onesimus: What then must I do? Go back? To crucifixion? Now I know of whom you spoke as I entered. Paul, you are a citizen of Rome and exempt from the cross.
> Paul: Of that there is no danger. Though he is not mature, Philemon is kind. If for fellowship's sake you go back to him, it will so impress him with the spirit of Christ in a slave, that it ought to, I believe it will, move his soul to give all his slaves their freedom (Cadoux 1952: 19).

Onesimus does go back to Philemon in Colossae with an epistle expressing his desires. The runaway slave is eventually reconciled to his master, but not before a confrontation takes place between Onesimus and the duplicitous Steward, who is accompanied by his sidekick Phlegon. Fortunately, Philemon witnesses his Steward threaten the runaway Onesimus with flagellation and crucifixion. Philemon intervenes and turns the tables on the Steward and Phlegon, threatening to inflict upon them the punishment they intended for Onesimus. Onesimus begs for mercy and Philemon relents, acknowledging the Christian character of Onesimus's actions.

The play closes on a hopeful note, with the dream of freedom from slavery realized for Onesimus, and a hint about his future life among the Christians in Colossae offered. The Epilogue has Philemon and Archippus together in the same room in which the play opened. The final words of the play are on the lips of Philemon, who reads Philemon 20–25, as the curtain falls.

k. *Elsie Parry's* Onesimus, The Church at Colossae *(1963)*

Another interesting play with overtly religious aims is Elsie Parry's *Onesimus, The Church at Colossae* (1963), which sets the drama against the backdrop of Paul's imprisonment in Rome. This play has thirteen characters, only five of which are based on people named within the letter of Philemon itself: Paul, Philemon, Onesimus, Apphia, and Tychicus. In this instance, Apphia is portrayed as the wife of Philemon, and Tychicus as a faithful companion of Paul; the play makes no mention of the third addressee of Paul's letter, Archippus.

The play contains seven Scenes spread over three Acts, and covers a period of about four months. Act One and Act Three are set in Philemon's house and estate in Colossae; Act Two is set in Rome, where Paul is under house arrest. No specific date is given for this imprisonment of Paul, although there is one mention of his having been in prison in Caesarea for two years prior to making an appeal to Caesar and being sent to Rome. In this regard, mention is made within the play to Claudius Lysias, the tribune who arrested Paul in Jerusalem and had him dispatched with a military escort to Caesarea (see Acts 23.26).

The city of Ephesus hovers in the background of the drama at several points, serving as a geographical mid-point, and narrative counterpoint, between events that take place in Colossae and Rome. Thus, Onesimus is noted to have been sold as a slave in Ephesus when he was sixteen, his family estate having been conquered by barbarians and the family members sold into servitude. Most importantly, Ephesus is also mentioned as the place where Paul first met Philemon and presented to him the gospel message. Philemon is also said to trade regularly in Ephesus, and both he and his wife Apphia are described as once having been devout worshippers at the famous temple of Diana in the city. Indeed tensions over the worship of Diana features as a key motif in the play, especially after Philemon becomes a Christian and begins to feel that such pagan worship is inappropriate for him (Apphia is not so convinced about this initially, and requires more time to agree with it). At one point Philemon sends orders from Ephesus to Onesimus in Colossae that he should destroy all the pagan images of Diana that are within the house. This Onesimus obediently does, but he is fearful of the consequences. Eventually this dread of divine wrath is the trigger for him stealing a bag of money and running away from Philemon's house; he fears all the while that he is now doomed to live as an accursed image-breaking slave.

Onesimus flees to Rome and tries to make a living as an accountant, but struggles to maintain himself since Rome is full of slaves looking for work. He is befriended by Tychicus, who invites him to Paul's house and suggests that his skills as an accountant and scribe might be put to good use within the Christian fellowship. Within the span of a few short weeks Onesimus proves himself to be a valuable asset to Paul and his work. He becomes a Christian and is welcomed as a brother into the life of the believers in Rome. Paul and Tychicus become aware that something is troubling Onesimus, although they are not sure what it is. Onesimus finally reveals the truth of his situation to them:

> Onesimus: Neither of you can understand how I suffer. You think me faithful. I am the most faithless servant on earth. I wronged a good master. I robbed him of what was his own by right of purchase, his own money ... and my own person!
> Tychicus: A slave!
> Onesimus: Worse than a slave. A runaway slave.
> Paul: In Christ there is neither bond nor free. We are all one.
> Onesimus: But I am a thief!
> Paul: So was the man, crucified with Jesus, who being penitent, was granted a place in His Kingdom.

And I, Paul, have to reckon with many bitter memories. You may speak freely, Onesimus. We have all fallen short of our high calling.

Onesimus: It will be a relief to speak of it. Ever since I was baptised, I have been harrassed by a sense of guilt. Something I have never experienced before. Then, two weeks ago, in the market place, I overheard some merchants talking. When they mentioned Colossae, I was paralyzed with fear, dreading that I might be recognised. Worse was to follow! I heard my master's name. They spoke in derision, "Philemon has turned Christian," they said. Then, suddenly I knew why he had sent that message from Ephesus, telling us to smash the shrine of Diana of the Ephesians ...

Paul: Philemon! Philemon, who has founded the Church in Colossae! I met him in Ephesus, and talked much with him, hoping to have the joy of seeing him join the Church of Christ, before I left. He spoke to me of his dear wife Apphia. And how I prayed that they might both come to know the power of the Risen Christ. News came at last that my prayers have been answered. It was not long before you came, Onesimus. And he was your master! Philemon was your master!

Onesimus: He still is my master, but if I go back, I face death. You know what can happen to a runaway slave.

Paul: Onesimus, you are my spiritual son. All these months I have watched your development with increasing joy, until this shadow came upon you. You must know what is expected of a Christian in such circumstance; yet, who am I, to bid you go or stay?

Onesimus: I think I know now, what I must do (Parry 1963: 17–18).

Tychicus accompanies Onesimus back to Colossae where he serves as a witness to Philemon about the runaway's conversion. Tychicus and Onesimus deliver two documents written by Paul to Philemon, a scroll for the church at Colossae and the personal letter addressed to Philemon himself. Interestingly, by this stage Philemon and Apphia are specifically said to be the leaders of the church in Colossae. After reading Paul's letter, and questioning Onesimus about its contents, Philemon welcomes him as a brother:

Philemon: A few minutes before you came, Onesimus, I was forbidding the mention of your name in my presence. How could I forgive one whom I had loved and trusted, and who had robbed me, deserted me, betrayed my trust?
Onesimus: I deserved such censure, my master.
Philemon: I, too, Onesimus, stand censured before my Master. God has revealed to me a deep truth concerning the Gospel of Christ's love! It is in forgiving, that we serve Him best: forgiving and forbearing! God has forgiven you. Who am I to withhold my pardon? We are brothers in Christ ... (Parry 1963: 22).

The stage is thus set for Onesimus to become a leader of the church in Colossae, serving alongside Philemon, the One Master, Jesus Christ the Lord. The play ends on a positive, up-beat note.

One of the most interesting features of the play is the way it attempts to weave the story of Philemon and Onesimus alongside the larger narrative of the life of Jesus Christ as revealed in the gospels. Paul's reference to the story of Jesus's crucifixion alongside a repentant thief (see Luke 23.32–43) was noted above, but there are some other interesting touches within the play which further suggest Paul's familiarity with the gospel accounts. For example, at one point Paul preaches to the crowds who assemble to catch a glimpse of him as he is escorted by his Roman guards to his house. During his sermon he alludes to Jesus's words in Matthew 18.20, mixing it with quotations of Jesus's declarations from John 8.32 and 10.10. At another point it is revealed that the Roman centurion responsible for Paul's prison guards is a Christian, and that his father was the centurion whose servant fell ill and was healed by Jesus in Galilee (see Matthew 8.5–13//Luke 7.1–10).

l. E.G. Nightingale's **Brother Onesimus *(1964)***

A third play with an overtly religious aim is E.G. Nightingale's *Brother Onesimus* (1964), which again sets the drama against Paul's imprisonment in Rome. This play has fourteen characters, only six of which are based on people named within the letter of Philemon itself: Paul, Philemon, Onesimus, Tychicus,

Archippus, and Apphia. In this instance, Philemon is an older man, a presbyter in the church at Colossae and a wealthy farmer. Meanwhile, Tychicus is an Ephesian Christian who was a companion of Paul during his Roman imprisonment; he is an acknowledged teacher-prophet within the wider Church. Apphia is portrayed as the wife of Philemon, and Archippus is their nineteen-year old son, who is a young Christian, rash and enthusiastic, with much to learn about himself and others.

The play contains four Scenes spread over three Acts: Act One is set in Paul's hired house in Rome, Act Two and Act Three take place in Philemon's house and estate in Colossae. The story is set in the year 62 CE, and Paul has at this stage been in prison for five years.

As the play begins Paul is in his house in Rome, accompanied by Onesimus the Phrygian slave, and attended by Marius, a Roman legionary, a member of the Praetorian Guard, responsible for Paul's incarceration. Paul is telling the story of his miraculous escape from the authorities in Damascus, and how he came to be let down in a basket from the city walls (see Acts 9.23–25). Marius soon tires of the story and steps outside, leaving Paul and Onesimus to talk on their own. Paul pressures Onesimus to tell him something about his background and his native Phrygia (his foreign accent gives him away). Onesimus is reluctant to do so, but with gentle questions Paul persuades him to reveal all.

Onesimus relates that he was a slave of the well-intentioned Philemon, and how he came to have a falling-out with Philemon's overseer, a wicked slave named Tertius. Onesimus was in love with a slave girl named Euodia, and when Tertius made improper advances on her Onesimus struck Tertius on the head with a shovel. Thinking he had killed his overseer, Onesimus took the money that Tertius had on him (money which belonged to Philemon) and fled from Colossae. He fled to Miletus, and from there to Corinth, where he spent the rest of his remaining money and booked a passage on a ship to Rome. The following exchange between Paul and Onesimus then takes place:

> Paul: A sad story and a terrible one, my son, but even in this I can see the hand of the Lord. Philemon is an old friend of mine. That will make it much easier when you go back.
> Onesimus (*Startled.*) Go back?

Paul: Yes, it all fits in beautifully. Tychicus is starting off to Colossae with the letter I wrote to the Church there tomorrow morning. You can travel with him and take a letter to Philemon. I'll write it now. What a good thing you told me your story tonight!

Onesimus (*Sulkily*.) I'm not going back ... I can't.

Paul: My son, you must go back. There's no question about that. You belong to Philemon, just as much as his land or his house or his furniture. The money you took was Philemon's money. You robbed him twice; once of yourself and then of his money. You can't be a disciple with a sin like that on your conscience. It's hard, I know, but you must go back (Nightingale 1964: 11–12).

Tychicus and Onesimus go to Colossae and meet with Philemon, who is pleased to learn that Paul has written him a personal letter, but less certain about it when he reads it. Philemon is primarily concerned with what impact that this will have on his situation as a master with over 50 slaves working in the fields alone. Still the challenge of Paul's appeal, 'receive him as my son, part of me' is powerful. Philemon admits, 'It's hard to refuse Paul anything, and when he puts it like that ... but it's difficult, very difficult' (Nightingale 1964: 18).

In Act Three the eruption of Onesimus's return has caused to Philemon's household is explored. In particular, the idea that Onesimus might be pardoned without reprimand has caused other local farmers to worry about their own situations. What if such ideas got out and affected others? How would social stability be maintained? A group of farmers (named Phlegon, Asyncritus, Nereus and Patrobas) try to persuade Philemon that he needs to act sensibly and punish Onesimus by making a public spectacle of him. Philemon points out that Onesimus is now a Christian, and a whole new range of questions are raised. How can Christian masters worship alongside Christian slaves? Apphia joins the conversation and suggests that each group should each be allowed to have their own worship service, at a place and time agreeable to them? This is perceived as an unacceptable compromise by the young, impetuous son Archippus. He joins the fray:

You're not facing up to the facts. Christians are all one brotherhood, one family. You can't have first-class

Christians and second-class Christians. Christ died for all, by His death he has broken down the middle wall of partition. Father, you've got to treat Onesimus one way or the other. If he's a Christian, he's one of us, and you've got to treat him just like any of the rest of us. If he's a slave, treat him like any other slave. Brand him. Then when Paul comes and asks 'where's my son Onesimus?,' you can say 'Oh, he's down in the fields somewhere. You can easily spot him by the big *F* I branded on his forehead.' Or go the whole hog. Crucify him, like Paul's friends crucified Jesus. Nail him up. What does fifty bob's worth of slave's flesh matter? It will be much easier, much simpler, save all the trouble in the Church. Asyncritus won't have to eat with a slave, and everybody will be happy ... till Paul comes back to visit us (Nightingale 1964: 26).

Archippus's brashness receives mixed responses among the assembled group, some admiring his courage; others doubting his wisdom. Philemon decides to invite all of the Christians in the area to an agape meal the next evening, and uses the occasion to make a public proclamation about Onesimus. The final Scene of the play has Philemon lead a communion service (the words of which are adapted from the rite as recorded in the *Didache* 9–10). As he offers the communion bread to his slave Onesimus, Philemon says, 'Take from my unworthy hands and eat, *Brother Onesimus*' (Nightingale 1964: 32). In this sense, the play resolves the awkward challenge presented by Paul to his friend Philemon, and intimates that the apostle's appeal for Onesimus's acceptance was successful.

One of the most interesting points arising within the play is a suggestion that Paul himself did not know exactly how slavery fitted within God's plans for human affairs. In the initial exchange with Onesimsus, when the runaway slave raised objections as to the unjust nature of one person owning another, and questioned how one brother in Christ can own another, Paul replies:

It is a thing I do not understand. I don't see how life can go on if there were no slaves. There have been slaves since the time of Abraham, and though the law gives Jewish slaves privileges that Gentile slaves do not have, neither the law nor the Prophets say anything about slavery being wrong. There have been slaves from the beginning and I suppose there will be till the Son of Man comes with the clouds of heaven. I don't think that will be very long now, Onesimus. (Nightingale 1964: 13).

Finally, it is worth noting that the word-play on the name *Onesimus* (see Philemon 10) is specifically mentioned at one point in the play. This occurs when Onesimus reveals to Paul that he had been given his double-entendre name as a back-handed compliment. He says, 'They called me Onesimus, Profitable, because I was always breaking things' (Nightingale 1964: 10).

3. Contemporary Conversations with Paul

Another interesting tack involves the imaginative recreation of fictional conversations between Paul and the ancient, or even contemporary, world. For example, Colin Morris's *Epistles to the Apostle, Tarsus Please Forward* (1974) juxtaposes selections from Paul's letters with imagined letters which may have been written from people in Paul's time. Thus he has a letter from Philemon written to Paul in Rome following the return of Onesimus to Colossae (Morris 1974: 41):

Dearest Paul,
    I got your letter safely, together with the Useful One—Onesimus—who brought it. I cannot believe the change that has come over him! Nor can any other members of the church here at Colossae. He is living proof of your claim that any man in Christ is truly a new man. He has become a tireless Christian evangelist and I am honoured to treat him not as a slave but as a friend because he is your friend. Though as far as I am concerned he can go free, he insists on serving me with diligence and loyalty. It's almost embarrassing! He is rapidly becoming a leader in the church here and I have no doubt that, taking you as a model, he will soon be carrying the Gospel throughout the world. Truly, he is as you described him "a faithful and beloved brother". He has no desire to be set free in the legal sense but I must take the necessary steps to make this possible so that he can move round the churches with greater freedom, for his testimony must be widely heard.

> From what Onesimus tells us of your plight and health in Rome, we worry greatly about you and you are constantly in our prayers. However, we have faith that God who has brought you safely through so many trials and dangers will preserve you and return you to us soon. As you requested, our guest room awaits you, together with a royal welcome from all your friends at Colossae.
> Your grateful friend,
> Philemon.

Similarly, Stephen Barton also has an attempt at reconstructing the addressees' point of view in a clever little article published in the journal *Theology* in 1990. Here Barton provides two imaginary letters, the first from Philemon to Paul after Onesimus has returned to him in Colossae. Onesimus has been baptised as a Christian and has begun to prove his usefulness within the life of the fellowship there. Nevertheless, Philemon has some questions to put to Paul, particularly after sister Apphia has pointed out to him that Paul's letter to him, if read carefully and between the lines, expresses the wish that Onesimus be set free. Philemon points out some of the practical difficulties that such an act would create, not least the fact that it goes against his (Philemon's) natural inclinations. Philemon continues:

> Onesimus might not want manumission. As a slave in my house he enjoys my protection and the company of my household. Then there is the problem of the other slaves. They would want their freedom too! What would become of us then? (Barton 1990: 99).

Nevertheless, Philemon concludes the letter on an amicable note, sending Paul greetings from the church and assuring him that a room has been prepared should his circumstances permit a visit.

The second letter is a reply from Paul to this letter from Philemon. Paul is still in prison in Ephesus, but he is thankful for the news about Onesimus being welcomed in the church. He reminds Philemon about some of the fundamentals of the faith, including the baptismal creed recorded in Gal. 3.27–28. He tries to address Philemon's misgivings, but eventually has to be rather blunt in his advice:

> Beloved Philemon, this is hard to bear I know. It was hard for Cephas when I confronted him in Antioch and showed

him that the unity of Jew and Greek was contradicted by withdrawing from Gentile table-fellowship. It has been hard for me to learn from my fellow-workers Phoebe and Nympha how short-sighted were the instructions I sent to Corinth about the place of women. So I do not expect it will be easy for you to see Onesimus as a slave no longer. It will require that you die again and rise again in your relation to him and he to you. And it will require that you die to the world of masters and slaves and rise to life in the Spirit (Barton 1990: 100).

A similar example is offered by Bert Jan Peerbolte in an interesting collection entitled *Yours Faithfully: Virtual Letters from the Bible* (2004). The volume contains 31 independent chapters, each dedicated to a careful examination of a specific portion of the Biblical text and attempting to hear the hidden narrative voices embedded within it. Peerbolte provides a five-page letter entitled 'Onesimus to Paul', and it is ostensibly written to the apostle Paul by the liberated servant Onesimus some time after he returned to his master Philemon in Colossae. Interestingly, the letter hints that Paul brought Onesimus to faith during an imprisonment in Ephesus, although nothing explicit is said about Onesimus's status as a *fugitivus* or about his having stolen from his master Philemon.

The letter is quite interesting in terms of how it fits within a reconstruction of Pauline chronology. It presumes that Paul was released from his house arrest in Ephesus, and that he enjoyed a period of further ministry strengthening the various churches he had helped establish in the East, as well as founding new ones in the West, before being rearrested and imprisoned in Rome. Onesimus gives details of what happened to him after his encounter with Paul in Ephesus:

After we had met in Ephesus I went back to my master, carrying the letter you had written for me. You remember, of course, how Philemon kindly and forgivingly received me and took me back as his servant. Since we had now become brothers in Christ I could serve him in a manner I had been unable to achieve formerly, and I remained in his house for seven more years. The costs of the damage I had caused him I have paid by the extra work I performed on his behalf. Furthermore, you know that after my liberation had been arranged, I remained a member of the church of Colossae. The power of the gospel of Christ has indeed created a new kind of freedom for me: a freedom to live my life as a servant of Christ, liberated from all worldly demands, and acting as a teacher for those in need of admonition or redemption (Peerbolte 2004: 142).

A great deal of theological reflection on the part of Onesimus is in evidence in the letter. The liberated Onesimus is presented as a man well-acquainted with Paul's life and ministry among the Christian churches; he knows of the churches in Ephesus, Thessalonica, Corinth and Rome, and of the work of Barnabas in Antioch. Onesimus also knows the distinctives of Paul's theology, for he cites, or alludes to, a number of Paul's letters, echoing key themes and theological ideas in language readily recognizable as Pauline in tone. The ministry of Onesimus in and around Colossae is brought out well within the letter, notably through the mention that 'the brothers in Laodicea have sent word from Nypha that their church, too, is in distress' (Peerbolte 2004: 144). Another indication of Onesimus's involvement in the churches of the Lycus valley is the way he arranges for practical support to be delivered to Paul in Rome:

> Several times I have tried to come to you in order to visit you, but each time Satan has held me back. Therefore I hope that Eutychus and Theophilus, who bring you this letter, will be able to envourage you and bring you our gifts. The churches of Colossae and Laodicea have raised the amount that will hopefully help you to obtain your freedom once again (Peerbolte 2004: 144–145).

There is no indication within Peerbolte's imaginative reconstruction that the liberated servant Onesimus is to be straightforwardly equated with Onesimus the bishop of Ephesus, at least not thus far within his career. Indeed, the letter appears to be written earlier in Onesimus's career, before he left Colossae and went to Ephesus. At one point Onesimus speaks of his intentions to relocate in Ephesus, perhaps even using that city as a springboard to come and visit Paul in Rome:

> If I will be granted the possibility, I will travel to Ephesus after Pentecost. An envoy from Ephesus brought me a letter in which the church has asked me to come and help them. It seems to me that I should answer God's call and relocate my workshop again. After all, in Ephesus more

than one door has been opened already. Perhaps I will be able to come to Rome after I have moved to Ephesus (Peerbolte 2004: 145).

Peerbolte cleverly includes reference to a number of individuals named within the Pauline letters and weaves them together into a plausible scenario within his letter. Somewhat surprisingly, the names of Apphia and Archippus (named in Philemon 2 and traditionally seen as Philemon's wife and son) are missing within the letter. However, the names of twelve others are included in a paragraph of concluding greetings. Five of these (Epaphras, Mark, Aristarchus, Demas and Luke) are listed as if they were present with Onesimus in the Colossae area and are sending their greetings to Paul. The remaining seven (Epaenetus, Urbanus, Stachys, Hermes, Hermas, Timothy and Tertius) are listed as if they are in Rome and Paul is asked to convey greetings from the Colossians to them when he next sees them. The effect of this is to give the impression that Onesimus is in contact with Paul's associates in Rome, or at least has access to a copy of his letter to the Romans (the seven names appear in the greetings of Rom. 16.5, 9, 14, 21, and 22).

There are several indications of Peerbolte's letter seems aware of the hermeneutical debates surrounding the Greek term *doulos*, for throughout the letter he uses the word servant, and only once does the word *slave* appear as an alternative rendering of the Greek word (in a quotation of Gal. 3.27–28).

In another example of a contemporary conversation, Bridget Plass in her *Dear Paul ... Am I the Only One?* (2001) constructs a dialogue between contemporary women who write letters to Paul in heaven and juxtaposes these with letters that contain the kind of things that Paul would write in reply. In one of these fictional replies Paul is made to mention of the incident involving Onesimus:

> When I sent Onesimus back to Philemon, I had no idea how my old friend would react. It was not usual for runaway slaves to be welcomed on their return as a 'dear brother'—which is how I urged Philemon to respond. I just knew it was right. Right for Onesimus to have a chance to ask for forgiveness and become whole and without fear. Right for Philemon to have an opportunity to forgive and look at the reasons why his slave ran away. Right for both of them to acknowledge their equal status before God as brothers in Christ and forgiven sinners (Plass 2001: 16).

Another interesting example is found in Brian J. Walsh and Sylvia C. Keesmaat's *Colossians Remixed* (2005), which suggests that Paul's letters were all expressions of his belief that Christianity as a movement challenged the foundations of the Roman imperial system. Although this book is concerned mainly with interpreting Colossians, there is an extended section dealing with the matter of Onesimus and the letter to Philemon. This occurs in connection with the *Haustafeln* of Col. 3.18–4.1, and comes in the form of a hypothetical letter that Onesimus wrote to Paul and reported what happened when he and Tychicus delivered the apostle's letters to the church at Colossae and to Philemon. In the midst of Onesimus's letter to Paul he gives an account of the church meeting:

> As you can imagine, every member of both house churches in Colossae was present for the reading of your letter. By God's grace Nympha was also present, since she was in Colossae to meet with one of her textile merchants. No small interest was generated by my presence, since everyone knew that you letter would address my status in the community. What would Paul suggest be done with Onesimus, runaway slave, supposed thief, betrayer of his master? As they listened to the letter I could feel that tension was building, along with bewilderment and unease.
>
> Then when you did finally mention Tychicus and described me as a good and faithful brother, the room erupted. Tychicus had to restore calm to finish the letter. As he did there was a look of blank disbelief. That's all? No *specific* advice to Philemon? Everyone looked disappointed—more than that, enraged—except for Archippus, who flushed and then went pale. He clearly knew what was up (Walsh and Keesmaat 2005: 202–203).

Interestingly, Walsh and Keesmaat suggest (on the basis of Philemon 1–2) that Archippus was given the difficult task of interpreting the radical implications of Paul's message to his slave-holding kinsman (or friend?) Philemon. They also expand the character Nympha within the overall plan of the book, having her present at the meeting of the church in Colosse where Paul's letter was read out. Indeed, Nympha is used as a narrative voice to raise key hermeneutical questions about issues relating to women which arise from the text.

8. Philemon at the Movies

A number of films about the life of Paul have been produced over the years, although most of these films simply avoid the story of Philemon and his runaway slave altogether. This was the case in one of the first attempts to present the life of the apostle Paul to film, a Milano Films production entitled *San Paolo Dramma Biblico* (1910). The film was the directed by the Italian film-maker Guiseppe De Ligouro, who cast himself in the starring role. Few details about this ten-minute film are known, although it was briefly discussed in *The Bioscope* 219 (1910), a reference magazine which discussed the early attempts of film-makers.

Another case in point was the series of 12 half-hour films collectively entitled *The Life of Paul,* which were produced by the Reverend James K. Friedrich for Cathedral Films in 1949–51. These were directed by John T. Coyle, and starred Nelson Leigh in the title role. The titles of the twelve films were: *Stephen the First Christian Martyr, Road to Damascus, Years of Apprenticeship, Return to Jerusalem, Ambassador for Christ, First Missionary Journey, Stoning at Lystra* (all 1949); *Second Missionary Journey, Vision to Corinth, Third Missionary Journey* (all 1950); *Trial at Jerusalem, Voyage to Rome* (both 1951). Interestingly, a shortened version of the project as a whole, lasting 80 minutes, was released in 1951 under the title of *Magnificent Adventure*. The final film within this series, entitled *Journey to Rome*, is the one that one might expect the Onesimus-Philemon episode to feature in. However, although the film's narrator briefly noted Paul's two-year imprisonment in Rome and stated that he wrote Ephesians, Colossians and Philippians during this house arrest, it fails to mention either Philemon or Onesimus by name.

In 1968 the Italian film director Roberto Rossellini completed an ambitious project entitled *Atti degli Apostoli*. This was a five-part dramatization of the book of Acts and was broadcast on Italian television between 6 April and 4 May 1969; it lasted

342 minutes, although a shortened version of 280 minutes was later released. Despite the fact that Paul, played by Edoardo Torricella, features prominantly in the second half of the series, the characters of Philemon and Onesimus do not appear at all. Two TV mini-series broadcast in the USA during the 1980s similarly featured Paul the apostle as a central character. The first is entitled *Peter and Paul*, first broadcast on 12 and 14 April 1981 by the Columbia Broadcasting System (CBS) as part of their Easter season. This film starred Robert Foxworth and Anthony Hopkins as the title characters Peter and Paul. The second is entitled *A.D*, a 10 hour mini-series first broadcast between 31 March and 4 April 1985 by the National Broadcasting System (NBC). This Emmy award-winning series was written by Anthony Burgess and included within its cast Philip Sayer as Saul/Paul. All three television series were based heavily on the Acts of the Apostles, so the omission of any reference to Philemon or Onesimus is understandable (neither figure appears in Acts).

Two recent films about Paul's life are also worth noting in this regard, for both similarly fail to include Philemon or his estranged slave Onesimus within their story-line. The first is Robert Marcarelli's *Paul: The Emissary* (1997), which does include a depiction of Paul's imprisonment in Rome and his execution at the hand of Nero's soldiers. Interestingly, the film has Paul citing sections of the Pastoral epistles as he is about to die, but nothing from Colossians or Philemon. The second is Roger Young's *Saint Paul* (2000), an instalment of the big-budget 'The Bible Series' distributed by Time-Life. The series as a whole boasts million dollar budgets and top-name actors and actresses in the title roles. Young's film offers an up-to-date interpretation of the life of the apostle, and contains several unusual fictional sub-plots, but like so many films about Paul before it, the characters of Philemon and Onesimus do not figure at all.

In fact, very few films about the life of Paul include the episode with Onesimus and Philemon within their story-line. One early exception from the silent-film era was a film entitled *As We Forgive* (1920), which was explicitly based on the letter of Philemon. This film was produced by the Historical Film Corporation of American as part of their ambitious plan to cover the whole of the Bible in a series of 52 two-reel films. *As We Forgive* was the only film completed before the company went bankrupt; unfortunately no copies of it appear to have survived.

A similar church-based venture is the series of films entitled *The Book of Acts*, produced in 1957 by Broadman Films of Nashville, Tennessee, an educational arm of the Southern Baptist Convention in the USA. *The Book of Acts* is a series of ten films, shot in colour and elaborately costumed, each lasting approximately twelve to fifteen minutes. The ten films are: *Endued with Power, A Faithful Witness, Light from Heaven, No Respecter of Persons, God's Care of his Own, Every Christian a Missionary, Salvation and Christian Fellowship, What Must I Do to Be Saved, Witness before a King,* and *Triumphant*. The film series has experienced a new lease of life for a DVD version was released as part of *The Living Bible Collection* by VCI Entertainment in 2004. Unfortunately, the cast of the film is uncredited, although the actor who played Paul was named Nelson Leigh. In the main the series does, as its title hints, follow the narrative of The Acts of the Apostles, but not slavishly so. This is particularly true in the final instalment of the series, an episode entitled *Triumphant*, which deals with Paul's arrival and imprisonment in Rome, notably his house-arrest under the watchful eye of Roman soldiers (as suggested in Acts 28.14–16). This segment creatively weaves in material from the Pauline letters to fill out the story-line of both Paul's imprisonment, and his eventual execution. It follows the popular scholarly suggestion that Paul was released from his initial house-arrest in Rome and enjoyed a period of further travel and missionary activity, supporting the churches he had helped found and composing the Pastoral Epistles. The film's narrator explains that sometime later (how much later is uncertain), Paul was re-arrested and again brought to prison in Rome. The film concludes with Paul, looking markedly older and white-haired, dictating 2 Timothy to Luke, his trusted and faithful companion. Although Paul's death at the hands of the Romans is not depicted in the film, it can be inferred.

At the beginning of *Triumphant* the narrator describes Paul's initial imprisonment in Rome as lasting two years, and states that Luke and Aristarchus accompanied Paul to the city. A number of scenes showing Paul ministering to Christian believers and writing letters from prison are offered. The narrator explains:

> He wrote words of counsel and comfort to the distant churches. He encouraged and instructed his Christian

brethren who sought him out in the house where he lived as a prisoner. And many were they who found their way to the little house in Rome. There was Timothy, Paul's adopted son, Epaphroditus of Philippi, Tychicus from Ephesus.

Included in *Triumphant* is an interesting sequence in which Paul composes the section of Eph. 4.6–10, dictating to Tychicus while carefully examining the unform an armament of one of his guards. More specifically for our concerns here, there is a scene in which Tychicus and Onesimus appear before Paul during his house-arrest. Tychicus is a tall, older man, and Onesimus a much younger colleague, and the two are dispatched by Paul with letters to the Lycus Valley. In the words of the voice-over narration:

> Paul continued to write the things God revealed. And active as his trusted messengers were Tychicus and Onesimus, the runaway slave transformed and regenerated. They were entrusted with the letters which Paul had written to churches in different cities, letter far-reaching in their effect.

Tychicus and Onesimus are then shown presenting Paul's letters to the church in Colossae. Tychichus reads aloud the words of Col. 3.1–3, 12–14 as the members of the congregation look on; Onesimus sits quietly by his side. Interestingly, there is no specific mention in the film of Onesimus's master Philemon, or of Paul's letter to him. Still, this short sequence (it lasts less than two minutes) is interesting in that it offers a small glimpse of the letter Philemon within a film ostensibly based on the Acts of the Apostles. This is something not often found in such films.

However, to find the figures of Philemon and Onesimus developed in any substantial way in film we must look elsewhere, beginning with a British pre-war venture.

1. Life of St Paul (1938)

In 1938 a series of five black-and-white films were produced by the Religious Film Society of England under the heading of the *Life of St Paul*. The five films relied heavily upon selected passages from the Acts of the Apostles and various letters of the Pauline corpus—at times the dialogue is taken verbatim from the New Testament texts. The five films, and the biblical texts which they sought to bring to the screen, were as follows: *On the Road to Damascus*—Acts 7.54; 8.3; 9.1–18 (13 minutes); *The Way of Salvation*—Acts 16.9–40 (25 minutes); *Faith Triumphant*—Acts 21.26–26.32 (20 minutes); *Grace and Forgiveness*—Acts 28.14–31, Ephesians, Colossians, and Philemon (28 minutes); *Crown of Righteousness*—Philippians 4; Rom. 8.35–39; 2 Tim. 3.10–11; 4.6–8 (20 minutes). The series as a whole were directed by Norman Walker for G.H.W. Productions in London. They were based on a script by Lawrence Barrett and were filmed largely at Nettleford Studios in Walton-on-Thames. The fourth film in the sequence, *Grace of Forgiveness*, most concerns us here for it is set in Paul's imprisonment in Rome and attempts to depict the circumstances surrounding the production of letter of Philemon. The film starred Gregory Stroud as Philemon and Thorley Walters as a youthful Onesimus in the central roles (see Figure 11). In addition, it cast Neal Arden as the Apostle Paul, Allan Jeayes as Burrus, Whitmore Humphreys as Gaius, Elliott Seabrooke as Tychicus, Kaye Seely as Epaphras, Trefor Jones as Aristarchus, Gerald Anderson as Timothy, and Lewis Broughton as Luke.

The film begins with Paul arriving in Rome under military guard, accompanied by his companions Luke and Aristarchus. Paul is escorted to the offices of the Roman administrator Burrus,

Figure 11: A youthful Onesimus and his master Philemon

the official, and is greeted by Timothy and Epaphras before being led away by the Roman soldier in charge. Epaphras and Timothy spot the youthful Onesimus loitering around outside the building. Epaphras describes him as 'that slave of Philemon's, he that stole from Philemon and made off in the night—Onesimus.' The two question between themselves how Onesimus came to be in Rome, and Epaphras suggests there is no safer place for such a runaway. Epaphras, in particular, is keen to catch Onesimus, who has wronged his own master Philemon, whom Epaphras describes as 'my good friend'. They make a move toward Onesimus, but he slips away in the crowd. Later, following a debate that Paul has with Jewish leaders in the city, Timothy approaches Paul and raises the matter of Onesimus: 'Master, thou rememberest that which Epaphras told you? How Philemon's slave Onesimus is in hiding in the city? He is out yonder, lurking on the terrace.' Paul takes his Roman guard with him and confronts Onesimus, asking him if he is ashamed to speak with him in public since he is in bonds. Onesimus replies, 'Thou art the friend of Philemon, my master. O sir, I care not what wrong thou hast done. I know thee to be a good man, whereas I am a slave, worthless, wretched with sin. But thou art good.' He explains to Paul that he remembered hearing Paul instruct Philemon about love and forgiveness. Paul invites Onesimus to stay with him, and promises that he would not send Onesimus back to Philemon against his will. Paul does make plans to send Tychicus and Onesimus to Colossae via Athens, charging Tychicus with delivering the letter to the church in Colossae. Onesimus has an exchange with Paul:

> Onesimus: O Master, if I were free I would stay with thee and serve thee forever. But I am Philemon's. And as thou said, I must return to him and beg for forgiveness.
> Paul: Thou art still afraid?
> Onesimus: O ask not that. Have I not wronged him? Hath he not power over my life with none to stay him?

Paul then turns to Timothy and instructs him to take down another letter which Onesimus shall take with him to Colossae. He dictates an abbreviated version of Philemon, consisting of vv. 1, 4, 7a, 8–10, 15, 16a (minus the phrase 'but more than a servant', 17–18, 19a (which Paul writes himself, taking up Timothy's quill for a moment and signing 'I will repay it'), 21b, 22, 23–25 (Figure 12).

Figure 12: Paul signs the letter to Philemon promising to repay any debt owed by Onesimus

The letter is then rolled up and given to Onesimus, with the instructions that he is to take good care of it, and deliver it safely. Paul also gives Tychicus the letter to the Ephesians with the instructions that it is to be read to all who desire to hear it.

On the journey to Colossae Onesimus is said to have read the letter to Philemon so often that he has memorized it by heart. Tychicus cautions him, 'If thou fingerest it more, Philemon will never be able to decipher it!' (Figure 13). To comfort Onesimus, Tychicus reads from Col. 3.1–2, 12–13a, 14–15, 17, 23–24a before the two enter Colossae.

Tychicus takes the lead when the two men come to the house of Philemon, instructing a slave who answers the door to say nothing to Philemon about Onesimus. Tychicus takes Paul's letter to Philemon from Onesimus and gives it to him, and Philemon examines it, reading aloud portions, including vv. 10, 15–16a, 17 (Figure 14).

Philemon then approaches Onesimus and the final scenes depict the reconciliation that takes place between them:

> Philemon: Onesimus!
> Onesimus: *[As he comes and kneels before Onesimus, taking his hand and kissing it.]* Master! Forgive thy servant. Forbid him not to serve thee.

156 *Philemon at the Movies*

Figure 13: Tychicus teases Onesimus about his incessant reading of Paul's letter to Philemon

>Philemon: Onesimus, thou knowest I forgive thee. *[He takes his hand and raises him from his knees.]* Come! For we are to gather together the brethren and examine the epistle which Paul hath written us. But first thou must eat with me.
>Onesimus: Nay, Master. May I not first call the brethren, and eat afterwards?
>Philemon: As thou wilt, my son.

The characters of Apphia and Archippus do not figure substantially within this film. Philemon is shown dining with a woman, presumably his wife Apphia, in one brief shot, and she speaks only one line; Archippus on the other hand does not appear at all. There is an interesting exchange between Paul and the Roman soldier Gaius, to whom he is chained. Gaius expresses an interest in the words of love and forgiveness Paul had been dictating to Timothy in the letter to the Ephesians and asks to hear them read again. Timothy reads them out and this moves Gaius to express his bewilderment about what his duties should be. Paul then looks at Gaius, decked out in his military armour, and dictates to Timothy the ending of Ephesians (incorporating imagery found in Eph. 6.10–11, 14–17).

2. The Runaway (2006)

In June of 2003 a charitable trust of Arab Christians registered in Nicosia, Cyprus and describing themselves as *Arab Vision*, announced plans to produce a new film project based on the life of Onesimus. Originally this was conceived as a 90-minute feature film, together with a TV series based on the film which consisted of 12 episodes each lasting approximately 25 minutes. The project was completed in late 2006 and was released under the title *The Runaway*; the title of the TV serialization is slightly different: *Onesimus: From Slavery to Freedom* (see Figure 15).

The film, which had expanded to 120 minutes, is in Arabic, although the DVD version provides subtitles in both English and Dutch. There are minor differences between the full-length film version and the TV series installments, and the English subtitles in the feature film are much better than those in the TV episodes, which often contain grammatical mistakes or spelling inconsistencies. The film was recorded in various countries in the Middle East, and was consciously designed to be a way for the Christian message to be brought to Arab people.

The film was directed by Yassen Esmail Yassen, and the screenplay was written by David Newton and Anis Attia. It stars

Figure 14: Philemon reads the letter from Paul as Tychicus and Apphia look on

Amr Abdel Galil as Onesimus, Seham Galal as Sofia, Sherif Khairalla as Yousef, Sabry Abdel Moneim as Philemon, Mostafa El Demerdash as Archippus, Mohamed Farid as Demetrius, Rehab El Gamal as Julia, Said El Rumy as Athamos, Raoulf Mostafa as Paul, Magda El Khatib as Apphia, the wife of Philemon, Zein Nassar as Sergius Gallus, Alaa Khamis as Timothy, and Akram Waziri as Brutus.

A summary of the film's plot is in order, for although it is clearly conversant with the traditional lines of interpretation of the letter of Philemon, there are some creative adaptations to it. Understandably, the film injects additional characters and extra sub-plots to help move the story along; some have a biblical foundation, and others do not. The story-line flits back and forth between two geographical focal points: Colossae, where Philemon and his family live, and Rome, where Paul is unprisoned and Onesimus runs away to seek a new life.

Figure 15: *The Runaway* (2006) – DVD cover

a. The story

The film opens in the market town of Colossae, near Laodicea, where the family of Philemon is introduced. Onesimus is presented from the beginning as the slave of Philemon, although from the outset he is presented as a person who desires his freedom like a bird enjoys the freedom of flight. Archippus is presented as the older brother of Philemon, a merchant, who has a daughter named Sofia. It is this Sofia, the niece of Philemon, who first introduces the idea of Christianity to Onesimus, emphasizing the freedom and equality that Christianity brings to human relationships. Philemon has a number of other slaves, notably the beautiful Julia, with whom Onesimus is in love and who he one day hopes to marry. Philemon also has an extrabiblical son, whose name is Athamos; he and Onesimus are roughly the same age and are childhood playmates.

However, in adulthood the relationship between Athamos and Onesimus is strained, partly because Onesimus has proven himself to Philemon to be capable in business in a way that the natural son Athamos is not. Athamos has a personal slave named Yousef, who encourages the tension betwen Onesimus and Athamos, manipulating it to his own advantage. In the end, Yousef will prove to be the villain of the film.

Paul the apostle is presented as being under house arrest in Rome, having survived two years in a prison in Caesarea and miraculously rescued from a shipwreck in Malta. He is anxious about the church in Phrygia and discusses this with his co-workers Epaphras, who helped foun the church in Colossae, and Timothy, who serves as his amanuensis.

Archippus returns to Colossae from Ephesus where he had been involved in some business negotiations. He and Philemon have been contemplating a business venture involving the shipping of grain to Jerusalem, a proposal which would also benefit the starving Christians there. However, money is in short supply, so Archippus suggests that they sell their slave Julia to gain money to finance the project. He notes that Christian girls are well known for their honesty and decency, and she should bring a high price in Rome. Sofia, with whom Julia has a close relationship, objects against the plan, saying it is against their Christian principles. Against Sofia's wishes Philemon decides to sell Julia in Rome, but wants her to visit Paul and tries to make sure she gets sold into a good family. Julia accepts her fate with tears, but when Onesimus hears of it and approaches Philemon about it a confrontation between them arises. Philemon reminds him that he is the master and Onesimus his slave. Archippus also joins the conversation, and reminds Onesimus that Philemon fed and housed him for many years, fully trusting him in all things. Later Onesimus suggests to Julia that they should run away, but she does not think this is the way to solve their problems. She suggests that God will solve their difficulties somehow. Archippus departs from Colosse with Julia, much to Onesimus's anger and regret.

Yousef, the slave of Athamos, plants the idea in Onesimus's mind about running away to Rome to be with Julia. For his part, Onesimus wants to apologize to Philemon and ask his forgiveness for their earlier argument and for embarrassing him in public over the situation with Julia. However, Philemon has other troubles to contend with, including tensions within the church in Colossae. Philemon gets into a debate with a Jewish leader named Moses who is circumcising men to make them Christians. A debate about Paul's teaching on freedom from the law ensues. The Jewish leader challenges Philemon, saying 'Are you giving us a lesson on freedom? Who else sold a sister of his to buy donkeys and slaves like you did?' This accusation prompts Onesimus to enter the room brandishing a knife to defend his master Philemon. At the family meal, Onesimus kneels at the side of Philemon and apologizes for his earlier actions over the Julia-affair, declaring that he is Philemon's slave and promising that he will do whatever is asked of him (see Figure 16). Philemon addresses Onesimus as 'my son', which causes Athamos to rise up in revolt. He angrily says, '*I* am your son, not him.'

Later, Athamos bewails his situation to Yousef, who plots with him to cause Onesimus's downfall. Meanwhile Onesimus meets Sofia, who explains that Philemon now loves him more than ever, given his spirited defence of his master in the face of the Judaizers. Onesimus explains to Sofia that although he was in love with Julia, his love for her came about because it was impossible to tell Sofia how he really felt about her (Sofia). Onesimus says that he loved Sofia since childhood but their slave/master situation prevented them from being together. Sofia proposes that she and Onesimus should flee and go to another city, have children (a small Onesimus and Olivia). Onesimus is hesitant, saying it is very dangerous to run away like this. Unfortunately, the scheming Yousef overhears their plan and begins to hatch an even more devious plot. Philemon decides to send Athamos and Onesimus to the north in order to hire some extra workers while Archippus is away in Rome attending to their business proposal. His plan is to put Athamos in charge of the money, but Onesimus in charge of buying and selling. On the evening before they are to depart, Yousef confronts Sofia about her plans to run away with Onesimus. He tells her that he knows that she and Onesimus belong to one another. When Sofia meets Onesimus next she tells him that Yousef knows their plans. They decide to leave that very night before Onesimus is sent away. Onesimus persuades Sofia to steal her aunt Apphia's jewelry, describing it as her (Sofia's) inheritance. The two then run away, stealing horses for their journey. Yousef, meanwhile, breaks into Philemon's office and steals his money. The next morning Yousef and Athamos convince Philemon and his wife that Sofia and Onesimus have stolen valuable property and run away, and they file a report with the local Roman officer Sergius Gallus to that effect.

Sergius Gallus and his junior officer Brutus decide to follow Sofia and Onesimus to Rome. Philemon and Apphia send their son Athamos to find the runaways and save embarrassment all

Figure 16: Onesimus asks Philemon for forgiveness and declares his loyalty

around. Athamos departs Colossae, taking his slave Yousef with him; Sergius and Brutus set out on the trail of Onesimus and Sofia, although they suspect that Yousef had planned their escape.

Back in Colossae, Philemon apologizes to Moses for his argument over the Jewish law, and renounces his leadership role over the Christian church in Colossae. They are told they can meet there whenever they want in Philemon's property. The church is exhorted to choose another leader. 'But Paul chose you, Philemon,' is their reply.

Athamos and Yousef find Onesimus and Sofia in Ephesus, but Onesimus manages to grab the stolen necklace and escape, continuing on his way to Rome. Sergius and Brutus also arrive and take Yousef with them as they continue on the trail; Athamos is deputed to escort Sofia back to Colossae. Onesimus arrives in Rome and rents a room, although he just misses a chance meeting with Archippus and Julia. Archippus manages to sell Julia into a Christian family of tentmakers, but grieves over the way the whole affair has been conducted. Meanwhile, Athamos and Sofia arrive back in Colosse and Philemon interrogates his niece about her running away with Onesimus. She admits that she stole the necklace, but claims that Yousef stole the money.

Back in Rome Sergius questions a disreputable contact named Demetrius about the whereabouts of Paul the apostle, hoping to track down Onesimus by this means. Playing a double-game Demetrius then meets with Onesimus, explains Paul's in-house arrest, and proposes a way that they together could rob him. At the time Paul is working with Epaphras in composing a letter to the church at Colosse, in part a response to news that Archippus had brought to them about the trouble Moses and his gang were causing in Colossae. Sergius and Brutus visit Paul, and accuse him of upsetting the Roman way of life. Sergius tells Paul of the trouble with the runaway Onesimus. Onesimus meets Julia in the marketplace in Rome and tries to persuade her to run away with him, but she says it is useless. She accuses him of acting irrationally and of wanting revenge against his slavemasters. Onesimus returns to his rented room and bemoans his situation, crying out aloud that he hates Jesus Christ. Back in Colossae, Athamos sets off again to Rome and Sofia and Apphia have a heart-to-heart talk about life and love.

Onesimus and Demetrius sneak into Paul's house while he is out in order to rob him. Onesimus searches the house and finds no money, but instead finds Paul's letter to Colossae, and a prayerful Epaphras. When Paul himself returns Demetrius threatens him, but Onesimus comes to the apostle's aid and knocks Demetrius out. This sets up the first meeting of Onesimus and Paul, and the runaway recounts the story of his journey to freedom. Paul questions whether it is a journey of freedom; he describes himself as a servant of Jesus Christ who does what his master bids. Paul then explains to Onesimus the meaning of the Christian faith and expounds to him the significance of the cross (see Figure 17). Paul arranges for Onesimus to meet Julia at a worship service at his house, but warns him that Sergius Gallus is looking for him; he invites Onesimus to stay with him in his house. Having recovered from the incident at Paul's house, Demetrius searches for the stolen necklace in Onesimus's room. Onesimus and Paul discuss further the nature of freedom and captivity, and Paul tells his life-story to Onesimus, explaining that Jesus paid the high price of salvation. Later Timothy and Paul discuss the problems that Onesimus presents as a runaway slave.

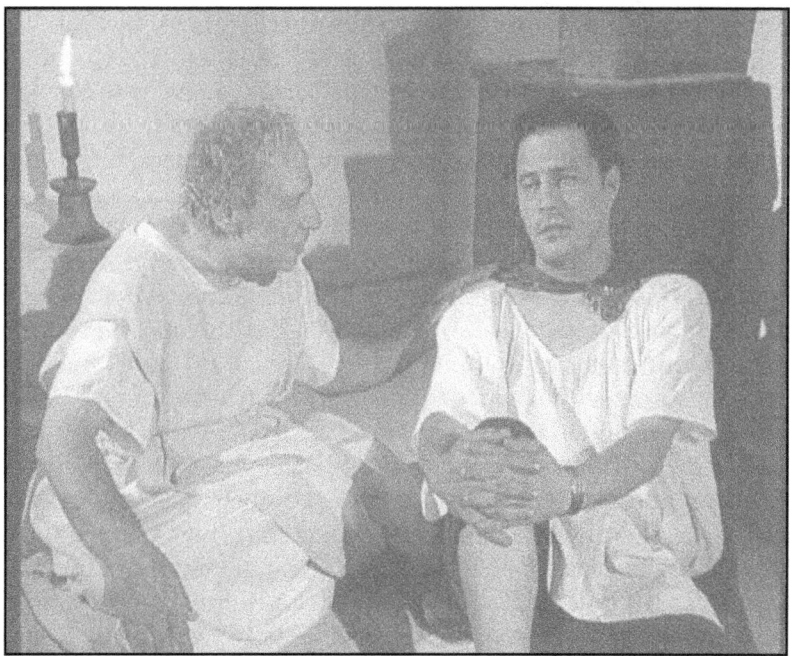

Figure 17: Paul explains the nature of the Christian faith to Onesimus

Back in Colossae Philemon and Archippus arrange harvest workers to get their crops to Ephesus. Philemon debates with Archippus whether he has acted correctly in the Onesimus/Sofia affair. For her part Sofia joins the Christian meeting, giving a moving account of her spiritual journey. At Paul's house in Rome, Onesimus listens as the apostle dictates more of the letter to the Colossians to Timothy. Athamos and Yousef join forces again and follow Julia, hoping to get the stolen necklace in order to win Philemon's trust. The Roman officer Sergius Gallus visits Paul and threatens him for having hidden a runaway slave. Later, Onesimus returns to Paul, admits his errors and says he wants to wake up from the false dream he has been chasing. Onesimus says he has believed in Jesus and found the real taste of freedom. Paul says that his own dream for Onesimus has now come true.

Impetuously, Onesimus visits Julia and declares his love for her. He also tells her of his decision to become a Christian and his intention to return to Philemon in order to ask his master's forgiveness. Sergius nearly captures Onesimus on Julia's balcony, but he escapes and runs away and is pursued by Sergius and his side-kick Brutus. Onesimus then returns to Paul and confesses he went to see Julia against Paul's advice. Onesimus gives Paul the stolen necklace and asks him to give it to Sergius; he explains that he wants to go back to Philemon with no outstanding matters separating them. Onesimus thanks Paul for all his help, and Paul calls Onesimus his 'son' in Jesus Christ. Tychichus is summoned and Paul gives him letters to take to Colossae and Philemon. He and Onesimus depart on horseback for their long journey eastwards. Shortly thereafter Sergius shows up at Paul's house and demands that the apostle tell him where Onesimus has gone. He orders that Paul be chained for six weeks and sets out after the runaway. Yousef and Athamos kidnap Julia and also set out after Tychicus and Onesimus.

On the journey to Colossae there is some friction between Tychicus and Onesimus. The two argue about the money Paul had given them, with Onesimus suggesting that Tychicus does not trust him to carry it. Interestingly the money is said to have been given by Paul *for Philemon*, in case Onesimus owes Philemon anything, no doubt a reference to Philemon 18 Eventually Yousef and Athamos catch up with Tychicus and Onesimus and a fight erupts between them. Yousef proves himself to be particularly duplicitous; he hits Tychicus on the head (seemingly killing him), he steals Tychicus's money. He then takes steps to make it appear that Onesimus was the murderer. He wounds Onesimus, and acts so despicably that Athamos decides to have nothing more to do with him. Yousef then rounds on Athamos, stabs him and throws him over a cliff. Meanwhile, Julia has escaped from Yousef's clutches and hides in the bushes. Yousef set off on horseback with Onesimus, planning to go on to Colossae and present the captured slave as the murderer of Athamos and himself as the hero responsible for capturing him. Julia discovers the wounded Tychicus and also comes to the aid of Athamos. They are soon joined by Sergius and Brutus, and together they all set out on the trail of Yousef and Onesimus.

Yousef and Onesimus arrive at Philemon's house and Yousef tells Philemon that Onesimus has killed Athamos. However, Athamos soon arrives with his escort and runs to the waiting arms of his mother and father. Athamos approaches Onesimus and the two are reconciled. Sergius presents the injured Tychicus and explains to Philemon that Tychicus has come as Paul's representative. Sergius further explains to Philemon that Onesimus had returned of his own free will; he further tells Philemon that as a Greek, he can judge his slave Onesimus as he wishes, although Romans might be more harsh in such matters. He hands over Paul's letters, sent with Tychicus, and returns the necklace to Apphia. Onesimus interrupts proceedings to ask Sergius about Paul's condition in Rome. The officer promises to give orders that Paul be set free, because he wants to ask how Paul could bring about change in someone as he did in Onesimus. Sergius plans to return to Rome, taking Julia and Yousef with him.

Philemon then begins to read the letter that Paul had written to him. His niece Sofia approaches and speaks words encouraging him to act in accordance with his Christian faith and promote reconciliation among all of his household members. With Paul's letter in his hand, Philemon goes to Onesimus, addressessing him as 'his son', and asks for his forgiveness, 'as a man, as a brother and as a human being' (see Figure 18). The remainder of Paul's letter is heard as a voice-over; vv. 21–22, 25 are read as the family all join together and enter Philemon's house.

A screen graphic in Arabic describes how increasing numbers of Christians brought trouble for Rome's slave system, creating brotherhood between slaves and masters. Included is a statement

Figure 18: With Paul's letter in hand, Philemon accepts Onesimus as his son and the two are reconciled

about Onesimus and his life and influence as a Christian leader. The English sub-title reads:

> As for Onesimus, the runaway slave, a few years after his return to his master Philemon he became the Patriarch of the new church in Ephesus. The old manuscripts tell us that in the year 95 AD Onesimus became a martyr at the hand of the Roman Emperor Domitian because he refused to reject Christ. Even after the most terrible persecutions, some of which continue to this day, churches all over the world celebrate the martyrdom of Onesimus. His life and death personify a lesson which remains true in our day and age. Nothing in life is more precious than knowing Jesus Christ, and experiencing the freedom we have throiugh Him. As for Paul, he too was martyred. The Roman emperor Nero had him beheaded in the year 64 AD. These heroes followed the steps of our Lord Jesus Christ, not only during their lives but also in their deaths. They are truly heroes of the faith.

b. Some Remarks and Observations

This is an ambitious, full-bodied undertaking, and there is much to commend within it. The film pays attention to the general scholarly conventions about the relationships between Paul, Onesimus and Philemon, and it attempts to provide a credible narrative structure for their story to be told. It opens with an on-screen graphic in Arabic which sets out the socio-political backdrop of the film. The English sub-title for this reads:

> Beginning in the year 91 BC, during the harsh rule of the Romans, there were 60 million slaves throughout the Roman Empire. But there was rebellion in the air and any such attempt was fought mercilessly by the authorities. At this time in the year 45 AD there was a new religion spreading on the Empire's borders. It was famous for encouraging masters to mingle with their slaves and to set them free.

The film asserts as a simple narrative fact that Onesimus was a slave of Philemon, although it does contain several scenes in which Onesimus struggles to come to terms with his situation. The traditional view that Paul's imprisonment took place in Rome is accepted here as a given, as are the ideas that Epaphras was instrumental in the establishment of the church in Colossae, and that Tychicus and Onesimus were responsible for delivering Paul's letters to the churches in the Lycus Valley. Needless to say, Pauline authorship of Colossians is assumed, and a great deal of the letter is presented as a narrative voice-over in the course of the film. The theological difficulties within the church at Colossae are imaginatively presented, and focus on a debate over the place that the Mosaic Law has within the life of the Christian believer. Not surprisingly then, that the name of the character who leads this Judaizing faction within the church at Colossae is Moses! A number of points commonly discussed within historical-critical investigations into the letter to Philemon feature within the film. For example, the word-play on Onesimus's name ('Useful') is mentioned several times within Paul's dialogue, and Philemon even alludes to it once in a remark made to Sergius Gallus. Onesimus's supposed theft of something valuable belonging to Philemon is given concrete expression in the form of the necklace belonging to Apphia. Interestingly, a selections from a variety of Paul's letters are cited, including a version of the hymn of Phil. 2.6–11 which Philemon recounts to the church at Colossae, and a recitation of the hymn in Col. 1.15–20 which Paul offers to the church in Rome during a worship service. Julia quotes from Rom. 8.28 as she accepts the prospect of being sold to a family in Rome, and Paul uses language drawn from 1 Corinthians when explaining the nature of the cross to Onesimus.

Other features of the film just do not work very well. For example, the geographical arrangements set out in the film are non-sensical. At times it seems as if Colossae and Rome are a merely a day or so apart, instead of the 1000 miles we know them to be. Impossibly, characters hop on their horses, ride for a few moments, and then end up at the other end of the Roman empire. This skewed sense of geography also contaminates the presentation of the passing of time. Indeed, the overall chronological sequence of the film is unspecified, and it seems impossibly compressed.

Other features within the story-line are unashamed fictional embellishments. The most important of these is the introduction of extra characters, notably Sofia, Julia, Athamos, Yousef and Sergius. Each of these characters is woven into the story-line, sometimes more successfully than others. At times they are injected in a rather ham-fisted manner which produces, in the end, an overly complicated, even impossible, plot. The love-interest, first between Onesimus and Julia, and then between Onesimus and Sofia, seems amateurishly scripted at best. The film works best when it sticks to the element which is at the heart of the drama, the soul-searching of Onesimus over the nature of his slavery to Philemon and of his submission to his spiritual master Jesus Christ. Having said that, there is also one very interesting use of the New Testament in the film which is especially worth noting. This concerns the story of the Woman Taken in Adultery from John 7.53–8.11, which is first mentioned in an exchange between Sofia and Apphia as the two women discuss the meaning of forgiveness. Later Sofia adopts this story as something of a model for her own life and sees herself in the role of the forgiven adultress. Most importantly, Sofia challenges her uncle Philemon with the story of the adulterous woman and suggests that here Jesus offered a demonstration on the nature of forgiveness. Philemon is wise enough to apply the story to his own situation, and following Sofia's gentle exhortation, goes to Onesimus and asks for forgiveness. Thus, the film's closing scene is one of reconciliation between a runaway slave and his master, but it is based on a gospel text, not a passage from Paul's letters.

Postscript

The letter of Paul to Philemon continues to exert its influence into the late twentieth and early twenty-first century world in a surprising number of ways. Some of the most characteristic cultural expressions of the West have also found themselves vehicles for the continuing story of Onesimus. A good example of this is the computer game entitled *Onesimus: A Quest for Freedom* produced by Ark Multimedia Publishing in the USA and released in 1992 (Figure 19).

Figure 19: *Onesimus: A Quest for Freedom* (1992)— an arcade computer game released by Ark Multimedia Publishing

This is a Super Nintendo™ type arcade game which uses the traditional interpretation of the story of the runaway slave Onesimus as its background. The game is developed by a Christian software company whose aim is to promote a better appreciation for the biblical text through such a popular format. The on-screen instructions offer an explanation:

> You are Onesimus, slave of Philemon. For months you have planned your escape from slavery. It is freedom you want. You can think of nothing else. One day while Philemon is away, you seize your opportunity. Stealing money from your master's house, you break away fleeing towards Rome. First you must escape the slave quarters, then sneak through Philemon's house without arousing suspicion. Along the way you must find keys to open doors and apples to maintain your health.
>
> Now free at last, you make your way towards Rome. Little do you know that at Rome you will meet the Apostle Paul, the great Christian preacher. Under Paul's teaching you will become a Christian. Only then will you discover true freedom. On your way to Rome, however, you must pass through treacherous areas. Besides keys and apples, you must also find other items necessary to complete your journey, including a knife to ward off dangerous animals.
>
> Even after arriving in Rome, you are restless until you find Paul, and through him Jesus. Then you are free at last.

The game, which is marketed for ages 6—Adult, contains some thirty levels of scrolling action, taking the runaway Onesimus through the forests of Colossae, across rivers and seas, up mountain fortresses, and down into Roman dungeons. Periodically, as Onesimus manages to escape from one danger or another and journey towards Rome, the text of the letter of Philemon pops up as a supplementary screen—a sort of reward for good progress made. As the promotional blurb on the packaging sums it up:

> If you've got what it takes to make it all the way to Rome, you will find refuge with a Roman citizen named Paul. He will unlock the mystery of the sacred writings that you have encountered on your journey and show you the meaning of true freedom.

Finally, we turn to consider one of the most intriguing examples of the use made of the letter of Philemon within social and political history. I am speaking of an artistic image, first forged in the heat of the abolitionist debate in the late 1780s, which built creatively on the text of Philemon 16: 'no longer a slave, but more than a slave, a beloved brother'. The text served as the inspiration for the seal of the Society for the Abolition of Slavery in England, and thus came under the guiding hand of the influential master potter Josiah Wedgwood (1730–1795), a member of that Society (J.R. Oldfield 1995: 155–61 discusses the circumstances of this). Wedgwood commissioned one of his designers, named William Hackwood, to assist in the creation of an official seal for the Society, an emblem which would visually capture its aims and intentions. The design executed by Hackwood was visually striking: it portrayed a black male figure, kneeling and bound in chains, surrounded by the legend, 'Am I Not a Man and a Brother.' This seal was adapted for use in Wedgwood's factories in Staffordshire and soon it was reproduced in various china patterns, cameos and medallions, many of which were given as gifts to people committed to the abolitionist cause. These medallions were often mounted in jewelry settings and worn as combs, tie pins, bracelets, and brooches. They quickly became fashion accessories and a valuable way of disseminating the abolitionist message.

Figure 20: Slave Token from 1792 showing a chained slave with the inscription 'Am I Not a Man and a Brother'

Figure 21: British £2 coin from 2007 issued to commemorate the 200th Anniversary of the Abolition of the Slave Trade

The distinctive image soon had an impact in the United States, and through a celebrated and well-respected agent. In February of 1788, Wedgwood sent a number of cameos to Benjamin Franklin, the eminent author and statesman, who was the president of the Pennsylvania Society for the Abolition of Slavery. This led to the issuing of an anti-slavery copper token in 1792 which was widely circulated in the United States and helped promote the abolitionist cause there. The obverse of the token portrayed the image from the Society's seal, including the legend based on Philemon 16, 'Am I Not a Man and a Brother.' The reverse of the token bears the clasped hands of brotherhood and the legend, 'May Slavery and Oppression Cease Throughout the World' (see Figure 20).

However, the impact of the abolitionist seal based on Philemon 16 did not end with the slave-tokens that were issued in 1792. For one thing, the token design was adapted by early feminists keen to link the demand for abolition with the demand for equal rights for women, partly in recognition of the role that women had played in the struggle against slavery. Not surprisingly, a companion version of the slave-token appeared in Britain in 1828 which depicted a kneeling slave woman under the suitably altered inscription from Philemon 16, 'Am I Not a Woman and a Sister'. The image of the kneeling slave woman became a potent symbol in the United States, and lent itself to endless adaptation by feminists who were active in the abolitionist movement (Yellin 1989: 3–26 offers an interesting discussion of this).

Moreover, the influence of this inscription, which was so important for the abolitionist movement, continues to be demonstrated to this day. In the United Kingdom a special coin was issued in 2007 which made deliberate use of the inscription made popular by Wedgwood. As part of the celebrations to mark the bicentenary of the abolition of slavery, the Royal Mint issued a £2 coin with the inscription 'An Act for the Abolition of the Slave Trade' (Figure 21). The reverse of the nickel-brass coin was designed by David Gentleman and has the date 1807 in the central field, together with a broken slave chain of five links (the third link doubles as the '0' in the 1807 date). Most importantly for our purposes here, the coin bears around its edge an inscription of the words from the original seal from 1787: 'Am I Not A Man And A Brother'.

This slogan became a popular rallying cry for the abolitionist movement and for many people it provided a biblical basis, even a mandate, for the manumission of slaves. In fact, the contribution that Philemon 16 made in this regard to the abolitionist campaign may well prove to be *the* most significant and enduring legacy of Paul's seemingly inconsequential letter to Philemon.

Bibliography

Abbott, Edwin A., *Onesimus: Memoirs of a Disciple of St Paul* (London: Macmillan, 1882).
Allen, David L., 'The Discourse Structure of Philemon: A Study of Textlinguistics', in David Alan Black (ed.), *Scribes and Scripture: New Testament Essays in Honour of J. Harold Greenlee* (Winona Lake, IN: Eisenbrauns, 1992), pp. 77–96.
Amling, Ernst, 'Eine Konjectur im Philemonbrief', *Zeitschrift für die neutestamentliche Wissenschaft* 10 (1909), pp. 261–62.
Anon, *America and her Slave-System* (London: Simpkin, Marshall & Co., 1845).
Arzt-Grabner, Peter, 'The Case of Onesimos: An Interpretation of Paul's Letter to Philemon Based on Documentary Papyri and Ostraca', *Annali di storia dell'esegesi* 18 (2001), pp. 589–614.
—*Philemon* (Papyrologische Kommentar zum Neuen Testament, 1; Göttingen: Vandenhoeck & Ruprecht, 2003).
Asch, Scholem, *The Apostle* (New York: G.P. Putnam's Sons, 1943).
Aune, David E., *The New Testament in Its Literary Environment* (Cambridge: James Clarke & Co., 1987).
Bahr, Gordon J., 'The Subscriptions in the Pauline Letters', *Journal of Biblical Literature* 87 (1968), pp. 27–41.
Barclay, John M.G., 'Paul, Philemon and the Dilemma of Christian Slave-Ownership', *New Testament Studies* 37 (1991), pp. 161–86.
Barnes, Albert, *An Inquiry into the Scriptural Views of Slavery* (Philadelphia: Perkins & Purves, 1846).
Barrett, C.K., *Paul: An Introduction to his Thought* (London: Geoffrey Chapman, 1994).
Bartchy, S. Scott, *First-Century Slavery and 1 Corinthians 7:21* (Society of Biblical Literature Dissertation Series; Atlanta: Scholars Press, 1973).
—'Philemon, Epistle to', in *ABD* 5 (1992), pp. 305–310.
—'Slavery (Greco-Roman)', in *ABD* 6 (1992), pp. 65–72.
Barth, Markus (and Helmut Blanke), *The Letter to Philemon* (Eerdmans Critical Commentary; Grand Rapids, MI: Eerdmans Publishing Co., 2000).
Barton, Stephen, 'Paul and Philemon: A Correspondence Continued', *Theology* 90 (1987), pp. 97–101.
Baur, F.C., *Paul: The Apostle of Jesus Christ* (2 vols.; London: Williams & Norgate, 1873, 1875).
Bentley, Richard, *Bentleii Critica sacra: Notes on the Greek and Latin Text of the New Testament Extracted from the Bentley MSS. in Trinity College Library* (ed. Arthur Ayres Ellis; Cambridge: Deighton, Bell & Co., 1862).

Binder, H., *Der Brief des Paulus an Philemon* (THNT, 11/2; Berlin: Evangelische Verlag, 1990).
Birdsall, J.N., 'Presbutes in Philemon 9: A Study in Conjectural Emendation', *New Testament Studies* 39 (1993), pp. 625–30.
Birney, James G., *Sinfulness of Slaveholding in All Circimstances; Tested by Reason and Scripture* (Detroit: Charles Willcox, 1846).
Blanchard, Jonathan (and N.L. Rice), *A Debate on Slavery Held in the City of Cincinnati, on the First, Second, Third, and Sixth Days of October, 1845, upon the Question: Is Slave-Holding in Itself Sinful, and the Relation between Master and Slave, a Sinful Relation?* (Cincinnati: William H. Moore, 1846). [Blanchard argues the Affirmative position; Rice the Negative.]
Blassingame, John (ed.), *The Frederick Douglass Papers, Series One: Speeches, Debates, and Interviews*. I. *1841–46* (New Haven, CT: Yale University Press, 1979).
—*The Frederick Douglass Papers, Series One: Speeches, Debates, and Interviews* Vol. 2. *1847–54* (New Haven, CT: Yale University Press, 1982).
—*The Frederick Douglass Papers, Series One: Speeches, Debates, and Interviews* Vol. 3. *1855–63* (New Haven, CT: Yale University Press, 1985).
Bornkamm, Günther, *Paul* (London: Hodder & Stoughton, 1971).
Bourne, George, *The Book and Slavery Irreconcilable* (Philadelphia: J.M. Sanderson & Co., 1816).
—*A Condensed Anti-Slavery Bible Argument* (New York: S.W. Benedict, 1845).
Boys, Thomas, *Tactica sacra: An Attempt to Develope and to Exhibit to the Eye by Tabular Arrangements a General Rule of Composition Prevailing in the Holy Scriptures*, 2 Parts (London: T. Hamilton, 1824).
Braxton, Brad Ronnell, *The Tyranny of Resolution: 1 Corinthians 7:17–24* (SBLDS, 181; Atlanta: Society of Biblical Literature, 2000).
Bruce, F.F., *Paul: Apostle of the Heart Set Free* (Grand Rapids, MI: Eerdmans, 1977).
—*The Epistles to the Colossians, to Philemon, and to the Ephesians* (NICNT; Grand Rapids, MI: Eerdmans, 1984).
Buttrick, George Arthur, 'The Epistle to Philemon: Exposition', in George Arthur Buttrick (ed.), *The Interpreter's Bible*, XI (Nashville: Abingdon Press, 1955), pp. 553–73.
Byron, John, 'Paul and the Background of Slavery: The *Status Quaestionis* in New Testament Scholarship', *Currents in Research: Biblical Studies* 3 (2001), pp. 116–39.
Cadoux, Arthur Temple, *Onesimus: A Play in Three Acts* (London: The Religious Drama Society of Great Britain, 1952).
Cadoux, C.J., 'The Dates and Provenance of the Imprisonment Epistles of St Paul', *The Expository Times* 45 (1933–34), pp. 471–73.
Caird, G.B., *Paul's Letters from Prison* (New Clarendon Bible; Oxford: Oxford University Press, 1976).
Callahan, Allen Dwight, 'Paul's Epistle to Philemon: Toward an Alternative Argumentum', *Harvard Theological Review* 86 (1993), pp. 357–76.
—'John Chrysostom on Philemon: A Response to Margaret M. Mitchell', *Harvard Theological Review* 88 (1995), pp. 149–56.
—*Embassy of Onesimus: The Letter of Paul to Philemon* (The New Testament in Context; Valley Forge, PA: Trinity Press International, 1997).

—'"Brother Saul": An Ambivalent Witness to Freedom', in *Slavery in Text and Interpretation* (Semeia, 83–84; Atlanta: Society of Biblical Literature, 1998), pp. 235–49.

—and Richard A. Horsley, 'Slave Resistance in Classical Antiquity', in *Slavery in Text and Interpretation* (Semeia, 83–84; Atlanta: Society of Biblical Literature, 1998), pp. 133–51.

—and Richard A. Horsley and Abraham Smith, *Slavery in Text and Interpretation* (Semeia 83–84; Atlanta: Society of Biblical Literature, 1998).

Calvin, John, *The Second Epistle of Paul the Apostle to the Corinthians and the Epistles to Timothy, Titus and Philemon* (Grand Rapids, MI: Eerdmans, 1964).

Chadwick, Henry, 'New Letters of St Augustine', *Journal of Theological Studies* 34 (1983), pp. 425–52.

Cheever, George B., *God against Slavery and the Freedom and Duty of the Pulpit to Rebuke It as a Sin against God* (Cincinnati: American Reform Tract and Book Society, 1857).

Chrysostom, John, 'Homilies of St John Chrysostom on the Epistle of St Paul the Apostle to Philemon', in P. Schaff (ed.), *A Select Library of the Nicene and Post-Nicene Fathers of the Christian Church*, XIII (New York: Christian Literature Company, 1889), pp. 545–57.

Church, F. Forrester, 'Rhetorical Structure and Design in Paul's Letter to Philemon', *Harvard Theological Review* 71 (1978), pp. 17–33.

Clark, Rufus W., *A Review of the Rev. Moses Stuart's Pamphlet on Slavery* (Boston: C.C.P. Moody, 1850).

Coleman-Norton, P.R., 'The Apostle Paul and the Roman Law of Slavery', in P.R. Coleman-Norton (ed.), *Studies in Roman Economic and Social History in Honor of Allan Chester Johnson* (Princeton, NJ: Princeton University Press, 1951), pp. 155–77.

Combes, I.A.H., *The Metaphor of Slavery in the Writings of the Early Church: From the New Testament to the Beginning of the Fifth Century* (JSNTSup, 156; Sheffield; Sheffield Academic Press, 1998).

Connolly, A.L., 'Onesimos', in G.H.R. Horsley (ed.), *New Documents Illustrating Early Christianity*, IV (North Ryde, NSW: Macquarie University, 1987), pp. 179–81.

Cope, L., 'On Rethinking the Philemon and Colossians Connection', *Bible Research* 30 (1985), pp. 45–50.

Corwin, Charles Edward, *Onesimus, Christ's Freedman: A Tale of the Pauline Epistles* (London: Oliphant, Anderson & Ferrier, 1901).

Courthion, Pierre, *Georges Rouault* (London: Thames & Hudson, 1962).

Cross, Timothy, *A Postcard from Paul: The Letter of Paul to Philemon* (Belfast: Ambassador, 1999).

Currier, Thomas Franklin, *A Bibliography of John Greenleaf Whittier* (Cambridge, MA: Harvard University Press, 1937).

Dames, Gregory W., '"But if you can gain your freedom" (1 Corinthians 7:17–24)', *Catholic Biblical Quarterly* 52 (1990), pp. 681–97.

Daube, David, 'Onesimos', *Harvard Theological Review* 79 (1986), pp. 40–43.

Davies, Margaret, 'Work and Slavery in the New Testament: Impoverishments of Traditions', in John W. Rogerson, Margaret Davies and M. Daniel

Carroll R. (eds.), *The Bible in Ethics: The Second Sheffield Colloquium* (JSOTSup, 207; Sheffield: JSOT Press, 1995), pp. 315–47.
Deissmann, Adolf, *Light from the Ancient East* (London: Harper & Brothers, revised edn, 1922).
—*Paul: A Study in Social and Religious History* (London: Hodder & Stoughton, 2nd edn, 1926).
Deming, Will, 'A Diatribe Pattern in 1 Cor. 7:21-22: A New Perspective on Paul's Direction to Slaves', *Novum Testamentum* 37 (1995), pp. 130–37.
Derrett, J.D.M., 'The Functions of the Epistle to Philemon', *Zeitschrift für die neutestamentliche Wissenschaft* 79 (1988), pp. 63–91.
Dibelius, Martin, *Paul* (edited and completed by Werner Georg Kümmel; London: Longmans, Green & Co., 1953).
Dodd, C.H., 'Philemon', in F.C. Eiselen, E. Lewis and D.G. Downey (eds.), *The Abingdon Bible Commentary* (New York: Abingdon Press, 1929), pp. 1292–94.
—*New Testament Essays* (Manchester: Manchester University Press, 1953).
Dodderidge, Philip, *The Family Expositor: or, a Paraphrase and Version of the New Testament*, V (London: John Wilson: 1756).
Doty, William G., *Letters in Primitive Christianity* (Philadelphia: Fortress Press, 1973).
Duncan, G.S., *St Paul's Ephesian Ministry: A Reconstruction* (London: Hodder & Stoughton, 1929).
—'The Epistles of the Imprisonment in Recent Discussion', *Expository Times* 46 (1934–35), pp. 293–98.
—'Paul's Ministry in Asia—The Last Phase', *New Testament Studies* 3 (1956–57), pp. 211–18.
—'Chronological Table to Illustrate Paul's Ministry in Asia', *New Testament Studies* 5 (1958–59), pp. 43–45.
Dunn, James D.G., *The Epistles to the Colossians and to Philemon* (The New International Greek Testament Commentary; Carlisle: Paternoster Press, 1996).
—*The Theology of Paul the Apostle* (Edinburgh: T. & T. Clark, 1998).
Eleen, Luba, *The Illustration of the Pauline Epistles in French and English Bibles of the Twelfth and Thirteenth Centuries* (Oxford: Clarendon Press, 1982).
Elliott, Neil, *Liberating Paul: The Justice of God and the Politics of the Apostle* (The Biblical Seminar, 27; Sheffield: Sheffield Academic Press, 1995).
Ellis, E. Earle, *The Making of the New Testament Documents* (Biblical Interpretation Series, 39; Leiden: Brill, 2001).
Farrar, Frederic W., *The Life and Work of St Paul* (London: Cassell & Company, 1913).
Fee, John G. *An Anti-Slavery Manual, or, The Wrongs of American Slavery Exposed by the Light of the Bible and of Facts* (New York: William Harned, 2nd edn, 1851).
Feeley-Harnik, Gillian, 'Is Historical Anthropology Possible? The Case of the Runaway Slave', in Gene M. Tucker and Douglas A. Knight (eds,), *Humanizing America's Iconic Book* (Chico, California: Scholars Press, 1982), pp. 95–126.

Finegan, Jack, 'The Original Form of the Pauline Collection', *Harvard Theological Review* 49 (1956), pp. 85–103.
Finseth, Ian Frederick, 'Introduction' to *A Narrative of the Adventures and Escape of Moses Roper*, in William Andrews (ed.), *North Carolina Slave Narrartives: The Lives of Moses Roper, Lunsforth Land, Moses Grandy and Thomas H. Jones* (Chapel Hill, NC: The University of North Carolina, 2003), pp. 23–34.
Fisk, Wilbur, 'Slavery Sanctioned by the Bible', *The Liberator* (9 January, 1837), p. 1.
Fitzmyer, Joseph A., 'The Letter to Philemon', in Raymond E. Brown *et al.* (eds.), *The Jerome Biblical Commentary 2* (Englewood Cliffs, NJ: Prentice—Hall, 1968), pp. 332–33.
—'The Letter to Philemon', in Raymond E. Brown *et al.* (eds.), *The New Jerome Biblical Commentary* (Englewood Cliffs, NJ: Prentice—Hall, 1990), pp. 869–870.
—*The Letter to Philemon* (AB, 34C; Doubleday: New York, 2000).
Foster, Stephen S., *The Brotherhood of Thieves, or, A True Picture of the American Church and Clergy* (New London: William Bolles Publisher, 1843).
Frilingos, Chris, '"For my Child Onesimus": Paul and Domestic Power in Philemon', *Journal of Biblical Literature* 119 (2000), pp. 91–104.
Funk, Robert W., 'The Apostolic *Parousia*: Form and Significance', in W.R. Farmer, C.F.D. Moule and R.R. Niebuhr (eds.), *Christian History and Interpretation: Studies Presented to John Knox* (Cambridge: Cambridge University Press, 1967), pp. 249–68.
Gamble, Harry, 'The Redaction of the Pauline Letters and the Formation of the Pauline Corpus', *Journal of Biblical Literature* 94 (1975), pp. 403–18.
Getty, Mary Ann, 'The Theology of Philemon', in Kent Harold Richards (ed.), *Society of Biblical Literature Seminar 1987 Papers* (Atlanta: Scholars Press, 1987), pp. 503–508.
Giltner, John, 'Moses Stuart and the Slavery Controversy: A Study in the Failure of Moderation', *The Journal of Religious Thought* 18 (1961), pp. 27–40.
—*Moses Stuart: The Father of Biblical Science in America* (Atlanta: Scholars Press, 1996).
Gnilka, Joachim, *Der Philemonbrief* (HTKNT, 10/4; Freiburg i.B.: Herder, 1982).
Godet, F., 'The Epistle to Philemon: The Oldest Petition for the Abolition of Slavery', *The Expositor*, Third Series, 5 (1887), pp. 138–54.
Goguel, Maurice, *Introduction au Nouveau Testament*, 4 vols. in 5 (Paris: Ernest Leroux, 1922–26).
Goodenough, Erwin R., 'Paul and Onesimus', *Harvard Theological Review* 22 (1929), pp. 181–83.
Goodspeed, Edgar J. *The Meaning of Ephesians* (Chicago: The University of Chicago Press, 1933).
—*An Introduction to the New Testament* (Chicago: The University of Chicago Press, 1937).
—'Paul and Slavery', *Journal of Bible and Religion* 11 (1943), pp. 169–70.
—*Paul* (Nashville: Abingdon Press, 1947).
—*The Key to Ephesians* (Chicago: The University of Chicago Press, 1956).

Bibliography 179

Gorday, Peter (ed.), *Ancient Christian Commenary on Scripture*. New Testament, IX. *Colossians, 1–2 Thessalonians, 1–2 Timothy, Titus, Philemon* (Downers Grove, IL: InterVarsity Press, 2000).
Green, Beriah, *The Chattel Principle: The Abhorrence of Jesus Christ and the Apostles; or, No Refuge for American Slavery in the New Testament* (New York: The American Anti-Slavery Society, 1839).
Greeven, Heinrich, 'Prüfung der Thesen von J. Knox zum Philemonbrief', *Theologische Literaturzeitung* 79 (1954), cols. 373–78.
Grimke, Angelina B., 'Appeal to the Christian Women of the South', *The Anti-Slavery Examiner* (September 1836), pp. 1–36.
Gülzow, Henneke, *Christentum und Sklaverei in den ersten drei Jahrhunderten* (Bonn: R. Habelt, 1969).
Guthrie, Donald, *New Testament Introduction* (Leicester: Inter-Varsity Press, revised edition, 1990).
Hahn, Ferdinand, 'Paulus und der Sklave Onesimus', *Evangelische Theologie* 37 (1977), pp. 179–85.
Hanson, Craig L., 'A Greek Martyrdom Account of St Onesimus', *Greek Orthodox Theological Review* 22 (1977), pp. 319–39.
Hanway, Jonas, *Virtue in Humble Life: Containing Reflections on Relative Duties, Particularly Those of Masters and Servants* (London, 1777).
Harrill, J. Albert, 'Ignatius, *Ad Polycarp*. 4.3 and the Corporate Manumission of Christian Slaves', *Journal of Early Christian Studies* 1 (1993), pp. 107–42.
—Review of Allen Dwight Callahan's *Embassy of Onesimus* (1997), *Catholic Biblical Quarterly* 60 (1998), pp. 757–59.
—'Using the Roman Jurists to Interpret Philemon: A Response to Peter Lampe', *Zeitschrift für die neutestamentliche Wissenschaft* 90 (1999), pp. 135–38.
—'The Use of the New Testament in the American Slave Controversy: A Case History in the Hermeneutical Tension between Biblical Criticism and Christian Moral Debate', *Religion and American Culture* 10 (2000), pp. 149–86.
Harris, Murray J., *Colossians and Philemon* (Exegetical Guide to the Greek New Testament; Grand Rapids, MI: Eerdmans, 1991).
—*Slave of Christ: A New Testament Metaphor for Total Devotion to Christ* (New Studies in Biblical Theology, 8; Leicester: Apollos, 1999).
Harrison, P.N., 'Onesimus and Philemon', *Anglican Theological Review* 32 (1950), pp. 268–94.
Harvey, A.E., *Companion to the New Testament* (Oxford: Oxford University Press, 1979).
Heil, John Paul, 'The Chiastic Structure and Meaning of Paul's Letter to Philemon', *Biblica* 82 (2001), pp. 178–206.
Hock, Ronald F., 'A Support for his Old Age: Paul's Plea on Behalf of Onesimus', in Michael White and O. Larry Yarbrough (eds.), *The Social World of the First Christians: Essays in Honor of Wayne Meeks* (Minneapolis: Fortress Press, 1995), pp. 67–81.
Horsley, Richard A., 'The Slave Systems of Classical Antiquity and their Reluctant Recognition by Modern Scholars', in *Slavery in Text and Interpretation* (*Semeia* 83–84; Atlanta: Society of Biblical Literature, 1998), pp. 19–66.
—'Paul and Slavery: A Critical Alternative to Recent Readings', in *Slavery in Text and Interpretation* (*Semeia* 83–84; Atlanta: Society of Biblical Literature, 1998), pp. 153–200.

—and Allen Dwight Callahan, 'Slave Resistance in Classical Antiquity', in *Slavery in Text and Interpretation* (Semeia 83–84; Atlanta: Society of Biblical Literature, 1998), pp. 133–51.

Houlden, J.L., *Paul's Letters from Prison: Philippians, Colossians, Philemon and Ephesians* (Pelican New Testament Commentary; Harmondsworth, Middlesex: Penguin Books, 1970).

Hoyt, Lauren M., *Onesimus the Slave: A Romance of the Days of Nero* (Boston: Samuel French & Co., 1915).

Jeremias, Joachim, 'Chiasmus in den Paulusbriefen', *Zeitschrift für die neutestamentliche Wissenschaft* 49 (1958), pp. 145–56.

Jewett, Robert, *Paul the Apostle to America: Cultural Trends and Pauline Scholarship* (Louisville, KY: Westminster/John Knox Press, 1994).

Johnson, Lewis, 'The Pauline Letters from Caesarea', *The Expository Times* 68 (1956–57), pp. 24–26.

Jones, Maurice, 'The Epistles of the Captivity: Where Were They Written?', *The Expositor*, Eighth Series, 10 (1915), pp. 289–316.

Jülicher, Adolf, *An Introduction to the New Testament* (London: Smith, Elder & Co., 1904).

Kim, Chan-Hie, *Form and Structure of the Familiar Greek Letter of Recommendation* (SBLDS, 4; Missoula, MT: Society of Biblical Literature, 1972).

Knox, John, 'Philemon and the Authenticity of Colossians', *Journal of Religion* 17 (1937), pp. 144–60.

—'The Epistle to Philemon: Introduction and Exegesis', in George Arthur Buttrick (ed.), *The Interpreter's Bible*, XI (Nashville: Abingdon Press, 1955), pp. 553–73.

—'A Note on the Format of the Pauline Corpus', *Harvard Theological Review* 50 (1957), pp. 311–14.

—*Philemon among the Letters of Paul* (London: Collins, 1960; original edition, 1935).

—'Acts and the Pauline Letter Corpus', in L.E. Keck and J.L. Martyn (eds.), *Studies in Luke—Acts* (London: SPCK, 1968), pp. 279–87.

Knox, Wilfred, *St Paul* (Edinburgh: Peter Davies, 1932).

Koch, Eldon W., 'A Cameo of Koinonia: The Letter to Philemon', *Interpretation* 17 (1963), pp. 183–87.

Koester, Helmut, *Introduction to the New Testament: History and Literature of Early Christianity* (2 vols.; Philadelphia: Fortress Press, 1982).

Kreitzer, Larry J., 'Living in the Lycus valley: Earthquake Imagery in Colossians, Philemon and Ephesians', in Jiří Mrázek and Jan Roskovek (eds.), *Testimony and Interpretation: Early Christology in its Judeo-Hellenistic Milieu, Studies in Honour of Petr Pokorny* (JSNTSup, 272; London: T. & T. Clark International, 2004), pp. 81–94.

Kümmel, W.G., *Introduction to the New Testament* (London: SCM Press, revised edition, 1975).

Lampe, Peter, 'Keine "Sklavenflucht" des Onesimus', *Zeitschrift für die neutestamentliche Wissenschaft* 76 (1985), pp. 135–37.

—'Onesimus', *ABD*, V (1992), pp. 21–22.

Leaney, A.R.C., *The Epistles to Timothy, Titus and Philemon* (Torch Bible Commentary; London: SCM Press, 1960).

Lewis, Lloyd A., 'An African American Appraisal of the Philemon—Paul—Onesimus Triangle', in Cain Hope Felder (ed.), *Stoney the Road We Trod:*

African American Biblical Interpretation (Minneapolis: Augsburg Fortress, 1991), pp. 232–46.
Lightfoot, J.B., *Saint Paul's Epistle to the Philippians: A Revised Text with Introduction, Notes, and Dissertations* (London: Macmillan & Co., 1885).
—*Saint Paul's Epistles to the Colossians and to Philemon: A Revised Text with Introduction, Notes, and Dissertations* (London: Macmillan & Co., 1916).
Llewelyn, S.R., *New Documents Illustrating Early Christianity* (North Ryde, NSW: Macquarie University, 1992).
Lohmeyer, Ernst, *Die Briefe an die Kolosser und an Philemon* (Göttingen: Vandenhoeck & Ruprecht, 8th edition, 1930).
—*Die Briefe an die Philipper, an die Kolosser und an Philemon* (Göttingen: Vandenhoeck & Ruprecht, 13th edition, 1964).
Lohse, Edward, *Colossians and Philemon* (Hermeneia Commentary; Philadelphia: Fortress Press, 1971).
Longstreet, Augustus Baldwin, *Letters on the Epistle of Paul to Philemon* (Charleston, SC: B. Jenkins, 1845).
Lüdemann, Gerd, *Paul: The Founder of Christianity* (Amherst, NY: Prometheus Books, 2002).
Lund, Nils W., *Chiasmus in the New Testament: A Study of the Form and Function of Chiastic Structures* (Chapel Hill, NC: University of North Carolina Press, 1942).
Luther, Martin, *Word and Sacrament*, I (Luther's Works, 35; Philadelphia: Fortress Press, 1960).
—*Lectures on Galatians 1535 (Chapters 5–6), Lectures on Galatians 1519 (Chapters 1–6)* (Luther's Works, 27; St Louis: Concordia Publishing House, 1964).
—*Lectures on Titus, Philemon and Hebrews* (Luther's Works, 29; St Louis: Concordia Publishing House, 1968).
—*Commentaries on 1 Corinthians 7, 1 Corinthians 15, Lectures on 1 Timothy* (Luther's Works, 28; St Louis: Concordia Publishing House, 1973).
Maclaren, Alexander, 'The Epistle to Philemon', *The Expositor*, Third Series, 5 (1887), pp. 270–80, 363–75, 443–53; 6 (1887), pp. 150–59, 180–91, 297–306.
Marshall, I. Howard, 'The Theology of Philemon', in Karl P. Donfried and I. Howard Marshall (eds.), *The Theology of the Shorter Pauline Letters* (Cambridge: Cambridge University Press, 1993), pp. 175–91.
Martens, John W., 'Ignatius and Onesimus: John Knox Reconsidered', *The Second Century* 9 (1992), pp. 73–86.
Martin, Clarice J., 'The Rhetorical Function of Commercial Language in Paul's Letter to Philemon (Verse 18)', in Duane F. Watson (ed.), *Persuasive Artistry: Studies in New Testament Rhetoric in Honour of George A. Kennedy* (JSNTSup, 50; JSOT Press, 1991), pp. 321–37.
Martin, Dale B., *Slavery as Salvation: The Metaphor of Slavery in Pauline Christianity* (New Haven, CT: Yale University Press, 1990).
—'Ancient Slavery, Class, and Early Christianity', *Fides et Historia* 23 (1991), pp. 105–13.
Martin, Ralph P., *Colossians and Philemon* (New Century Bible; London: Oliphants, 1974).
McDonald, J. Ian H., *The Crucible of Christian Morality* (London: Routledge, 1998).

McKeen, Silas, *A Scriptural Argument in Favor of Withdrawing Fellowship from Churches and Ecclesiastical Bodies Tolerating Slaveholding among Them* (New York: American & Foreign Anti-Slavery Society, 1848).

Meeks, Wayne A., 'The "Haustafeln" and American Slavery: A Hermeneutical Challenge', in Eugene H. Lovering, Jr, and Jerry L. Sumney (eds.), *Theology and Ethics in Paul and his Interpreters: Essays in Honor of Victor Paul Furnish* (Nashville: Abingdon Press, 1996), pp. 232–53.

Metzger, Bruce M. *A Textual Commentary on the Greek New Testament* (London: United Bible Societies, 1971).

Meyer, F.B., *Paul: A Servant of Jesus Christ* (London: Marshall, Morgan & Scott, 1953).

Mitchell, Laura, '"Matters of Justice between Man and Man": Northern Divines, the Bible, and the Fugitive Slave Act of 1850', in John R. McKivigan and Mitchell Snay (eds.), *Religion and the Antebellum Debate over Slavery* (Athens, GA: The University of Georgia Press, 1998), pp. 134–65.

Mitchell, Margaret M., 'John Chrysostom on Philemon: A Second Look', *Harvard Theological Review* 88 (1995), pp. 135–48.

Mitton, C.L., *The Formation of the Pauline Corpus of Letters* (London: Epworth Press, 1955).

Morris, Colin, *Epistles to the Apostle, Tarsus Please Forward* (London: Hodder & Stoughton, 1974).

Morrison, Larry R., 'The Religious Defense of American Slavery before 1830', *Journal of Religious Thought* 37 (1980–1981), pp. 16–29.

Motyer, Stephen, 'The Little Epistles of the New Testament—1: Philemon', *Evangel* 4 (1986), pp. 2–6, 14.

Moule, C.F.D., *The Epistles of Paul the Apostle to the Colossians and to Philemon* (Cambridge Greek Testament; Cambridge: Cambridge University Press, 1957).

Murphy-O'Connor, Jerome, *Paul: A Critical Life* (Oxford: Oxford University Press, 1996).

Neilson, Winthrop and Frances, *Letter to Philemon* (St Louis: Concordia Publishing House, 1973).

Nightingale, E.G., *Brother Onesimus* (London: Epworth Press, 1964).

Nordling, John G., 'Onesimus Fugitivus: A Defense of the Runaway Slave Hypothesis in Philemon', *Journal for the Study of the New Testament* 41 (1991), pp. 97–119.

—*Philemon* (Concordia Commentary; St Louis: Concordia Publishing House, 2004).

Oates, Stephen B., *The Fires of Jubilee: Nat Turner's Fierce Rebellion* (New York: Mentor Books, 1975).

O'Brien, Peter Thomas, *Introductory Thanksgivings in the Letters of Paul* (Supplements to Novum Testamentum, 49; Leiden: E.J. Brill, 1977).

O'Connell, J.B. (ed.), *The Roman Martyrology* (London: Burns & Oates, 1962).

O'Donnell, Matthew Brook, *Corpus Linguistics and the Greek New Testament* (New Testament Monographs, 6; Sheffield: Sheffield Phoenix Press, 2005).

Oesterley, W.E., 'The Epistle to Philemon', in W. Robertson Nicoll (ed.), *The Expositor's Greek Testament*, IV (Grand Rapids, MI: Eerdmans, 1974), pp. 205–17.

Oldfield, J.R. *Popular Politics and British Anti-Slavery: The Mobilisation of Public Opinion Against the Slave Trade 1787–1807* (Manchester: Manchester University Preess, 1995).
Ollrog, W.-H., *Paulus und seine Mitarbeiter* (WMANT, 50; Neukirchen: Neukirchener Verlag, 1979).
Osiek, Carolyn, 'The Ransom of Captives: Evolution of a Tradition', *Harvard Theological Review* 74 (1981), pp. 365–86.
—*Philippians, Philemon* (Abingdon New Testament Commentaries; Nashville: Abingdon Press, 2000).
Owen, Christopher H., *The Sacred Flame of Love: Methodism and Society in Nineteenth-Century Georgia* (Athens, GA: The University of Georgia Press, 1998).
Parry, Elsie, *Onesimus, The Church at Colossae: A Play in Three Acts* (London: National Sunday School Union, 1963).
Parry, Thomas, *Paul, Philemon, and Onesimus, or, Christian Brotherhood; Being a Practical Exposition of St Paul's Epistle to Philemon, Applicable to the Present Crisis of West Indian Affairs* (London: J.G. & F. Rivington, 1834).
Patterson, Orlando, *Slavery and Social Death: A Comparative Study* (Cambridge, MA: Harvard University Press, 1982).
Patzia, Arthur G., *Colossians, Philemon, Ephesians* (Good News Commentary; San Francisco: Harper & Row, 1984).
—'Philemon, Letter to', in Gerald F. Hawthorne and Ralph P. Martin (eds.), *Dictionary of Paul and his Letters* (Leicester: Intervarsity Press, 1993), pp. 703–707.
Payne, Daniel Alexander, *Recollections of Seventy Years* (Nashville, TN: Publishing House of the A.M.E. School Union, 1888).
Pearson, Brook W.R., 'Assumptions in the Criticism and Translation of Philemon', in Stanley E. Porter and Richard S. Hess (eds.), *Translating the Bible: Problems and Prospects* (JSNTSup, 173; Sheffield Academic Press: Sheffield, 1999), pp. 253–80.
Peerbolte, Bert Jan, 'Onesimus to Paul', in Philip R. Davies (ed.), *Yours Faithfully: Virtual Letters from the Bible* (London: Equinox, 2004), pp. 141–45.
Perkins, Pheme, 'Philemon', in Carol A. Newsom and Sharon H. Ringe (eds.), *Women's Bible Commentary (Expanded Edition)* (Louisville, KY: Westminster John Knox Press, 1998), pp. 453–54.
Petersen, Norman R., *Rediscovering Paul: Philemon and the Sociology of Paul's Narrative World* (Philadelphia: Fortress Press, 1985).
Peterson, Beverly, 'Stowe and Whittier Respond in Poetry to the Fugitive Slave Law', *Resources for American Literary Study* 26 (2000), pp. 184–99.
Pickard, John B., *John Greenleaf Whittier: An Introduction and Interpretation* (New York: Barnes & Noble, 1961).
Plass, Bridget, *Dear Paul ... Am I the Only One?* (Oxford: BRF, 2001).
Plumptre, E.H., 'Paul as a Man of Business', *The Expositor*, Fifth Series, 1 (1875), pp. 259–66.
Polaski, Sandra Hack, *Paul and the Discourse of Power* (Biblical Seminar, 62; Sheffield: Sheffield Academic Press, 1999).
Pollock, John, *The Apostle* (London: Hodder & Stoughton, 1969).
Porter, Stanley E., 'Is Critical Discourse Analysis Critical? An Evaluation Using Philemon as a Test Case', in Stanley E. Porter and Jeffrey T.

Reed (eds.), *Discourse Analysis and the New Testament: Approaches and Results* (JSNTSup, 170; Sheffield: Sheffield Academic Press, 1999), pp. 47-70.

Preiss, Théo, *Life in Christ* (Studies in Biblical Theology, 13; London: SCM Press, 1954).

Rapske, Brian M., 'The Prisoner Paul in the Eyes of Onesimus', *New Testament Studies* 37 (1991), pp. 187-203.

Reicke, Bo, 'Caesarea, Rome and the Captivity Epistles, in W.W. Gasque and R.P. Martin (eds.), *Apostolic History and the Gospel: Biblical and Historical Essays Presented to F.F. Bruce on his 60th Birthday* (Exeter: Paternoster Press, 1970), pp. 277-86.

Riesenfeld, Harald, 'Faith and Love Promoting Hope: An Interpretation of Philemon 6', in M.D. Hooker and S.G. Wilson (eds.), *Paul and Paulinism: Essays in Honour of C.K. Barrett* (London: SPCK, 1982), pp. 251-57.

Richardson, William J., 'Principle and Context in the Ethics of the Epistle to Philemon', *Interpretation* 22 (1968), pp. 301-16.

Robertson, A.T., 'Philemon and Onesimus: Master and Slave', *The Expositor*, Eighth Series, (1920), pp. 29-48.

—*Epochs in the Life of Paul* (Nashville: Broadman Press, 1974).

Robertson, James Alex, *The Hidden Romance of the New Testament* (London: James Clarke & Co., 1920).

Robinson, John A.T., *Redating the New Testament* (London: SCM Press, 1976).

Roper, Moses, *A Narrative of Moses Roper's Adventures and Escape from American Slavery* (London: Darton, Harvey & Darton, 1837). [Another edition with 'Letters to the Author' was published in England in 1848.]

Russell, David M., 'The Strategy of a First-Century Appeals Letter: A Discourse Reading of Paul's Epistle to Philemon', *Journal of Translation and Textlinguistics* 11 (1998), pp. 1-25.

Sanders, E.P., *Paul* (Oxford: Oxford University Press, 1991).

Schenk, Wolfgang, 'Der Brief des Paulus an Philemon in der neueren Forschung (1945-1987)', *ANRW* (*Aufstieg und Niedergang der römischen Welt*) 2.25.4 (1987), pp. 3439-95.

Schmithals, Walter, *Paul and the Gnostics* (Nashville: Abingdon Press, 1972).

Schoedel, William R., *Ignatius of Antioch: A Commentary on the Letters of Ignatius of Antioch* (Hermeneia; Philadelphia: Fortress Press, 1985).

Schrage, Wolfgang, *The Ethics of the New Testament* (Edinburgh: T. & T. Clark, 1988).

Schubert, Paul, *Form and Function of the Pauline Thanksgivings* (BZNW, 20; Berlin: Alfred Töpelmann, 1939).

Scott, E.F. *The Epistles of Paul to the Colossians, to Philemon and to the Ephesians* (Moffatt New Testament Commentary; London: Hodder & Stoughton, 1930).

Shanks, Caroline L., 'The Biblical Anti-Slavery Argument of the Decade 1830-1840', *The Journal of Negro History* 16 (1931), pp. 132-57.

Shapiro, Samuel, 'The Rendition of Anthony Burns', *The Journal of Negro History* 44 (1959), pp. 34-51.

Shaw, Graham, *The Cost of Authority: Manipulation and Freedom in the New Testament* (London: SCM Press, 1983).

Smith, Gail K., 'Reading with the Other: Hermeneutics and the Politics of Difference in Stowe's *Dred*', *American Literature* 69 (1999), pp. 289-313.

Smith, H., Sheldon *In his Image, But ...: Racism in Southern Religion 1780–1910* (Durham, NC: Duke University Press, 1972).
Snyman, A.H., 'A Semantic Discourse Analysis of the Letter to Philemon', in P.J. Hartin and J.H. Petzer (eds.), *Text and Interpretation: New Approaches in the Criticism of the New Testament* (New Testament Tools and Studies, 15; Leiden: E.J. Brill, 1991), pp. 83–99.
Soards, M.L., 'Some Neglected Theological Dimensions of Paul's Letter to Philemon', *Perspectives in Religious Studies* 17 (1990), pp. 209–19.
Steele, Richard, *A Discourse Concerning Old-Age* (London, 1688).
Stevens, Charles Emery, *Anthony Burns: A History* (Boston, 1856).
St John, Patricia, *Twice Freed* (Basingstoke: Pickering & Inglis, 1970).
Stowe, Harriet Beecher, *Uncle Tom's Cabin, or, Life among the Lowly* (London: Penguin Books, 1982; first published in 1852).
Stowers, Stanley K., *Letter-Writing in Greco-Roman Antiquity* (Philadelphia: Westminster Press, 1986).
—'Paul and Slavery: A Response', in *Slavery in Text and Interpretation* (Semeia 83–84; Atlanta: Society of Biblical Literature, 1998), pp. 295–311.
Stuart, Moses, *Conscience and the Constitution* (Boston: Crocker & Brewster, 1850).
Stuhlmacher, Peter, *Der Brief an Philemon* (Evangelische-Katholischer Kommentar zum Neuen Testament; Zürich: Benziger Verlag 1975).
Thompson, Marianne Meye, *Colossians and Philemon* (The Two Horizons New Testament Commentary; Eerdmans: Grand Rapids, MI, 2005).
Vincent, Marvin R., *The Epistles to the Philippians and to Philemon* (ICC; Edinburgh: T. & T. Clark, 1897).
Vos, Craig S. de, 'Once a Slave, Always a Slave? Slavery, Manumission and Relational Patterns in Paul's Letter to Philemon', *Journal for Study of the New Testament* 82 (2001), pp. 89–105.
Walsh, Brian J., and Sylvia C. Keesmaat, *Colossians Remixed. Subverting the Empire* (Bletchley: Paternoster, 2005).
Wansink, Craig S., 'Philemon', in John Barton and John Muddiman (eds.), *The Oxford Bible Commentary* (Oxford: Oxford University Press, 2001), pp. 1233–36.
Webb, Lance, *Onesimus* (Nashville: The Upper Room, 1980).
—*Escape from Ephesus* (Nashville: Thomas Nelson, 1991).
—*Onesimus: Rebel and Saint* (Nashville: The Upper Room, 1988).
Weizsäcker, Carl von, *The Apostolic Age of the Christian Church* (2 vols; London: Williams & Norgate, 1894, 1895).
Welch, John W., 'Chiasmus in the New Testament', in John W. Welch (ed.), *Chiasmus in Antiquity: Structures, Analyses, Exegesis* (Hildesheim: Gerstenberg Verlag, 1981), pp. 211–49.
White, John L., 'The Structural Analysis of Philemon: A Point of Departure in the Formal Analysis of the Pauline Letter', *Society of Biblical Literature Seminar Papers 1971* (Missoula, MT: Society of Biblical Literature, 1971), pp. 1–47.
—*The Form and Function of the Body of the Greek Letter: A Study of the Letter-Body in the Non-Literary Papyri and in Paul the Apostle* (SBLDS, 2; Missoula, MT: Scholars Press, 2nd edn, 1972).
Whittier, John Greenleaf, 'A Sabbath Scene' *National Era* (27 June, 1850), p. 102.

—*A Sabbath Scene, with Illustrations by Baker, Smith and Andrew* (Boston: John F. Jewett & Company, 1854).
Wickert, Ulrich, 'Der Philemonbrief—Privatbrief oder apostolisches Schreiben?', *Zeitschrift für die neutestamentliche Wissenschaft* 52 (1961), pp. 230–38.
Wiles, Gordon P., *Paul's Intercessory Prayers: The Significance of the Intercessory Prayer Passages in the Letters of St Paul* (SNTSMS, 24; Cambridge: Cambridge University Press, 1974).
Wilson, Andrew, 'The Pragmatics of Politeness and Pauline Epistolography: A Case Study of the Letter to Philemon', *Journal for the Study of the New Testament* 48 (1992), pp. 107–19.
Wilson, A.N., *Paul: The Mind of the Apostle* (London: Sinclair—Stevenson, 1997).
Wilson, Joseph Ruggles, *Mutual Relation of Masters and Slaves as Taught in the Bible: A Discourse* (Augusta, GA: Steam Press of Chronicle & Sentinel, 1861).
Wilson, R. McL., *A Critical and Exegetical Commentary on Colossians and Philemon* (ICC; Edinburgh: T. & T. Clark, 2005).
Winstanley, Edward William, 'Pauline Letters from an Ephesian Prison', *The Expositor*, Eighth Series, (1915), pp. 481–98.
Winter, Sara B.C., 'Methodological Observations on a New Interpretation of Paul's Letter to Philemon', *Union Seminary Quarterly Review* 39 (1984), pp. 203–12.
—'Paul's Letter to Philemon', *New Testament Studies* 33 (1987), pp. 1–15.
—'Philemon', in Elisabeth Schüssler-Fiorenza (ed.), *Searching the Scriptures: A Feminist Commentary* (London: SCM Press, 1994), pp. 301–12.
Wire, Antoinette Clark, 'Reading Our Heritage: A Response', in *Slavery in Text and Interpretation* (Semeia, 83–84; Atlanta: Society of Biblical Literature, 1998), pp. 283–93.
Wright, H.C., 'Moses Stuart of Andover Seminary', *The Liberator* (30 June, 1837), p. 106.
Wright, N.T., *The Epistles of Paul to the Colossians and Philemon* (TNTC, 12; Leicester: Intervarsity Press, 1986).
Yellin, Jean Fagan, *Women and Sisters: The Antislavery Feminists in American Culture* (New Haven, CT: Yale University Press, 1989).

Index of References

Old Testament

Exodus
21.2	79
21.5-6	79
21.16	82

Deuteronomy
15.12	79
15.16-17	79
23.15-16	78, 79, 82, 99, 102

Jonah
	13

New Testament

Matthew
8.5-13	139
18.20	139

Luke
7.1-10	139
10.1	52
23.7	24
23.11	24
23.32-43	139

John
7.53-8.11	168
8.32	139
10.10	139

Acts
	3, 53, 67, 112, 130, 149, 150, 151, 152
7.54	153
8.3	153
9.1-18	153
9.23-25	140
12.12	29
12.25	29
15.37-39	29
16.9-40	153
18-19	40
19.23-41	130
20.4	29
21.26-26.32	153
23.26	136
23.33-26.32	3
24.27	108
28.14-31	153
28.14-16	151
28.11-31	3

Romans
	107
1.7	20
8.28	26, 168
8.35-39	153
16.3	3, 20
16.5	147
16.7	3
16.9	20, 147
16.14	147
16.20	30
16.21	20, 147
16.22	147

1 Corinthians
	15, 107, 111, 127, 168
1.3	20
4.1	23
4.4-15	23
4.15	14
4.17	14
7.20-23	110
7.21	29, 82, 86, 102, 105
7.23	102
15.30-32	3
16.21	28
16.23	30

2 Corinthians
	15, 107, 111
1.2	20
1.8	34
2.12	34
5.20	23
6.12	22
6.13	23
8.23	20
11.23	3
13.13	30

Galatians
	17, 107
1.3	20
3.27-28	132, 144, 147
4.4	27
4.19	14, 23
6.11	28
6.18	30

Ephesians	53, 54, 58, 59, 60, 109, 115, 119, 149, 153, 155, 156	3.12-13	155	2 Timothy	150, 151
		3.12	22	1.8	19
		3.14-15	155	1.16-18	58
		3.17	155	3.10-11	153
		3.18-4.1	59	4.6-8	153
		3.23-24	155	4.10	29, 60
1.2	20	3.22-4.1	16	4.11	29, 30
3.1	19	3.25	59	4.22	30
4.1	19	4.7-9	24, 60, 67, 98		
4.6-10	152			Titus	150
6.5-9	103	4.9	32, 45, 48, 113	3.15	30
6.9	60				
6.10-11	156	4.10-14	29	Philemon	
6.14-17	156	4.10	29, 60	1-19	134
6.20	23	4.11	32	1-3	5, 9, 10, 11, 64
6.24	30	4.12-13	20		
		4.12	34, 45	1-2	19, 32, 55
Philippians	107	4.13	109		
1.1	19	4.14	29	1	21, 23, 28, 31, 32, 40, 45, 56, 154
1.2	20	4.15	35, 120		
1.8	22	4.16-17	34		
2.1	22	4.16	33, 54, 119		
2.6-11	167				
2.22	23	4.17	19, 35, 45, 54, 55, 74, 109, 110, 131	2	13, 19, 20, 31, 32, 33, 34, 35, 64
2.25	19, 20, 37, 64				
4	153				
4.23	30				
		4.18	28, 30	3	9, 20, 31
Colossians	16, 17, 18, 54, 55, 58-60, 108, 109, 122, 150, 153			4-7	5, 9, 11, 12, 20, 22
		1 Thessalonians	107		
		1.1	19	4-6	10
		1.2	20	4-5	21
		3.2	20	4	20, 154
		5.28	30	5	20, 21, 28, 29, 31, 40
1.1	19				
1.2	20	2 Thessalonians			
1.6-7	34	1.1	19	6	4, 21
1.7-8	20	1.2	20	7	10, 21, 24, 28, 36, 154
1.7	34	3.18	30		
1.15-20	168				
2.21-23	130			8-20	5, 22
3.1-3	152	1 Timothy	150	8-16	12
3.1-2	155	1.9-10	82	8-14	64
3.12-14	152	6.21	30	8-11	10

Index of References   189

Philemon (cont.)
8-10	11, 154	19-25	101, 104	epistolam ad
8	9, 22, 31	19-20	6	Philemonem 1
9-10	9	19	28	
9	4, 14, 19, 22, 31, 45, 46, 71		2, 5, 9, 27, 28, 29, 31, 40, 57, 66, 154	Clement *Epistle to Rome* 5.6 3
10-19	105	20-25	136	*Didache*
10-16	51	20-22	11	9-10 142
10-12	23	20	9, 10, 22, 24, 28, 31, 46	Eusebius *Ecclesiastical History* 3.25 1
10	9, 14, 23, 31, 36, 45, 46, 56, 143, 155	21-25 21-22	5, 9 10, 28, 165	Ignatius *Ephesians*
11-13	11		13, 154	1-6 58
11-12	9	21	9, 29, 34, 108, 154	1.3 48, 54, 57
11	9, 24, 28, 46, 68	22		2.1 57
12-15	10	23-25	10, 11, 29, 154	6.2 57
12	22, 24, 57, 93	23-24	9	*Letter to Polycarp*
13-16	9	23	28, 29, 31, 34	4.3 76
13-15	9		20, 29, 31, 32, 60	Jerome
13-14	25	24		*In epistomam ad Philemonem* 1
13	9, 25, 36, 45, 46			
14	9, 11, 25, 93, 104	25	9, 20, 30, 31, 165	Justin Martyr *Apology* 67.6 76
15-17	11			
15-16	25, 155			*Letter to the Laodicaeans* 2, 54
15	9, 25, 26, 57, 61, 71, 79, 92, 154	**Early Christian Writings**		
16-17	10	*Anti-Marcionite Prologue to Philemon* 2		*Martyrdom of St Perpetua and St Felicitas* 119
16	9, 26, 27, 28, 65, 87, 89, 99, 101, 154, 173			
17-22	12	*Apostolic Constitutions* 7.46.1, 3-5 48 4.9.2 76		*Muratorian Canon* 1
17-18	27, 154			
17	7, 9, 27, 36, 66, 155			Origen *Homily in Jeremiah* 1
18-19	9, 10, 11	Chrysostom		
18	8, 68,	*Homiliae in*		

The Roman Martyrology 42-44, 49

Shepherd of Hermas
8.10　　76

Tertullian
Against Marcion
5.42　　1

Theodore of Mopsuestia
In epistomam ad Philemonem 1

Other Ancient Documents

Codex Vindolonensis
　　50

Pliny the Elder
Epistula
9.21　　6

Oxyrhynchus PTurner
41　　7

Hierocles
On Fraternal Love　　66

Josephus
Life of Josephus
298　　28

Jewish War
2.18.10　　124

Philo
De virtutibus
124　　62

Philostratus
The Life of Apollonius of Tyana　　66

Plutarch
On Brotherly Love　　66

Suetonius　　130

Tacitus　　130
Annals
14.27　　36

Index of Names

Abbott, E.A. 116, 119
Alleine, J. 73
Allen, D.L. 7
Amling, E. 31
Anderson, G. 153
Arden, N. 153
Artz-Grabner, P. 18, 34, 36, 114
Asch, S. 113, 115
Attersoll, W. 70, 71
Attia, A. 157
Augustine of Hippo 76
Aune, D.E. 5

Bahr, G.J. 6
Barclay, J.M.G. 67, 68, 69, 78
Barnes, A. 81, 84, 86, 88
Barrett, C.K. 107
Barrett, L. 153
Bartchy, S.S. 63, 77, 102
Barth, M. 3, 14, 18, 78
Barton, S. 144, 145
Baur, F.C. 1, 112
Bentley, R. 14
Binder, H. 3, 35
Birdsall, N. 3, 14
Birney, J.G. 98
Blanchard, J. 84
Blanke, H. 3, 14, 18, 78
Blassingame, J. 89, 90, 92
Bornkamm, G. 108

Bourne, G. 65, 100, 102, 105
Boys, T. 8, 9
Braxton, B.R. 15, 76, 102
Broughton, L. 153
Bruce, F.F. 1, 3, 41, 56, 58, 62
Burgess, A. 150
Burns, A. 82
Buttrick, G.A. 76
Byron, J. 69

Cadoux, A.T. 132, 136
Cadoux, C.J. 3
Caird, G.B. 3, 32, 35, 56, 57, 58, 78
Caldwell, T. 112
Callahan, A.D. 6, 26, 27, 35, 38, 65, 66, 67, 79, 102
Callot, J. 50, 51
Calvin, J. 33, 56
Chadwick, H. 76
Cheever, G.B. 99, 100
Chrysostom, John 1, 2, 32, 36, 45, 53, 66, 70
Church, F.F. 6, 7, 12
Clark, R.W. 93
Clement of Rome 3
Cole, J. 149
Coleman-Norton, P.R. 38
Combes, L.A.H. 15, 76
Connolly, A.L. 114
Cope, L. 55

Corwin, C.E. 119, 122
Courthion, P. 47
Cross, T. 31
Currier, T.F. 94

Dames, G.W. 102
Daube, D. 67
Davies, M. 78
Deissmann, A. 3, 6, 35, 74, 111
De Ligouro, G. 149
Demerdash, M.E. 158
Deming, W. 102
Derrett, J.D.M. 67
Dibelius, M. 3, 108
Dodd, C.H. 3, 33
Dodderidge, P. 46
Doty, W.G. 5
Douglass, F. 89, 93
Duncan, G.S. 3
Dunn, J.D.G. 3, 34, 36, 39, 46, 63, 78, 110

Eleen, L. 41
Elliott, N. 17, 67, 77
Ellis, E.E. 3
Epictetus 117, 118
Eusebius of Caesarea 1
Eveleigh, J. 84

Farid, M. 158
Farrar, F.W. 6
Fee, J.G. 65, 84, 104, 105

Index of Names

Feeley-Harnik, G. 12, 13
Fillmore, M. 90
Finegan, J. 16
Finseth, I.F. 83
Fisk, W. 91, 92
Fitzmyer, J.A. 3, 6, 7, 17, 18
Foster, S.S. 91, 97
Foucault, M. 13
Foxworth, R. 150
Franklin, B. 172
Friedrick, J.K. 149
Frilingos, C. 6, 14
Funk, R.W. 66

Galal, S. 158
Galil, A.A. 158
Gamal, R.E. 158
Gamble, H. 16
Gambol, J. 57
Garrison, W.L. 91
Gentleman, D. 173
Getty, M.A. 2, 13
Giltner, J. 77, 91
Gnilka, J. 3, 17, 46, 58
Godet, F. 1, 3, 7, 41, 44, 56, 76, 77, 112
Goguel, M. 3
Goodenough, E.R. 3, 62
Goodspeed, E.J. 33, 53, 54, 55, 85, 108, 109, 110
Goodwin, J. 71
Gorday, P. 1, 32
Green, B. 77, 91
Greeven, H. 58
Grimke, A.B. 78, 79, 101
Grotius, H. 6
Gülzow, H. 35
Guthrie, D. 55

Hackwood, W. 171

Hahn, F. 56
Hanson, C.L. 50
Hanway, J. 72
Harrill, J.A. 6, 15, 76, 77, 79, 85, 102
Harris, M.J. 3, 15, 102
Harrison, P.N. 3, 56, 58
Harvey, A.E. 6
Heil, J.P. 3, 11
Hock, R.F. 4, 14
Hopkins, A. 150
Horsley, R.A. 13, 15, 38
Houlden, J.L. 3, 35, 36, 57
Hoyt, L.M. 122, 124
Humphreys, W. 153

Ignatius of Antioch 48, 54, 76

Jay, W. 90
Jeayes, A. 153
Jeremias, J. 10
Jerome 1, 2, 32, 70
Jewett, R. 17
Johnson, L. 3
Jones, C.C. 81
Jones, M. 3
Jones, T. 153
Josephus 28, 124
Jülicher, A. 77
Justin Martyr 76

Keesmaat, S.C. 148
Khairalla, S. 158
Khamis, A. 158
Khatib, M.E. 158
Kim, C.H. 5
Knox, J. 3, 6, 16, 23, 33, 34, 53, 54, 60, 63, 64, 77
Knox, W. 3, 36

Koch, E.W. 6
Koester, H. 3, 6, 56, 77
Kreitzer, L.J. 36
Kümmel, W.G. 3, 32, 35, 78

Lampe, P. 3, 62, 63, 109
Leaney, A.R.C. 3
Leigh, N. 149, 161
Leo XIII 76
Lewis, L.A. 17
Lightfoot, J.B. 3, 11, 16, 33, 39, 41, 66
Lincoln, A. 76
Lingard, E. 83, 84
Llewelyn, S.R. 7
Lohmeyer, E. 3, 62, 77
Lohse, E. 3, 14, 78
Longstreet, A.B. 88, 89
Lüdemann, G. 3, 6, 111, 112
Lund, N.W. 10
Luther, M. 3, 33, 70

Maclaren, A. 18, 33, 78
Marcarelli, R. 150
Marshall, I.H. 34
Martens, J.W. 58
Martin, C.J. 8
Martin, D.B. 15
Martin, R.P. 56
McDonald, J.I.H. 75
McKeen, S. 98, 99
Meeks, W.A. 85
Metzger, B.M. 4
Meyer, F.B. 36
Michelangelo 18
Mitchell, L. 93
Mitchell, M.M. 66
Mitton, C.L. 16, 53
Moneim, S.A. 158

Morris, C. 143, 144
Morrison, L.R. 79
Mostafa, R. 158
Motyer, S. 36, 78
Moule, C.F.D. 3, 4, 14, 58
Murphy-O'Connor, J. 109, 110

Nassar, Z. 158
Neilson, F. 128, 130
Neilson, W. 128, 130
Newton, D. 157
Nightingale, E.G. 139, 143
Nordling, J.G. 3, 18, 67, 68, 69

Oates, S.B. 82
O'Brien 3, 8, 56, 78
O'Connell, J.B. 44, 49
O'Donnell, M.B. 8
Oesterley, W.E. 78
Oldfield, J.R. 171
Ollrog, W.H. 39, 56
Origen 1
Osiek, C. 32, 34, 56, 76
Owen, C.H. 80, 81, 88

Parry, E. 136, 139
Parry, T. 85, 86
Patterson, O. 15
Patzia, A.G. 3
Payne, D.A. 91
Pearson, B.W.R. 6, 61, 62, 69
Peerbolte, B.J. 145, 147
Pelagius 32
Perkins, P. 4
Petersen, N. 4, 7, 13, 67, 77
Peterson, B. 94

Pickard, J.B. 97
Plass, B. 147
Pliny the Younger 6, 7, 68
Plumptre, E.H. 36
Polaski, S.H. 13, 78
Pollock, J. 115, 116
Polycarp of Smyrna 58
Porter, S.E. 5, 8
Preiss, T. 12, 62

Rapske, B.M. 62, 63
Reicke, B. 3
Reisenfeld, H. 4
Rice, N.L. 84
Richardson, W.J. 14
Robertson, A.T. 3, 35, 76
Robertson, J.A. 56, 67, 124, 126
Robinson, J.A.T. 3
Roper, M. 83, 84
Rossellini, R. 149
Rouault, G. 47
Rumy, S.F. 158
Russell, D.M. 7, 78

Sanders, E.P. 107
Sayer, P. 150
Schenk, W. 3, 34, 62
Schmithals, W. 16
Schoedel, W.R. 58
Schrage, W. 75
Schubert, P. 8
Scott, E.F. 3, 32, 33, 35, 36, 56, 76, 110
Seabrooke, E. 153
Seely, K. 153
Shanks, C.L. 98
Shapiro, S. 82
Shaw, G. 12
Smith, G.K. 94
Smith, H.S. 79
Snyman, A.H. 7

Soards, M.L. 6, 61, 70
Steele, R. 71
Stevens, C.E. 83
St John, P. 126, 128
Stowe, H.B. 94, 105, 106
Stowers, S.K. 5
Stroud, G. 153
Stuart, M. 76, 77, 91, 92, 95, 97
Stuhlmacher, P. 3, 6, 17, 35, 56, 58, 60
Suetonius 130

Tacitus 36, 130
Tertullian 1
Theodore of Mopsuestia 1, 32, 70
Theodoret 4
Thompson, M.M. 3, 6
Torricella, E. 150
Turner, N. 81

Vincent, M.R. 1, 3, 32, 61
Vos, C.S. 6, 78

Wagerin, W. 112
Walker, N. 153
Walsh, B.J. 148
Walters, T. 153
Wansink, C.S. 64
Waziri, A. 158
Webb, L. 130, 132
Webster, D. 92, 95, 97
Wedgwood, J. 171, 172
Weizsäcker, C. von 31
Welch, J.W. 9
White, J.L. 5
Whittier, J.G. 93, 94, 97
Wickert, U. 13, 14
Wilberforce, W. 74, 75, 76

Wiles, G.P. 8, 56
Wilson, A. 8, 12
Wilson, A.N. 35
Wilson, J.R. 102, 104
Wilson, R. McL. 3, 65
Wilson, W. 102
Winstanley, E.W. 3
Winter, S.B.C. 3, 13, 23, 34, 39, 55, 56, 61, 63, 64, 65, 69, 113
Wire, A.C. 15
Wright, H.C. 91, 92
Wright, N.T. 3, 14
Yassen, Y.E. 157
Yellin, J.F. 173
Young, R. 150

www.ingramcontent.com/pod-product-compliance
Lightning Source LLC
Chambersburg PA
CBHW050148170426
43197CB00011B/2010